THE ART

OF CREATIVE

RESEARCH

Chicago Guides
to *Writing*, Editing
and Publishing

Permissions, A Survival Guide by Susan M. Bielstein

The Craft of Research by Wayne C. Booth, Gregory G. Colomb, Joseph M. Williams, Joseph Bizup, and William T. FitzGerald

The Chicago Guide to Fact-Checking by Brooke Borel

Immersion by Ted Conover

The Architecture of Story by Will Dunne

The Dramatic Writer's Companion by Will Dunne

Getting It Published by William Germano

From Notes to Narrative by Kristen Ghodsee

Storycraft by Jack Hart

A Poet's Guide to Poetry by Mary Kinzie

The Writer's Diet by Helen Sword

A Manual for Writers of Research Papers, Theses, and Dissertations by Kate L. Turabian

THE ART
OF CREATIVE
RESEARCH

A Field Guide for Writers

PHILIP GERARD

The University of Chicago Press
Chicago and London

The University of Chicago Press, Chicago 60637

The University of Chicago Press, Ltd., London

© 2017 by Philip Gerard

Published 2017.

Printed in the United States of America

26 25 24 23 22 21 20 19 18 17   1 2 3 4 5

ISBN-13: 978-0-226-17977-3 (cloth)

ISBN-13: 978-0-226-17980-3 (paper)

ISBN-13: 978-0-226-17994-0 (e-book)

DOI: 10.7208/chicago/9780226179940.001.0001

Library of Congress Cataloging-in-Publication Data

Names: Gerard, Philip, author.

Title: The art of creative research: a field guide for writers / Philip Gerard.

Other titles: Chicago guides to writing, editing, and publishing.

Description: Chicago; London : The University of Chicago Press, 2017. | Series: Chicago guides to writing, editing, and publishing | Includes bibliographical references and index.

Identifiers: LCCN 2016036902 | ISBN 9780226179773 (cloth: alk. paper) | ISBN 9780226179803 (pbk: alk. paper) | ISBN 9780226179940 (e-book)

Subjects: LCSH: Authorship. | Research. | Creative writing.

Classification: LCC PN146 .G47 2017 | DDC 808.02—dc23 LC record available at https://lccn.loc.gov/2016036902

♾ This paper meets the requirements of ANSI/NISO Z39.48-1992 (Permanence of Paper).

CONTENTS

Prologue: On Fire for Research (an Homage to Larry Brown)   *vii*

1   What Creative Research Is and How to Use It   1

2   Preparing a Research Plan   22

3   The Tools of the Trade   38

4   Archives: What They Are, Where They Are, and How
    Best to Use Them   57

5   It Must Be True—I Saw It on the Internet   73

6   The Archives of Memory, Imagination, and
    Personal Expertise   83

7   The Warm Art of the Interview   98

8   Walking the Ground and Handling the Thing Itself   130

9   Troubleshooting, Fact-Checking, and Emotional Cost   149

10 Breathing Life into Facts and Data on the Page   170

Afterword   203   Acknowledgments   209
Selected Sources for Quotations and Concepts Addressed in This Book   211
Index   215

PROLOGUE: ON FIRE FOR RESEARCH

(AN HOMAGE TO LARRY BROWN)

*I have chosen this thing to do, away from my family, the doors
closed, characters who form in my head and move to the paper, black
symbols on a white sheet, no more than that. It may
seem senseless to anybody else, but I know there is a purpose
to my work. . . .—Larry Brown, On Fire*

I love getting in my car in the predawn darkness, watching the dashboard glow blue and silver and red as I turn the ignition, feel the neighborhood stillness all around me.

They're all asleep, my neighbors, and I'm awake and stealing away on an adventure. I back out of the driveway slowly and roll up the street, the GPS beaming on the dashboard, toward a destination two hundred miles away, where I will talk to a stranger—an old moonshiner, who, in his wild youth, drove fast cars down twisting midnight roads on the adventure of his life—and hope that he will tell me what he knows and I need to know, some clue that will help me make sense of the history of half a million restless people and their descendants. And I don't even know what that is.

It's the *not* knowing that always gets me, the surprise waiting at the end of the road. I love the feeling of excitement tinged with anxiety, the anticipation of a new encounter, of knowing that by day's end I will be rocketing back home along country roads with the goods in my notebook, my digital recorder, my camera, to be unpacked and mulled over and formed into words that will create an experience in the imaginations of strangers, sometime in the indeterminate future.

Maybe. With a little luck.

If I am good enough to make it happen.

And I love it that sometimes I am good enough to make it happen.

I love the moment when someone tells me something he or she never intended to say, the look of wonder and discovery in their eyes, the smiling tears of memory, the clutch in the throat that carries all the story you'll ever need to hear. The pang of good-bye, leaving a stranger who has just confided his most precious secret, hoping you will honor it—I don't love that, I never get used to that. Yet afterward, how I do cherish the memory of it.

Every conversation is a story, and every story is an adventure, and every adventure takes me out of my small life into a larger one, and I love that. I love that it catapults me out into the world, outdoors, in all seasons, to places I have only dreamed of going—or maybe never dreamed of going—places where they speak in different accents, different languages even. Where the air smells different, and the skyline is unfamiliar, and the landscape is a brand-new map.

I love finding historical markers on remote country lanes, pulling to the side of the road and stepping into weeds brushed by an October wind. Then walking up a long winding path to ground where something has been fought over, decided, the struggle mapped into the ground: earthworks, entrenchments, graves.

I love the hush of those deserted places, those old battlefields, always so breathtaking, as if we, as a species, have decided to struggle only in beautiful places. And listening to the ghosts moan among the last leaves of autumn, seeing their shapes rise up in uniforms: Union blue, Confederate gray, British red and scarlet, the motley of Revolutionary militias, the painted flesh of Iroquois.

There is treasure in the ground—the body of British General Edward Braddock, haughty and dismissive, cut down by ambush in the Pennsylvania woods, buried secretly and the grave tracked over by his surviving troops so it could never be found and desecrated.

The things that men dropped in their frenzy to retreat— they're in the ground, too: bullets and swords and muskets and haversacks. It is all there still, and their voices rise on the wind, an eternal chorus. Just as at Cowpens and Guilford Courthouse, Antietam and Gettysburg, Manassas and the little village of Averasboro, North Carolina, where the unknown Confederate dead are fenced into a little flat graveyard—barefoot boys from Alabama and Mississippi and Georgia who were still fighting after Robert E. Lee's surrender and never made it home.

On a transatlantic trip hunting the ghosts of World War II soldiers, on Omaha beach at Normandy, I walk from the gray rumbling sea across a broad pebbled bar to the first hump of sandy cover, feel the steep distance in my legs, slip a smooth pebble into my pocket, a hard nugget of memory. How did men ever cross that ground and live?

Later I climb a rocky village churchyard among miniature stone sepulchres, the repositories of children dead from the Black Death. The tiny sepulchres are fitted into the crowded graveyard like puzzle pieces.

In Poland I climb a long hill called Jasna Gora, Hill of Light, to reach the fortified monastery at the top. In the year 1655, beset by an invading army of 10,000 Swedes, the monastery was saved by the intercession of the Black Madonna—captured in an image painted by St. Luke on a tabletop built by Jesus of Nazareth himself and displayed inside the cathedral.

So they say.

Now on the Feast of the Assumption, a high mass is being celebrated on the parapet by a score of bishops, monsignors, priests, and acolytes. Tens of thousands of pilgrims are climbing the hill on their knees—old men in tattered wool suits, nuns in black Reeboks, schoolgirls wearing bright badges identifying their schools. I reach a door in the wall, for some lucky reason unlocked, and enter. A stone staircase brings me to the parapet, a few yards from the mass, and I gaze out over a crowd that can be measured in acres. I love that moment on the parapet, peering out into the Middle Ages.

And I love libraries and the still windowless rooms of Special

Collections—even the name is exciting: *Special Collections*, an invitation to view the extraordinary. Letters are the best—love letters, letters of regret or exultation, scolding letters, letters asking for a new shirt, boots that aren't rotten, candy, fresh eggs. A letter of reply. The thin brittle paper under my linen gloves is stained with sweat and coffee and dew and whiskey and tobacco juice and blood. The handwriting is curlicued and cramped and at times illegible, enlivened by whimsical spelling and inky devil's teardrops dotting each "i." Some give off a faint whiff of mildew or tobacco or perfume.

And I love opening the diary of a young soldier fresh from a horrific battle and watching a dried flower fall out—proof that the meadow where he camped was blooming, a moment of promise amid the madness.

And the stern sepia portraits in the deck of cartes-de-visite, a whole regiment's worth, taken just before going into battle the next day, when the regiment would be wiped out almost to a man.

I love the weight of old objects in my hands: a rosewood and spruce parlor guitar made by hand in the 1890s, the brass field glasses my grandfather owned for no good reason, the bone saw used by a Civil War surgeon, some colonial farmer's rude-handled shovel or ax, the rusty shackles that once bound a slave. I love exploring forts and old houses and ruined factories, crawling through a World War II bomber whose passages are so tight that it must have been designed for miniature men, and descending into a played-out copper mine in Arizona on a narrow-gauge railroad into eternal darkness.

And dioramas—how I love those! The miniature towns with their railroads and harbors, their lighted windows and tiny citizens frozen in the act of unloading a barge or cutting firewood or hanging laundry on a backyard line.

And topographical tables, how the mountains rise out of the plain and the river valley cuts a canyon. Scale models, how cool are they? A whole roomful of windjammers at the Smithsonian, a railroad layout complete with a working carnival at an old freight shed on the Erie Canal. And the dim secretive museum light, like the stingy light inside a haunted house.

And reenactments, actors dressed in period costume, all their accessories so ridiculous and quaint and real. I love the ammoniac smell of their horses and the reek of old saddle leather and the acrid burn of black powder gun smoke wafting across the meadow.

At a museum in Maryland, I walk among antique fire engines, gaudy as circus wagons, their company names scrolled in gold leaf, their steam boilers decorated in vivid oil-painted tableaux of heroism. An old fireman docent sounds an antique alarm, and the switchboard inside the alarm house lights up and sends its signal out to all the right stations, ranged along the walls. On the flickering kinescope, a team of horses that have been dead for a century wheels into harness at the sound of a silent bell and heave the engine out the double doors of the firehouse in a herky-jerky motion, a little spotted dog leaping aboard at the last second. I want to go to that long-ago fire with them. I want to buckle on a canvas turnout coat and leather helmet and feel the heat and listen to the little dog yap with joy at the flames.

I want to be where all the important moments of history happened: Runnymede, Old North Church, the Alamo, Independence Hall, Appomattox Court House, the Bennett Farm—where the Civil War really came to an end.

I love standing at a table where something important was signed, like a surrender.

I love the little notebooks that fit in my back pocket, bound with an elastic band, the fistful of pens that snug into a row of khaki sleeves like spare cartridges, the camera and digital recorder and snacks and water bottle that live in my vest when I know I will be in the field for a long day. And don't forget the binoculars, how I love them! They help me see what is invisible—a bald eagle soaring above the tree line, a house snuggled into the distant mountainside, and far out at sea, a breaching whale. Like the magnifying glass in my pocket that reveals the soft indentation of a fountain pen nib on rag paper, and the spotlight in the console of my SUV that illuminates addresses and turn-offs at night on unfamiliar country roads.

The SUV is a rolling office, and I love packing it for any emergency, any adventure: spare batteries, first aid kit, hazard lights, jumper cables, tools, a spare toiletry kit, bottled water and blankets, foul weather gear, even a harmonica in the glove compartment to pass the slow times.

At highway rest stops, I can't help but wonder where everyone else has come from and where they are bound: the chic couple in the red convertible sports car, the rowdy family with all the wild kids pouring out of the camper, the pensive loner hurrying back from the restroom with his hands jammed tight in his windbreaker pockets. I want to get in all their cars with them and go someplace else, anywhere but here, and find out why: Why are they going? What's waiting at the end of the road?

I never watch a boat shove off from a dock without wanting to climb aboard, never see a canoe disappear around a river bend without wanting to paddle after it, never see the contrail of an airplane overhead without wondering who is aboard and where they are going and why, and wishing I was going somewhere too. And often enough, I do climb aboard—ships, planes, trucks, trains, kayaks, my own two legs—and rattle off on an adventure that will someday live on pages.

After the adventure, I love going somewhere quiet and just listening to the world be quiet, the story settling on me like grace, or like a snowfall, accumulating weight and shape and even beauty.

The words are already there, buckets of them, notebooks full of them. They're in my ears, a hubbub of words, and when I make it home again, they will visit my dreams, as will the faces and the stony churchyard and the wooded path to a hidden grave and old rough-handled tools and the soughing breeze that sounds like spirits awake and restless among the trees.

I love all that, and the words are already trying to find my fingers, trying to turn fact and impression and color and tone of voice into something true—as in straight, plumb, level, and square, a carpenter's truth.

That's what this thing is for me, this thing the scholars call *research*.

That's the thing I want you to share—the adventure of finding out and the excitement of turning that knowledge into the right words to somehow touch your reader, a stranger, who follows and trusts you, and somehow was always there at your side on that airplane, in that archive, on that river, sharing that weather, during that interview.

And it doesn't really matter what genre you choose to work in. The thrill is the same whether it results in an authentic poem or a true-crime book or a personal essay or a novel. Knowing about the world with specific accuracy changes everything about the creative process. It enlarges the borders of your imagination exponentially, allowing you to write about science, history, the natural world, society, politics, medicine, business, technology, personal relationships, and human nature in ways that will delight and surprise both you and your reader—which is, after all, the point.

Research can take you to that golden intersection where the personal meets the public, the private crosses the universal, where the best literature lives. It is deeply rooted in the writer's heart, yet blossoms out into a larger thing that includes the world.

It's a lot of work, and it takes some gumption, but it sure is a thrill.

1 WHAT CREATIVE RESEARCH IS AND HOW TO USE IT

The only things I can't write about are things that I am ignorant
about, and that can always be changed. —Jacob Bateman, poet

Somewhere in our schooling, the idea of research got separated from
our creative impulse. The kids who went into science do research.
Maybe the historians and social scientists, too. And, of course, we
all suffered through writing the required "research" paper in high
school or college, in which we rounded up a specified number of
reputable sources to splint the bones of our argument. And maybe
journalists need to quote sources for the sake of credibility. But poets?
Novelists? Personal essayists? Don't we just reach deep into the well of
our imaginations and subconscious minds and produce art? Well, not
exactly. Sometimes it's not enough simply to peer intently into your
own soul. Sometimes you have to look out the window and see the
world in all its complicated glory.

Think of Rita Dove's haunting book of poems, *Thomas and Beulah*,
based on the lives of her African American grandparents. True, she
achieves poetic power by imagining herself into their lives and by creating a living sense of them for us on the page. But to do that, she first
had to discover all she could about them. Her declared intent was to
remind us that these were *real* people, that their lives actually hap-

pened and were not just artistic constructs, that those lives contained both mystery and beauty along with hardship and suffering. Drawing from the actual known details of their lives would honor them. Think, too, of Carolyn Forché's mesmerizing book of poems, *The Country Between Us*, based on her experience on the ground during the time of the death squads and impending war in El Salvador, using poetry to try to understand the savagery she witnessed—and make it known to the world in a more powerful and lasting form than a daily news story.

Lavonne J. Adams had published scores of personally inspired poems before she wrote an enchanting cycle of poems about women on the Santa Fe Trail, *Through the Glorieta Pass*—a breakthrough experience that opened up a whole new dimension in her poetry. A simple assignment that she gave to her poetry class prodded her to venture so far afield in search of subject matter—an assignment designed to jar students away from writing only what was familiar and comfortable. She describes the experience this way:

Students of poetry, in the initial stages of the development of their craft, often write about their own experiences, which is an unarguable means of claiming authority in the writing. During a semester in which an intermediate workshop group shared an inordinate number of poems about romance-gone-awry, I pondered ways that I might encourage them to consider other topics. I wondered if shifting from subjects in which they had a strong emotional stake, to others that might be less personally inspired or traumatic, would allow these poets the distance that they need to focus on craft. My hypothesis was that they could then return to more personal poetry with greater insight and mastery over imagery, language, voice, and form.

Adams goes on, "The assignment was simple: choose a topic and research, write a poem about that topic. I began to write in this vein along with my students, delighted in the temporary liberation from my own life, or thoughts on life in general, within my poetry."

Like so many writers, Adams often finds that the surprises, even the disappointments, inherent in research often turn out to be the most inspiring moments. As she recounts:

Though I've found that traveling for the sake of research isn't a necessity, it can certainly enrich the experience for the author, as well as provide another level of engagement in the resulting creative work.

For example, while investigating the life and art of Georgia O'Keeffe, I was able to take a brief trip to Lake George, New York, where O'Keeffe and husband Alfred Stieglitz spent many summers. My first day there, I wandered the heart of the village, examining buildings, noting trees, the way light struck the lake and the surrounding mountains. I was frustrated when an unexpected afternoon storm swept across the lake, forcing me to take shelter. The next day, I visited a quaint brick building with spires, the former county courthouse, which now houses the Lake George Historical Association & Museum. There, I studied artifacts, read placards that described how quickly storms formed, the impressive number of resulting wrecks found lying at the bottom of the lake. When I saw a photograph of O'Keeffe's painting, *Storm Cloud, Lake George*, all of these elements combined to create a rendition of an ill-fated afternoon on the lake, when Stieglitz and O'Keeffe witnessed two boys drown.

Adams gains an important grounding in such factual events, but ultimately the facts are only as interesting as the poet can make them, as she turns them into something larger and more meaningful, actions and images that resonate beyond the historical moment and even beyond the poem. She says, "But real authority is something more craft-oriented—the engagement of the poet with the subject matter."

When Stephen Crane wrote his novel *The Red Badge of Courage*, the Civil War was already settled history. His research took place at the feet of old veterans reminiscing on porches, and he listened carefully. When he wrote "The Open Boat," a short story, he was drawing on his own (unintended) research of being shipwrecked off Florida while en route to cover the rebellion in Cuba in 1896. In fact, he first wrote a reportorial nonfiction account of the incident and then shaped the raw material of fact into fiction. Mark Twain earned direct personal experience as a riverboat pilot, but he also closely—and intentionally—observed legendary river men like Horace Bixby to write *Life on the Mississippi*. Ted Conover rode the rails across America for a season to find out about the hobo life by living it for his book *Rolling Nowhere*, as complete an immersion experience as one can imagine. Later he reprised part of his hobo trip with his grown son, adding a new lens to the experience—and also using the journey to deepen his understanding of fatherhood.

It's not hard to come up with a pretty impressive list of writers of all genres who intentionally addressed public events, history, science, technology, and all manner of other subjects through research, including deliberately creating an experience to write from. The nonfiction writers are obvious: Tracy Kidder (*The Soul of a New Machine*), Joan Didion (*Miami*), Randall Kenan (*Walking on Water: Black American Lives at the Turn of the Twenty-First Century*), Barry Lopez (*Arctic Dreams*)—the start of a long and distinguished list. But on reflection, so are the novelists: Charles Frazier (*Cold Mountain*), Joyce Carol Oates (*Blonde*), Larry McMurtry (*Lonesome Dove*), David Guterson (*Snow Falling on Cedars*), Thomas Keneally (*Schindler's List*), Toni Morrison (*Beloved*)—another lengthening list.

As for poets, Emily Dickinson may have spent a lot of time indoors, but she was constantly in touch with the public figures of her day and deeply affected by the wholesale death of the Civil War, which she followed in the newspapers and from the personal accounts of friends, and which informs a large portion of her work with an unsettling darkness. Her contemporary Walt Whitman went south to witness the suffering for himself as a hospital worker, then wrote *Drum-Taps*, a sequence of forty-three poems about the human side of the conflict—and more in *Leaves of Grass*. Documentary poetry has usually come to the fore during times of crisis and social unrest—such as the Great Depression, which gave us Archibald MacLeish's *Land of the Free*, featuring gritty photographs and poetic social comment; or the Harlem Renaissance, which gave us Langston Hughes, among many other poets addressing history and justice ("Remember / The days of bondage"). In more contemporary times, poets are resurrecting this documentary impulse, voicing deeply informed lines about race, genocide, war, justice, history, and contemporary culture. Not all write about deeply controversial social subjects. The late William Matthews, for instance, wrote passionately and knowingly about jazz.

So creative research is a matter of discovery of both the facts of the world that can be turned to artistic purpose and the method of finding out those facts, which in itself is a creative act. The journey of research is a drama all its own. The discoveries don't just fill in a few blanks to make a piece feel authentic; rather they often inspire the creation of a poem, an essay, or a story to somehow contain the discovery—a work of art not previously envisioned by the writer. The act of creative research begins the moment the writer decides to venture into the world beyond his or her own knowledge and experience.

THE ACTUALITY AND THE ZONE OF NOISE

A nonfiction writer may be trying to pin down exactly the complicated facts of an event or life. A poet or novelist may be after authenticity—a reliable feel for a historical period or profession or place that he or she can then transform through invented characters or imagery.

Think of a true fact as a pencil point in the middle of a blank page. Now draw a small circle around that point. Inside this first circle are all the sources that directly touch what we'll call the "Actuality": physical evidence, eyewitness accounts, film, video, or audio of the event in real time; letters and diaries written by the people involved; police reports, maps, medical charts, or birth certificates written at or very close to the moment in question by people directly involved in the event—including, perhaps, you the author. Call these primary sources. The next circle out gets bigger and more encompassing. It contains reputable scholarship; contemporaneous journalism or other reporting; scientific studies; official investigations; trial transcripts; oral histories or memoirs created long after the fact; theories and analysis and informed speculation—all of them one big step removed from direct contact with the people and events of the actuality. These are secondary sources. Beyond that is what I call the Zone of Noise—the largest circle. This zone contains material far removed from direct contact: tradition, family lore, rumor, popular culture, blogs, opinion, and so on. It contains a measure of truth—but also distortion, falsehood, misinterpretation, irrelevancies, propaganda, and just plain fiction.

Your job as a researcher is to pass through the Zone of Noise—if need be tied to the mast like Odysseus, with wax stuffed in your ears to keep out the siren call of convenient drama. Then, guided by the clues and sources embedded in the second circle, you do your best to penetrate into the first circle of primary data. To get as close to the Actuality as you can. But the process is likely to be analogous to celestial navigation. The art of celestial navigation posits that, for every moment in time, you can plot your exact point on the Earth's surface, through the use of a sextant and some trigonometry. True enough, but rare is the navigator who, on the pitching deck of a small boat, using imperfect gifts and prone to mathematical errors, can pinpoint his or her position exactly. The best navigators, after long practice, using three stars or sun sights can locate their vessels inside a small triangle of ocean a few square miles in extent—a triangle that gets smaller and smaller with diligent practice.

The navigator approaches the knowledge of exact location and with practice gets closer and closer in that approach. But even when he or she is perfectly mathematically correct, it is unlikely that the navigator can be any more certain than at other times. That is, even when you have hit on the exact truth, you are unlikely to be certain if that is indeed the case. Still, if the navigator can steer a safe passage between the rocks and into a harbor, the calculation has proved accurate enough. So, too, the writer. With practice, you'll learn when to trust an eyewitness account and when it strikes you as fishy; you'll become adept at "triangulating," the way a navigator does—locating the truth somewhere in the intersection of several conflicting accounts; you will recognize that when a story seems too good to be true, it usually is. You will find yourself so close to the Actuality that you can feel it present in your words on the page and know you have approached as closely as you are ever likely to come to the literal truth of what was said or done. Then you can use that truth to your own artistic purpose.

Here a word about primary sources—the stuff in that first circle. Whether a source is primary depends to a large extent on how you are using it, what it is there to "prove." So a newspaper account written during the time of the event may contain many errors—may even be deliberately falsified, as were many journalistic accounts of Civil War battles, to either underestimate the losses of one side or overstate the losses of the other or to plump the reputation of a patron general. So they are not necessarily reliable primary sources for how many men died or were wounded—or even which side won the battle. But they stand as excellent primary sources for the way in which the war was reported, for the kind of language and sentiment that made its way into the public square.

Likewise, a trial transcript is essentially a secondary source as it relates to the events at the heart of the crime or lawsuit. The conflicting theories of the crime, as put forward by the lawyers on both sides, are essentially hypotheses to be tested by evidence, logic, and testimony. Both cannot be true at once. Remember, the whole American judicial process rests not on measures of certainty but on *degrees of doubt*. But embedded within the transcript are many primary sources—the exact charges or grievances; the applicable statutes; documents or physical evidence entered into the record; the testimony of eyewitnesses, experts, and the accused; facts independently verified regarding weather, location, and other matters of context. And here it's worth noting that the court reporter is perhaps the only person on the public payroll whose job it is to produce an exact, unabridged, truthful record of what is spoken by all parties in an encounter—in this case, in the courtroom. Even sustained objections and matters to be stricken from the record and disregarded by the jury remain in the official transcript, in case of review by an appellate court, which may need to take them into account in its deliberations.

So the transcript is a reliable primary source about the trial itself. But it remains one important step removed from the Actuality. You can know exactly what a witness said, but how do you know if he or she is telling the truth? Misremembering? Leaving out important details? Trial lawyers know this well. All the circumstantial evidence that's available can point to the "obvious" guilt of a completely innocent person. Different juries, reviewing the exact same evidence, can arrive at completely opposite decisions regarding guilt or innocence.

In the title essay of her book *The Partly Cloudy Patriot*, Sarah Vowell proclaims a truth I have come to know well in writing about the Civil War and other American adventures: "American history is a quagmire, and the more one knows, the quaggier the mire gets." She is addressing the complicated nature of events and motives, as well as the sheer difficulty of knowing anything—even the seemingly most basic fact—for sure. Every new thing you find out tends to contradict the last thing you found out. Facts, evidence, clues—whatever you want to call them—are only as true as the story we use them to tell. And I use the term *story* loosely to mean the vital stuff of human behavior, whether it winds up in narrative or a lyric poem or an essay of ideas. A poem or fictional story is "true" if it offers insight into the way human beings actually behave, feel, think, aspire, dream. For the nonfiction writer, "true" also means truthful to the most verifiable version of events.

As writers we find our material in what we have experienced and in what we know. Sometimes the experience, as it happens by chance and circumstance, is enough to fuel a body of work. But often the writer deliberately seeks out experience and knowledge of some kind in order to enlarge the scope of his or her canvas. Sometimes the facts point to an obvious story. But more often there is a larger true thing, a Big Fact behind the Facts of the Case. It is this fact behind the facts that determines the meanings of all the other facts, creates a context for interpreting what our eyes are seeing and what our informants are telling us, and dictates the true *syntax* of a story.

THE SYNTAX OF STORY

A story is a created thing—whether we're trafficking in fiction or nonfiction. It is the artful manipulation of facts, events, emotions, characters, time, and language to convey human experience that is authentic—not cartoonish or formulaic. And every story, like every sentence, has a syntax, a dynamic cohesion that determines meaning, based on three qualities that every word in a sentence has—as does every element of a story:

1. Sequence: in what order the elements are arranged (which may differ from the order in which they occurred), and where in that sequence any particular element fits.
2. Priority: the importance of any element relative to any other element.
3. Relationship: a special connection to each other element and to the story as a whole.

You can see at once that *priority* involves a *sequence* of subordination—this thing is more or less important than that other thing. And of course to say that implies a *relationship* or lack thereof between any two elements—and assumes you have discovered all the elements, including that first big fact that colors all the others individually and collectively.

Finding the fact behind the facts is crucial in both public and private stories. Sometimes the implications are personally important, as in a wonderful student memoir I once read. The writer remembered a childhood without a mother in which her father did his best by her—but kept her from contact with his estranged wife, her mother, whom she missed terribly. Rather than simply wallow in her bittersweet memories, she approached her own childhood story as an investigator: she interviewed her father, other family members, former teachers, the neighbor woman who used to babysit her after school while her father was still at work. She learned that in reality her father had been shielding her all those years from a dangerously unbalanced, drug-addicted mother who might have harmed her in all sorts of ways. Her father had sacrificed heroically and without complaint to give her a childhood free of crisis and damage—her calm, safe, happy childhood was a gift of love from her father, at a significant cost to him. This was the controlling fact behind all the other facts of the story that lent context and meaning. Her memoir, like all true memoirs, turned out not to be simply a scrapbook of memories to brood over or cherish, not a highlight reel of her life, but a meaningful *reckoning*.

Memory can be warped. It lies. It tells us what we want to hear. So another part of the lesson is to work beyond personal knowledge and thus beyond memory, to test that memory against the other evidence of the world. Memory will rarely match that other evidence very neatly, but this is a good thing for the writer. Discrepancy between memory and other evidence—like discrepancy between any researched "facts"—is not a problem. It's the point. The reckoning, the true story, lives in the space between the contradictions.

Bronwen Dickey—a journalist who writes for *Outside*, the *Oxford American*, *Newsweek*, and many other magazines—is alert to the challenge of finding out verifiable facts, the bedrock satisfaction of knowing something for sure. In researching *Pit Bull: The Battle over an American Icon*, she has come to regard the breed as "the world's biggest Rorschach test." Everyone she talks to is absolutely certain about "facts" that have absolutely no basis in reality. Even peer-reviewed medical journals turn out to be sourced from popular media, which have been sourced from urban legend or myth. "Never ever lose your sense of skepticism—benevolent skepticism, but skepticism," Dickey warns. "As a writer, the most important tool in your toolbox is the question: How do you know that?"

Whenever possible, track the information back to a primary source, then ask yourself: How reliable is that source? Whatever form this search for knowing takes, it is research. It becomes *creative* when the writer applies imagination and artfulness to the manner in which it is pursued—and then incorporated into the work. That is, the writer doesn't just Google a few facts or read a couple of books, but rather designs a research plan to get to the bottom of something in a profound way, then uses that knowledge to shape the form and content of the writing—not as mere decoration, but as deeply embedded, founding truth. Sometimes the very lexicon of the subject being researched becomes the language of the creative work.

In creative research, crucial and relevant information may be discovered in places where others forget to look, in sources that require some ingenuity to discover. Creative research is both a process and a habit of mind, an alertness to the human story as it lurks in unlikely places, in the forgotten words of witnesses, in the connections a sharp observer makes between two disparate caches of knowledge. So part of this book will be devoted to the practical skills of finding and acquiring relevant knowledge. And part will address the ways in which a writer can incorporate such knowledge into poems and stories, both factual and fictional, to make more profound art. Just as true suspense in a story is achieved by what the writer *reveals*, not *conceals*, the artistic use of facts, information, knowledge, and ideas can create dramatic tension; can infuse a line of poetry with authority and power; can endow a fictional character with absolute plausible authenticity. Deep and broad knowledge of the world can enlarge you as an artist, no matter what your chosen genre—and likely in the course of your writing life, you'll work in more than one.

To use all those ingredients, you first have to find them. The aim of this book is to help you figure out ways to find them.

FIRST PRINCIPLES

In writing this book, I have considered deeply the question of who can benefit from reading it. My answer is that I want to address writers at various stages of their careers. In my very long experience of teaching at large state institutions and at a small liberal arts college, leading conference workshops, writing for newspapers and magazines, as well as pursuing book-length projects and television and radio pieces, I have learned never to discount first principles. That is, over and over again, I have seen seasoned writers overlooking very basic matters, habits, and techniques that would seem to be no-brainers for anyone who has been writing for a while. Indeed, I have to remind myself constantly of the need to listen, to be fluent in whatever technology I plan to use, and so on. No matter how experienced a writer is, he or she should, from time to time, revisit first principles.

Likewise, it's clear that most younger writers—digital natives—don't need to be reminded to access social media, which of course changes constantly. Or at least to use it in familiar ways. But social media and Internet databases are revolutionizing culture and our access to it, and we need to be creative with it, to use it for more than the usual interactions. More important is that I have learned not to underestimate novice or undergraduate writers. Being a novice doesn't mean that a writer can't tackle an important or challenging subject. Undergraduate students of mine have frequently pursued challenging projects, and their success was as much a matter of their ingenuity and determination as any particular talent. And often they do this close to home. One recent student went searching among the archives in the local historical society and found the record of the first victim of the yellow fever epidemic in Wilmington, North Carolina, in 1862—a young seaman visiting a waterfront brothel. She also traced the young woman from the brothel, a Confederate officer who was having an affair with another local woman, a spy, and other real-life figures. Then she crafted a beautiful historical novel weaving together all their stories into an epic of love, tragedy, betrayal, and war.

Other undergraduates have sought out elderly family members and interviewed them in order to write memoirs, short stories, and poems. And while most of them can't afford to travel to pursue a story, plenty of them have incorporated research into trips they were taking anyway, on family vacations or semesters abroad, and this, too, is a good lesson for the writer: if you're going to be in an interesting place for other reasons, take advantage of the chance to find its stories.

Whatever project you are contemplating, start with a couple of simple precepts. First, variety of experience is your ally. There are lots of ways to do valuable research, and there is almost always more than one way to find out what you need to know. Second, you probably come to any new project knowing more than you realize—and part of your research is to figure out what you already know and how to use it. We'll talk more about this "narrative intelligence" later on in the chapter. And third, whether you are a total novice or an experienced writer, you need to dare a little—to push beyond your comfort zone.

There is—in my book at least—no such thing as a "student writer." Every writer is dead earnest about his or her project, and nobody cuts an inexperienced writer any slack—that writer must live up to the demands of the material. But it's also true that every writer is a student of his or her current project and must pay close attention to it, let it teach us what we need to know in order to tackle it.

Writers tend to be experienced in the various aspects of the craft to differing degrees. A memoirist might feel right at home baring secret thoughts but intimidated about interviewing a distant relative whose memories could illuminate her personal story. A seasoned reporter might know how to discover any elusive fact held in an archive but has never tried to fashion such facts into a narrative. A poet might be brilliant with language but scientifically illiterate. A novelist might have a well-honed sense of human ambition but lack an understanding of the social history that brought his characters to entertain such ambitions.

Like many young writers, I chose my original genre—fiction—too early and somehow absorbed the notion that writing short stories and novels meant sitting alone and consulting my imagination, to the exclusion of anything else. That doing what journalists call "reporting" (and I simply think of as "research") was somehow cheating, that it meant my imagination wasn't large enough to produce great stories out of my own genius. And it was true—my imagination wasn't yet large enough. But imagination isn't static. We aren't born with a certain finite amount, and that's that. Like talent and memory, imagination must be nurtured and cultivated through use. One way to apply imagination is to explore places, lives, events, subjects of all kinds that lie outside our direct personal experience. Deliberately venturing out into the world to learn its secrets fuels the imagination and enlarges it, creates a feedback loop as the knowledge you have gained catalyzes with your own native intelligence and leads you to further exploration of things and ideas. Your imagination grows and becomes more nimble. But I grant you, it can be daunting, especially the first time you take that big leap of faith and embark on a journey that may test your resources.

During the Solidarity revolution in Poland, I got a notion to see for myself how my grandfather's homeland was enjoying its new freedoms. I took a flier, queried a magazine, and drummed up an assignment for two long stories—one of them focused on locating any family who had survived World War II, the other exploring the national veneration of the Virgin Mary, a movement that had aided Pope John Paul II in breaking the hold of the communist government on his native country. I knew no one in Poland, couldn't speak the very difficult language, and was traveling on a very modest budget into a country where the national currency, the *zloty*, was in free fall. I was advised to carry cash in small denominations, so I stuffed a money belt with US$3,000 in tens and twenties. I took a deep breath and drove to New York, almost surprised to find that the promised airplane ticket was waiting for me at JFK airport.

I roamed the cities and countryside of Poland for ten days on slow trains and trams and in rattletrap private cars, walked the dark avenues of Warsaw and the shambles of the Gdańsk waterfront. Through a chance encounter with a stranger on a train, I located long-lost cousins; and through a translator, I interviewed members of Solidarity in their Gdańsk headquarters. I even saw Lech Walesa at his home. I was simply astonished at how well the trip had gone, how all the obstacles had somehow melted away, how I already had the two magazine stories in my notebook and a short story forming in my imagination.

When I returned from Poland, still jet-lagged, to the Bread Loaf Writers Conference in Vermont, I confided this to my longtime friend Bob Reiss, who has traveled every continent in search of material for both true stories and novels. He said, "Yeah, it's amazing, isn't it—how often the only difference between not doing something and doing it is *doing* it." It was a lesson I never forgot. We can hem and haw and make up all the reasonable excuses in the world—no contacts, lack of funds, hard to get time off work, don't speak the language, don't have any experience, can't get a publisher in advance so maybe the whole thing will wind up in my desk drawer—but in the end, if we want to pursue a story, for whatever reason, we can find a way. We can go where it lives and hunt it down and—as they say—bring it back alive.

NARRATIVE INTELLIGENCE

Remember, when you're at the very start of a project, any project, during that limbo moment when you're not sure whether to proceed, whether you'll remain interested long enough to see it through, whether the story or poem will even pan out: You do not begin in blank ignorance. You already have a store of what I call *narrative intelligence*. It is axiomatic that all writing is autobiographical—that is, it springs from the life experience and character of the writer. This is obviously true in memoir and personal essay, but the writer is equally if more subtly present in reportage and other kinds of third-person narrative, including and especially fiction. And the poet is certainly present in every line of his or her poem.

Tracy Kidder and Richard Todd ask and answer a basic question in *Good Prose: The Art of Nonfiction*: "What happens when you begin reading a book or an essay or a magazine story? If the writing is at all interesting, you are in search of the author. You are imagining the mind behind the prose. No matter how discreet or unforthcoming writers may be, they are present, and readers form judgments about them."

Narrative intelligence is my term for talking about the ineffable way in which an author inhabits a piece of writing, the way in which the work itself becomes an embodiment of personality in highly distinctive ways—or, occasionally and oddly, not at all. Narrative intelligence in this sense is the soul of the work. When we say we recognize the work of an author simply by reading his or her sentences, we are actually talking about something deeper than style that results in style. Narrative intelligence conveys the sense that the author is thinking below the lines, that the unfolding story is not merely a list of events, however vividly presented, not merely experience accurately recounted, nor merely a catalog of information, however useful, or vivid and original images; rather it is ballasted by a matrix of interlocking ideas, informed by a system of values, and carried along by an urgent logic, underpinned by a lifetime of knowledge—all of which is quite personal to the author, in sum as identifiable as a fingerprint.

So you don't start from scratch. You start with motivation that derives from your passions. You start with a set of skills and practical assets. Once you have settled on a subject, you can get to work in earnest.

FREEING THE WRITER

One of the great advantages of writing from research is that it frees us from the burden of our own self-consciousness. What I mean is that while devoting our attention to another subject—people, events, phenomena—we escape the constant scathing introspection that can bring on emotional exhaustion and a kind of paralysis that we mistake for writer's block. For the relatively inexperienced writer still getting control over basic elements of craft, as well as for the deeply introspective writer who regularly mines his or her own personal experience, writing from research can offer an emotional respite. That doesn't mean that the writer doesn't invest emotion in the subject, only that the investment is of a different kind—active empathy for other lives—that takes us out of ourselves in a useful way. When we come back into ourselves, we do so with a new perspective.

Instead of struggling to master both the meaning of his own life and the craft of fiction, say, a young writer can turn the focus of his craft away from his own life and toward another's—mastering storycraft but not simultaneously having to also master the deepest traumas of his own life. He can do that once he has more confidence in his craft. And in fact, I would argue, in so doing, he might very well come to terms with extremely personal issues by a side door, obliquely, since none of us can escape inhabiting the pages we write. Likewise the seasoned poet or memoirist who has spent years examining her own personal experience might lose her self-consciousness while exploring the lives of others in very unfamiliar circumstances—and in so doing discover a whole new vein of creative ore. Such a change of pace can refresh the imagination and spirit and, of course, whatever the apparent subject the writer engages, she is always also writing about herself. She is just finding a new part of herself, a new way of addressing her passions, through history or science or the biography of another.

As with any new activity, the very act of trying a new slant can jolt the writer into discoveries, unlock hidden talents. As a poet, you might never have conducted an interview—that's what *reporters* do, you say. Yet poetry is all about *voice* in every sense, and what better way to understand voice than by listening to the voices of others— their tone and cadence and idiom? It may turn out that you have great instincts as an interviewer. And cultivating the art of listening is about as good a way as I can think of to internalize the nuances of different voices.

As an essayist, you love ideas and events and might balk at examining, say, a budget—yet a budget is a statement of the values of whatever organization adopts it, as well as an expression of hope that the future will turn out according to a given prediction expressed in numbers. A budget is an expression of philosophy—ideas—and also a blueprint for future events. It expresses an ethical stance. It makes sense that we reveal our priorities by what we are willing to spend our money on—and how much: Battle tanks or famine relief? Affordable housing or a new sports stadium? A special education teacher or another administrator? You just have to practice reading such a dry document and learn to tease out its inherent drama. Once you have trained yourself to do that, you have essentially learned a whole new language with which to listen to stories. Likewise census data or medical statistics might make your eyes glaze over, yet these also express human truths: how many people were living in a given house in a certain year, what are the chances that a child will outlive infancy, the cash value of a teenaged female slave in 1860, and so on. Hidden in the numbers are real people and real experience, and with a little effort and patience you can unlock them and—just as important—connect them to other truths.

The kinds of tools found in any scientist's field bag—binoculars, magnifying glass, thermometer, scale, calipers, tape measure, and so on—might seem irrelevant to a novelist, until she finds herself examining an heirloom Victorian pendant she wants her character to wear, or determining her shoe size from a museum artifact, or knowing how much a whalebone corset weighs—all of which might be part of the intimate reality of her character. The true role of research is to help you discover what can be known about something, which can then shape how you think about it and value it—and ultimately how you explore its meaning in words. Like a detective, the good researcher follows where the evidence leads—without prejudice or assumptions. This is how we enlarge ourselves as writers and humane individuals.

So, in fact, there is an ethical dimension to the art of research. The literary researcher—no less than the scientist or historian—is committed to finding truth based on evidence rather than mere bias. We write our novels or essays or poems not simply to "prove" what we believe to be true but to venture into unknown territory, to test our beliefs and assumptions and knowledge on the laboratory of the page. The actual facts of the world are by turns remarkable, fascinating, troubling, frightening, and ennobling, and we honor them by writing factually, by writing fiction that creates scenarios in which those facts fuel drama or that explores alternatives to those facts, or by using the language of poetry to celebrate those facts in ways that can be uplifting, troubling, inspiring, challenging, and beautiful. And in ways that always enlarge the reader's vision of the world.

There is one important caveat: Research is an exciting and even seductive process. Indeed, one of the chief dangers is to fall into the temptation of continuing a line of research forever, never getting around to the actual writing of the creative piece. But among the many temptations available to the writer, it is probably the most useful, that creative tension between the urge to find out and the urgent need to disclose the discovery to the reader. Court that temptation, and then resist it.

LOOKING OUTWARD

The process of research begins with the act of lifting up your eyes and looking out at the world, of paying attention and noticing, of listening alertly, of practicing the habit of inquiry and investigation of common things that leads to uncommon discoveries. There are no boring facts—not once you learn to decode them. Remember: you do not begin in blank ignorance but with a formidable well of knowledge and experience waiting to be brought to bear on your project. And while it is true that much of what we do and know has little direct relevance to many of the projects we pursue, it's also true that pretty much everything we do in life, as well as everything we take the trouble to learn, somehow traces back to our governing passions, which are rooted in our identity—both the one we inherited (race, gender, ethnicity, age, family background) and the one we have cultivated (education, political philosophy, religion, taste, etc.).

So a useful first step calls for a little directed daydreaming— taking a kind of mental and emotional inventory of just who you are, what skills you possess, what experiences you have had, and how they might be linked to the project at hand. Sometimes the connections are obvious: you were given up for adoption as an infant, and for years you have longed to know who your birth mother is, what kind of family and background you sprang from. So it's no great stretch to understand your drive to pursue this story, to settle pressing questions of identity and origin. Or you were a competitive swimmer whose best memories include the bond between coach and athlete, and you feel powerfully drawn to put that experience into words— especially since you yourself are now a coach. In both cases, the writer has discovered not just motivating passions but also expertise: the first writer is an expert on being adopted, the second on what it's like to be on both sides of the athlete-coach relationship.

Other times the connection is hiding in plain sight—hidden from you, but perhaps obvious to anyone looking over your shoulder. You find yourself drawn to writing about an order of Catholic nuns, and it's clear to someone who knows you well that it's not religion or vows of chastity and poverty that have captured your imagination but the ideal of a community of shared values, the support of strong, humane, like-minded women for each other—because you grew up in a world of estranged brothers and a widowed father. And there are of course the projects that capture us heart and soul for no reason we can define until well into the work—maybe even after the work has been completed. Sometimes we never actually get to the bottom of our fascination, but we are forced to recognize it and reckon with it in the future.

The ethic informing every sentence of this book is simple: Don't write what you already know—write what you passionately want to find out about. This doesn't mean you must be wholly ignorant of a subject. On the contrary, the very fact that it intrigues you is a sign that you already know something about it—maybe even a lot. So what do you want to find out about? You haven't even begun researching—you're just daydreaming the thing into life, sneaking up on it before announcing yourself. Even so, you are starting with imagination, the key to everything.

Prompt #1: "See and Also Observe." Go through a familiar routine (drive to work, morning breakfast, interaction with friends). Notice at least three new things. Write them down, mull them over, and then write a couple of sentences about what thoughts these new facts inspire.

Prompt #2: "Personal Inventory." For a project you are considering, inventory your skills and experience, and list ten assets that can help you in your research. Then list ten potential drawbacks or obstacles from that same inventory. Next, identify ways in which the items on the first list can help you overcome the ones on the second.

Prompt #3: "Beyond a Shadow of a Doubt." Choose a "fact" and devise a way to prove it beyond a shadow of a doubt. A fact can be defined as any material element of a narrative—a detail, an action, an event, spcken words, a piece of environmental or historical or personal context, and so on. This fact should have three qualities:

1. It is not trivial but rather matters to your larger project. It may be that a seemingly trivial fact—for example, the color of a woman's hat—takes on significance in a specific context, such as a murder trial, and if so this kind of fact is fair game.
2. It is not conveniently documented in the public domain. That is, it did not occur in the light of public scrutiny, on audio- or videotape, or in some other manner that leaves no doubt about the essential nature of the fact. Remember that a fact can occur in front of many witnesses, including technologically advanced monitors, and still be in dispute.
3. It was not witnessed personally by you.

2 PREPARING A RESEARCH PLAN

Maybe most important, this research journey has imbued me
with a commitment to the project. No longer a vague "someday"
idea, my novel is now a living, breathing work-in-progress.
—Diane Sorensen, fiction writer

Being artistic and making a plan are not incompatible. In fact, the great painters of history typically made numerous studies of important works before they settled on exactly the approach they would take. Sculptors make numerous drawings and scale models. So it's clear that the writing itself—the art—can profit from a plan. If it's worth doing, it's worth planning to do. Think of the research as part of the artistic process, and it makes sense to plan it—knowing, of course, that all plans are provisional, subject to change based on surprise and circumstance.

We often imagine research as directed toward finding out a particular set of facts. But research can be free-form—that is, not simply directed to find a specific fact or detail for a predetermined use. An interview might indeed yield the anticipated profile or personal portrait, but it also might inform your own personal biography with, say, a facet of your parents' life that you didn't know. So research isn't just a tool in service of a given piece of writing. The very act of research can lead you in creative directions, can help you discover not just a subject worth writing about but a way of writing about it. Research opens rather than narrows the writing process. It can inspire a new piece of fiction, poetry, or creative nonfiction. So think about research not just as a process for informing a preconceived project with an authentic underpinning—which it often is—but also as one that can yield a new approach, a whole new subject even, and actually inspire the artistic process in a new direction. Thus you want to form a plan that has a chance to do that: it will have specific objectives, but whether or not those are met, it is bound to yield something interesting and probably surprising.

Before you come up with an elaborate research plan, it's often useful to play around a bit with various possible subjects, seeing if one or another sustains your interest. Sometimes a promising subject turns out to be too small or limited to keep your passion for it, or you realize it cannot sustain a whole book and must be contained in a shorter work—which is fine. But it may affect how much time, money, and emotional energy you are willing to expend on it. Or you quickly discover that there is very little information out there in the world that you can reasonably discover, or that your access is blocked in some insurmountable way—by an individual, an organization, a government. Especially if you are planning a long project—a book, a long-form narrative, or a cycle of poems—you want to plumb the subject a bit before you commit yourself to it for weeks, months, or even years. Make sure it will hold up. Reassure yourself that the archives you can tap will likely yield useful stuff. Do some casual browsing on the Internet or at a library. Push and tug the subject a little, testing its durability, its sustaining interest. Consult any acquaintances who may be helpful, and see if they can provide any leads. You're not yet committed to anything, so you can browse as much as you like and walk away from the project at any time without remorse.

This phase constitutes a kind of foundational research—seeing what's out there, where the information is located, how easy or hard it will be to access, who has been there ahead of you. Check out online booksellers to find out what's been written lately about your subject. Especially if you're working in nonfiction, this is crucial: if one or two prominent books have been published in the last two years addressing exactly what you want to explore, then your chances of finding a receptive publisher are diminished. This point would also seem to be true for short-form works, but not always. If lots of people are writing about the dangers of addiction to prescription opioids, say, that could signal a demand for pieces on that subject, at least up to a point. Short-form pieces are more perishable in every sense.

FINDING YOUR PASSION AND YOUR SUBJECT

Let's pause to consider how to define "subject." It may be very specific public event: a crime that shocked a community; a moment of athletic triumph; a groundbreaking political maneuver. Or it may be an event that is quite personal: your mother's decision to give up her first child for adoption; the suicide of a close friend; the summer afternoon when your brother, a lifeguard, saved a drowning swimmer.

But your subject also may be much more general, at least at first. You may be interested in how fine furniture is made, or what goes on in a hospital emergency room, or whether there are any authentic cowboys left in the West. You may—for reasons you cannot yet articulate—harbor a latent interest in the circus, Irish dancing, hip-hop culture, the history of money, how gay high school kids coped in the 1950s, what became of all the polio kids living in iron lungs, epidemics in general, the culture of makeup and cosmetics, punk music, your Cuban heritage, and so on and on.

At the outset of a project, it's okay, even desirable, to cast a broad net. Part of what you will do first in this early stage is to *locate yourself inside the subject*. This means two things. First, you will immerse yourself in it enough to gain a general knowledge of its scope and depth. You'll read some books or articles that provide an overview, tap the brain of anyone you know who is connected to your subject, look at pictures and video—in short, consult any readily available source that can teach you the basics of the subject you are planning to pursue.

At this stage you are not ready to invest a great deal of money or time—you're just setting a foundation in place. Having already determined that there's no recent book that covers the same ground you plan to cover, you can begin the process of imagining where your work might fit into the general literature of this subject, what new special insight it might contribute. This will happen on nobody's schedule but your own. That is, sometimes we noodle around with a subject for months or years before committing to it. Other times, a few hours or days are all it takes to arrest our whole attention and give us our bearings.

I believe this schedule is driven in some important way by the second aspect of locating yourself in the subject: *finding yourself in it*. As writers, we are curious beings, but all of us are curious about different things, and that curiosity is usually rooted deeply in our individual life experience and our natures. The task is to drill down through the various layers to locate the root of your passion. For example, a writer I knew once said he wanted to write about minor league baseball stadiums. All well and good, but why? Well, he said, some of them are very picturesque ballparks, and in them you can get closer to the action. There are no bad seats in a minor league ballpark. It's much more like the old days, before sports got to be such a corporate megabusiness. Again, all well and good, but that simple nostalgia didn't explain the passion he was clearly bringing to the project. He then described how gratifying it was to see fathers and sons—sometimes also grandfathers—all together, rooting for their home team. So now we had gone from a picturesque sports experience to heartfelt nostalgia to families united across generations. He made one more leap: really, he would be writing about his own experience as a son and father, how as a son he had missed the kind of father-son experience he witnessed at all those quaint minor league ballparks, how hard he was striving to be a good father himself. So his apparent subject was minor league ballparks, but that was only a way of getting his arms around matters that were much more profound and universal. He had located himself inside his subject.

Sometimes this recognition of your location inside the subject is elusive and doesn't come right away—maybe it comes only once you are very far along into the project. You just can't predict. All you can do is keep on peeling back layers, looking at your subject from different angles, letting it work on you until your passion reveals itself. At the point when you are firmly located inside your subject, you can write with a kind of relaxed confidence that comes with self-knowledge. Thomas French, a narrative journalist who teaches at Indiana University, says, "Sometimes there's a pattern in your choices that you don't see when you're making them. Like I found out much later in my reporting life that I was drawn to writing about people who get back up." So whatever his purported subject was, he was also writing about the resilient human spirit, the stubborn refusal to stay down. You can review your own work periodically to see what patterns, if any, emerge, clues to your ongoing interest in certain themes.

A SIMPLE PLAN

At the point when you decide to pursue a subject in earnest, it can be useful to make a research plan, especially if you are relatively new to the research process. Don't make this too complicated—better to have a simple plan that you will actually follow than a perfect detailed one that you won't. Start by asking some basic questions—the kind of questions that are so basic we often forget to ask:

- What do I need to find out?
- Why do I want to know it?
- Who knows what I want to know, and how can I find them?
- Where is the information I need located, and how can I access it?
- What are the obstacles to finding out what I need to know?
- How do I plan to use it? What form might it take on the page?

Sometimes the answer to the last question is obvious from the start, but other times the answer might be "I don't know exactly—I'll wait and see how the story wants to be told, what it teaches me along the way. Then I'll know what form it will take."

Next, formulate a simple research plan in three parts:

- Draft a timeline, realistically projecting the duration of research and specific dates on which you can devote yourself to pursuing it. This should take into account other obligations, interruptions for work or family responsibilities, the duration of a college semester, etc.
- Locate specific tasks to accomplish along that timeline: published works to consult, archives to visit, interviews to conduct and transcribe, a place or activity to experience, even time off to review your notes and recharge your emotional batteries.
- Budget for the anticipated costs, both direct and indirect: travel and meals, tools or equipment, fees, time off work, child care, etc. If you're pursuing the project as part of a class or independent study, realize that it might draw time and effort away from other challenging classes, perhaps present scheduling conflicts. Sometimes there are special fees or insurance requirements for students pursuing field projects, so find out what they are in advance.

Let's say, for example, you want to write about the circus—as I once did. When I was a young reporter, I was invited by the Clyde Beatty–Cole Bros. Circus to perform a couple of shows as a clown. I'd get a feature story that the circus people hoped would generate publicity for the show. Many years later, I went in search of that circus again to write about its head clown, Jimmy James, who had trained me in basic clown-craft and rose to become ringmaster. Maybe you're interested in how the elephants and other performing animals are treated, or who the people are who swing on the trapeze and walk the high-wire, or how a lion tamer is trained, or maybe even why the circus still exists at all, in our age of digital magic and gargantuan theme parks.

It's early spring, say, the start of the touring season. You do some basic browsing on the Internet and find out that a circus will perform in a town four hours away from your home three weeks from now. You begin your timeline next week and give yourself two weeks to do some basic reading on the history of the circus. You locate the public relations agent for the circus, headquartered in Florida, through the circus's website, introduce yourself, and explain your project in an e-mail. The agent writes back that you should arrive at the circus grounds three hours in advance of the performance and she will arrange an interview with the head clown and the ringmaster. You can tour the back lot with a guide. She also sends you some promotional and background literature on the circus.

Your timeline might continue with a trip to the circus museum in Baraboo, Wisconsin, the following week (it just happens to be a vacation week for you). Again using the Internet, you find out what is in the museum, what are its hours of operation, and so on. You contact the curator and arrange for an interview. So far, so good. Maybe that's all you need to plan for at present. You've got dates, and you've got tasks: whom you will interview, what you will observe, time scheduled for transcribing your interviews.

Now figure out costs. If you need to drive to the circus, calculate mileage or fuel cost (MapQuest, Google Maps, or any of a number of other programs can help you both map the route and calculate fuel costs). Any tolls? You'll likely need a hotel for the night, unless you want to drive four hours home after a long day, so add that in. You'll probably need some meals. Figure in the admission cost, even though they might waive it. What about the museum trip? Does that require an airplane ticket? Add in travel, meals, and finally some funds to cover miscellaneous costs, often unexpected: photocopies, a useful book from the gift shop, fixing a flat tire. And don't forget other costs. If you don't have a digital recorder (we'll discuss tools of the trade in the next chapter), maybe now is the time to buy one—or at least upgrade to a smartphone that has a good voice app (and test it—some are not very useful at all). Are there any indirect costs? Oh, yeah—you need a dog sitter for two nights, and you'll miss one shift waiting tables. Maybe you can trade for another shift and so not lose a whole night's tips.

Common sense and some forethought can yield practical knowledge about how to structure and budget the experience of research so that it yields what you need and leads to a creative work. The research plan is a drama all its own, with its own promise and payoff. Good preparation can help you succeed while having a memorable and even inspiring experience that may lead to other writing projects—just as my first piece on clowning led ultimately to a much later follow-up that was focused in a very different way: I went in search of Mr. James and was on hand for the last season during which the roustabouts used elephants to raise the Big Top, an amazing spectacle of choreographed animal muscle.

Your plan is likely to need constant updating, but that's okay. Maybe the circus performance for that city is canceled at the last minute because of a tornado watch and you have to drive to another place farther away a month later. Maybe the clown is in a rotten mood the day of your visit, and you wind up interviewing a tightrope walker instead. So prepare yourself to improvise. Just plant the thought in your head that *something interesting* is going to happen. Maybe it will be exactly what you have planned—or maybe a sudden storm will cancel the performance. But one way or another, you'll come home with something to write about. So relax and relinquish a little control to circumstances. Recall John Steinbeck's opening observation in *Travels with Charley*: "We find after years of struggle that we do not take a trip; a trip takes us."

LETTING THE TRIP TAKE YOU

This is good news. You are not driving the bus; you are along for the ride. You have planned as much as you are able. You have done your homework. You have packed whatever tools you think you'll need. You have already allocated the time and the budget. And you have your wits about you, your senses on high alert. In any case, the plan gives you an armature to build on, a kind of scaffold on which you can stand to pursue your project with some confidence that it will pan out.

During the wars in Iraq, Kirsten Holmstedt—then a graduate student and small-town journalist—started wondering about the lives of American women who, for the first time in history, were deployed to the front lines of combat. Each woman warrior she found led her to others, and while holding down a full-time job—working nights, weekends, and holidays—Holmstedt made a plan to seek out each one. She made connections via e-mail, sat in kitchens on military bases, chalked up hours of phone conversations. Then she went aboard the ships they served on, strapped herself into the cockpit of a fighter jet one of them flew, watched an Al-Qaeda video of one of them being blown up by an IED while driving convoy duty—with the wounded veteran herself.

Holmstedt never expected to achieve such intimate access, but through diligent and imaginative research, she was able to write their stories: *Band of Sisters: American Women at War in Iraq.* Holmstedt's experience points out one really important truth about the process: big things start small. Don't be intimidated by the scope of your project or overwhelmed by its complexity. The first contact leads to the second, and so on. The first fact yields another, and that takes you to a new area of inquiry, on and on to the end. Your plan is a guide, as much a work-in-progress as whatever you write from it.

Holmstedt is not the first writer to be amazed at where the journey of research can lead. Even I have been lifted out of my quiet life into remarkable experiences. Besides performing with the circus, I've jumped out of helicopter with amphibious marines, listened to a federal judge in a Philadelphia courtroom deliver a ruling on a landmark school desegregation case, cinched Brahma bulls in a rodeo, steered a replica 1812 era schooner in a minor gale at sea, loaded and fired a Revolutionary era musket, patrolled Times Square with the Guardian Angels, shared beers with rollicking Polish soldiers on the overcrowded night train to Warsaw, rode an elephant at a logging camp in northern Thailand, listened to a choir of Hmong village kids singing at their school, sampled legal and illegal moonshine, and rode along with cops on high-speed calls to armed robberies.

Other research is less about immersion in experience and more about immersion in paper archives—for example, in some of the kinds of archives discussed in chapter 4. You may need to closet yourself in a special collections library and pore over letters, old newspapers, police reports, land deeds, court transcripts—as Carrie Hagen did in discovering the bizarre facts of the first kidnapping for ransom in U.S. history (*We Is Got Him: The Kidnapping That Changed America*).

Some research, of course, is accidental or simply accrued through life experience, but you can also shape an intentional research experience to address family projects and personal memoir. In writing about her experiences working in an inner-city African American funeral home during her teenaged years, Sheri Booker drew on vivid memories gained over several years of hands-on work—including tense times when handling arrangements for gang victims. But she also interviewed her mother and other family members, as well as an embalmer—since she herself had never performed that particular task. All of it informs *Nine Years Under: Coming of Age in an Inner-City Funeral Home*.

A different project might require that you interview a person in jail, or in a far-flung rural place, or on a literal journey. The interview—and we'll talk extensively about the art of the interview in chapter 7—may be a one-shot conversation, or it might require multiple installments over time. Some projects will require extensive travel and planning for it: Who's going to water the plants while you're gone? How about your day job? Will it cost you vacation days? Maybe some portion of your research will be conducted in the comfort of your home or office, using the Internet, Skype, FaceTime, cell phone, e-mail, texting, and all the other high-tech avenues of connection.

One of the most interesting days of research I ever had was spent sitting at the dining room table of the home where I grew up and interviewing my own father with a tape recorder. I was in my late twenties, and he was nearing sixty. We had been tiptoeing up to this moment for years, when I would be mature enough to see him not just in relation to myself, as *my* father, but as a poor boy who grew to manhood during a desperate and thrilling time, who had a whole previous life that didn't include me but did include a colorful hardscrabble boyhood on the wrong side of the tracks in an immigrant neighborhood, who had a job in the regional Civilian Conservation Corps, then a stint in the Army Air Corps on Oahu, Saipan, and Okinawa during World War II. The novel inspired by our talk sits on my shelf, unpublished, but the interview also turned into a radio essay, and the lesson was worth every hour of writing: sometimes starting at home, in the place where you live with the people you love, can lead you to the far reaches of the world.

Imagine the research you need, then figure out a realistic way to pursue it—so you can make it come true on the page. And always have a Plan B. Robin Hemley based his book *Do-Over!*—in which he revisits key occasions of his life and takes another try at them—on a simple plan. "For me, a do-over wasn't a correcting of karmic imbalance, though there was some of that. It wasn't always a matter of my choices, my wrongdoings either. It was a matter of roadblocks. What were the roadblocks in my life that I had never completely negotiated?" He would reprise those events that in some way remained unfinished business, moments when he wished he had done things differently, and this time he would try to get them right: prom night, a school play, taking a standardized test, summer camp, even kindergarten. "After I created my list," he writes, "I resolved, when possible, to do over the original event in its original place, though this wouldn't always be feasible." He had to balance out the need to continue meeting the obligations of his teaching job with the need to experience extended moments in some far-flung places.

Diane Sorensen faced the same issues while still an MFA student in search of her Danish immigrant ancestors for a novel based on their adventures in America. She writes, "Given my other classes and responsibilities, I couldn't go until April 10th, which compressed all of the travel and work for the interview and final assignments into 20 days. But I'd planned to go to Nebraska anyway, only during summer break. So I took the plunge and booked the tickets." Her deadline happened to be for a class, but it could just as well have been for an editor. "I was in a bit of a panic about making the best possible use of my time while I was there. After all, it took five days out of schoolwork time, and it cost nearly $1,500 to go and take my husband, Doug (for moral support and driving assistance). I didn't want to waste any of it. I put together an itinerary, which included far more than we could possibly do in five days, but it gave us choices. We ended up doing most of it."

In my research classes, I insist that each of my students not only designs a research experience—a plan that includes a timeline for finding out what they need to know, where they need to go to find it, whom they need to talk to, and what form the final project might take—but also a detailed budget: Will they miss work and lose wages? Do they need to buy a plane, train, or bus ticket? Will they need local transportation—a rental car, taxis, subway fare? How about gas money and tolls? A hotel room? Are there supplies or equipment they will need to buy—special clothing, a recorder, gifts for a host? Any fees to enter historic sites, national parks, or museums? Will they need to hire a translator, a fixer, a backcountry guide? How about photocopy costs at archives? Internet access? For various writing projects, I have bought items as diverse as the following: special boots, recording equipment, a kayak, a Civil War officer's cap, a sextant, a money belt, boxes of cigars to trade, Moleskine notebooks, travel adapters for electronics, dry bags, a digital camera, a photojournalist's vest, a Colt .45 Peacemaker, even oceangoing foul weather gear.

There is a cost to research, and you may as well acknowledge it up front and prepare to pay it, or else figure out how to cut some of the cost. Planning for the cost will remove a lot of anxiety from the experience and allow you to be as cost-efficient as possible. So, for instance, for a certain book I needed a document located at the Dwight D. Eisenhower Presidential Library in Abilene, Kansas. I couldn't justify a plane ticket, taxi, meals, and a couple of days in a hotel for just one document, so I got in touch with one of the archivists, who graciously found me the document and mailed me a photocopy. And not only that, he included in his package copies of several other related documents he thought might interest me—and which I didn't even know existed and that proved extremely valuable to my project—all for zero cost.

SPECULATIVE RESEARCH

Bob Reiss, who writes both fiction and nonfiction, talks about the difference between researching for the respective genres. For nonfiction, he usually wants to conduct all his research—or at least as much as possible—before writing the book, then check facts and follow up on issues that come up in the writing. "But for speculative fiction, the kind I write," he says, "you're trying to come up with something nobody's thought of before. So if you just go on what has already happened, you're going to learn that it never happened. But that's the whole point—to find out a way that it *could* happen."

Reiss plotted a thriller called *Salt Maker* on the premise that the president of the United States is being tried for treason because he refuses to launch nuclear missiles against the Soviet Union after early warning systems indicate that the Soviets have launched a missile at the United States. To make sure his scenario was plausible, he sought out two experts on constitutional law: Samuel Dash, former Chief Counsel for the Senate Watergate Committee, and Alan Dershowitz, the famous First Amendment champion and constitutional lawyer. These were cold calls—he didn't personally know either man. Both of them gave him all the reasons why such a trial would never happen. But Reiss was dogged and called back several times. He tried several different scenarios for triggering such an event, but each time the experts told him it could never happen. Then, after months of such back-and-forth, he called Dash and ran the newest scenario by him. "There was a long pause, and then in a little voice, he told me, 'Well, that could happen.'" When Reiss called Dershowitz, he thought he sounded annoyed that Reiss was still pursuing the original premise. "I ran it by him," Reiss says. "There was a long pause on the other end of the phone, then he said, '*That* could happen.'" His point is that an author who is trying to create an alternative world, to posit how things work in that world—in this case the world in which a sitting president is on trial for treason, something that has never happened in history—he or she cannot simply take the word of experts. Research may actually hinder the creative process until the writer has a specific scenario to test, a hypothetical reality that never happened but is not just possible but plausible.

So research is not just about what has *already* happened, established facts and historical events. It's also about how to combine facts into new ways of understanding the world—whether it is speculating on the "what ifs" of history or extrapolating from settled knowledge into future events. All the most remarkable events of history—which seem so comprehensible in retrospect—seemed utterly unpredictable at the time. The *Titanic* sunk on her maiden voyage? Preposterous. Pearl Harbor attacked on a peacetime Sunday morning? Never happen. Commercial aircraft hijacked and used as missiles to take down the World Trade Center and the Pentagon on the same day? A bad movie script. Yet in retrospect, all those horrific events seem eminently predictable. So that's another lesson of research: it matters what you're researching *for*.

ACCESS—THE KEY

One key component of your plan, naturally, is *access*, which usually means locating a person who can take you inside the subject in some crucial way: an eyewitness, a person who participated in the event, the gatekeeper of a vital archive, or an expert who can be your "rabbi" or guide to the world you want to explore.

Michelle Boyajian had the germ of an idea for a novel in which a mentally handicapped young man goes on trial for killing one of his caregivers, whom he loves, for a noble but mistaken reason. How would guilt be assigned? *Lies of the Heart* turned out to be a complex and fascinating tale of mistaken perceptions and tragically misguided actions. She knew she would have to write a very convincing narrative of the young man's trial, but she was not herself an attorney and knew very little about criminal law—especially as it applied to the mentally handicapped. She recounts the role serendipity played in setting her on the right track. She was working out at her health club one day and talking about her project with the brother of the local district attorney, Ben David, who also happened to have a membership at her club. "I met his brother at the gym," she recalls. "He said, 'You should really talk to Ben.' And then he said those magic words: 'He's about to start a murder trial.'" She was able not just to witness a murder trial but to have access to the expertise of the prosecutor and his team in understanding what she was seeing, at every step of the long process. She was after authenticity, and she knew she couldn't fake it. She'd have to write from exact knowledge. "I don't want to be the lawyer who watches a lawyer show and gets disgusted, or the medical student who watches *Scrubs* and gets pissed off," she says. "I wanted it to be authentic."

Gaining access can be one of the most daunting challenges of beginning any project—most often not because gaining access is so hard, but because even experienced writers may *think* it is so hard. Now, of course, there are going to be occasional cases in which access turns out to be impossible: the person at the heart of the story simply refuses to talk to you, or the government records you need are top secret. But those tend to be outliers, unusual cases. Mostly the keys to access are two: *First, ask for it—nicely.* This step presumes that you have identified someone to ask, and that person may or may not be obvious. So always keep in mind step two: *Be persistent and patient.* You may get passed from one person to another. You may have to call or e-mail twenty people before you find the first one who is at all helpful.

If you don't know where to start, start somewhere. Boyajian could have visited the office of the clerk of court to find out if any murder trials were on the docket, and, except in rare cases, criminal trials are open to the public. She could have called the District Attorney's office and requested an interview, during which she could have laid out her project and asked for his help. Sometimes a lower-level person in the office can assist you or steer you to someone else who can. Be courteous but be persistent. Ask politely—again and again. Be prepared to provide some kind of credentials—a copy of something else you've written to assure the person that you are not out to write a hatchet job. A website or social network site that lists professional credentials and affiliations and perhaps includes a link to other publications can help establish your bona fides.

While in Boston to research Paul Revere for a novel, I wanted to climb to the top of the Old North Church so I could set a scene there on the night of his famous ride to warn the Middlesex militias in 1775 that the British regulars were marching out of Boston on a surprise raid. Revere arranged for the sexton, Robert Newman, to hang either one or two lanterns in the church tower when the British marched. To the Sons of Liberty watching from Charlestown, one lantern would indicate the soldiers were marching out by Boston neck—the long way—and two lanterns that they were crossing in boats to Cambridge—the short route. The signal would get the word across the river to other Patriots, whether Revere himself made it safely out of the city or not. It was his Plan B.

The guide told me that the church tower was closed to the public. I asked to see her boss, who also politely said it was closed. I asked to see his boss, and when I explained my project, she personally escorted me all the way to the top, climbing the ever-narrowing series of stairs and ladders in her high heels. At the top she opened the windows onto a breathtaking vista of Boston Harbor and Back Bay that I could never have imagined in its strategic grandeur. There laid out below was the entire landscape of Revere's ride, with Bunker Hill—the final refuge for the British regulars after their bloody rout from Concord—just across the water. The tower provided, quite literally, a new panoramic point of view on the action.

Divers have a saying to keep them safe in the water: *Plan your dive, then dive your plan.* This doesn't mean you stick foolishly to a preconceived itinerary. Just the opposite: working from a clear plan, you are in a better position to improvise and innovate when circumstances change, because you have actually envisioned the enterprise in advance. If you don't have a plan, how can you know when things are working out according to plan, or veering wildly off track? Anticipate the adventure as much as you can, ever ready to go to your backup plan.

Prompt #4: "Plan Your Dive." Prepare a simple plan and budget for a research project. This should include a *timeline*, specified *tasks* to accomplish along that timeline, and the anticipated direct and indirect *costs* you will bear.

3 THE TOOLS
OF THE TRADE

The train stopped yet again on the south side of Cheyenne.
And here, for the first time, I appreciated what a profound
difference it made to ride a freight train with a smartphone.
Google Maps let us see exactly where we were relative to
both yards. —Ted Conover, *"Rolling Nowhere*, Part Two"

Good researchers start with not just a plan but a well-stocked tool-box. They may reach for different tools for different projects, or at different stages of the same project, but they come prepared for what they expect to encounter so they don't have to rely on memory alone. Your first big tool is of course the habit of *noticing*, of paying attention. It's a habit you can practice very moment of every day—being present and aware of what is going on around you: what people are saying, what the landscape or cityscape looks like, what's ordinary or unusual, what the weather is doing. Beyond that, your choice of tools will depend on what you need to accomplish in your research. Some likely tools and their uses:

- Interviewing: a notebook, pen, and highlighter; a digital sound re-corder; a camera to photograph the subject and the surroundings (recorder and camera—including video capability—are likely to be avail-able on any smartphone.)
- Archival work with manuscripts, letters, other documents: a magnify-ing glass or reading glasses available at any drugstore (indispensable

in reading cursive handwriting and discerning the hidden detail in a photograph); a laptop or tablet to make notes (pens are typically not allowed in special collections; the alternative is to use pencil and paper, which means you have to type all your notes later); a portable scanner (if allowed—this will vary based on the nature of the document and the particular archive, and sometimes a photo can serve; the alternative is to request and pay for either electronic scans furnished by the archive or physical photocopies).

- Observation of exterior or interior site: binoculars (for closing distance); measuring tape (scaled to your project—a crime scene might require a 20-foot tape, while a larger space might require a laser measure, if you want to know exact dimensions, or even a pedometer when walking any distance; measuring small objects might be done with just a six-inch scale etched into the handle of a Leatherman or similar tool, or a cheap ruler).
- General purpose: a telescoping walking stick (useful for establishing scale in photographs); a calculator (for converting currency, metric to decimal, etc.; also calculating all the amounts, sums, percentages, dimensions, etc., that inform a story and figuring out how best to relate them to the reader); a Leatherman or similar tool (which can open any battery case and fix just about anything); good maps of all sorts (both a source and a tool—for guiding you through the physical topography of a story).

Let's walk through some ideas for using these and other tools in your research.

THE TOOLS OF TECHNOLOGY

Many good writers still work with just a notebook and pen—old school. This may seem anachronistic in our digital age, or maybe a signal that the writer is too set in his ways to adapt to changing technology. But, in fact, I know a lot of younger writers who are finding that in some situations the old-fashioned notebook is the most reliable and useful way to create a record that won't be accidently erased, doesn't rely on a battery charge, fits into a pocket, can survive a drenching, and can be accessed anywhere. But technological tools can offer many advantages, and a good researcher learns how to use them effectively. Let me begin with the caveat that technology changes all the time, too fast, in fact, for even this book to remain a reliable guide to which digital tool or website best serves the writer. But you will want to pay attention to new devices, programs, or apps that can support your work, and while not being beguiled by every new gadget that comes along, choose those that can genuinely improve the quality of your research.

Electronic tools have the virtue of miniaturizing your toolbox—giving you less to carry. In pre-digital days, I would routinely carry a whole camera bag full of fresh film and extra lenses and batteries. Now even my smartphone has a high-quality lens with zoom capability and can hold hundreds of digital photos. And I can upload them to program such as Evernote remotely (more on that later). Likewise, I don't need to carry a separate calculator—each of my devices has one built in. The iPad gives me high-resolution photographs and video, as well as the means to communicate remotely with family or sources using Skype. I wear a watch not specifically to keep time (my smartphone is more accurate) but because it also has a dual stopwatch, a tide clock, a compass, a differential barometer, even an altimeter. In fact, if you carry around a smartphone or some sort of tablet, you are already holding most of the basic tools you'll need. You can download free voice recording apps for your phone, though not all are created equal and they change all the time, so try out the app before you rely on it for a crucial interview.

If you are recording for broadcast, you're probably going to need a higher-quality recorder than your smartphone—best to work from the end-use backward. Sound quality for a blog or other Internet use can be lower than for, say, radio, though this is changing fast and it is likely that before long such consumer-grade devices will provide broadcast-quality sound. The same is true of photographs. The quality varies greatly both with the device and the settings you choose on the device, so do your homework. If you are photographing, as I do, mainly so that you can sharpen your memory weeks or months after conducting the research, go for the convenience of the device. One advantage of a smartphone is that we carry them everywhere without a second thought, so ours is likely to be available when a surprising opportunity arises. (I carry mine in a shatterproof Otter case that clips to my belt).

But if the photo is intended for publication, it will have to have a high resolution, and you need to know ahead of time what that standard is and if your device can meet it. And it will matter how much you plan to enlarge your photos for viewing, what level of sharpness and detail you'll require, since low-resolution photos degrade considerably when you enlarge them. Typically, publications require a PPI (pixels per inch—a measure of the resolution of the printed image) of 300. So if, for instance, you plan to blow up the pictures as big as possible in search of hidden elements—an animal or bird camouflaged in the undergrowth, the lettering on a railroad car a hundred yards in the distance—you have one answer. (I used a digital Sony to collect photos for a book chronicling a journey down the Cape Fear River, and one photo, taken in the wetlands of a rice plantation, clearly revealed an alligator lurking in the weeds a hundred yards away— invisible while I was actually on the scene.) If all you want is a general sense of the place, of color and weather, maybe the shape of a particular storefront or architectural feature, you have another answer.

If you plan to publish the photo of a person or use his or her recorded voice, you'll want to get permission. A signed release for the photo is usually sufficient. For audio or video, having the person agree on record to being recorded for publication or broadcast is generally acceptable, though you should check in advance with whatever site or broadcast outlet is going to use the material to make sure you meet its standards. Whenever practicable, I ask my interviewee if I can take his or her photograph. Then when I am sitting at my desk a month later listening to the recorded interview, I have the person's face to match with the voice. And when I write about him or her, I don't have to rely on memory or notes that always turn out to be missing some crucial physical detail to describe their appearance, their eye color or hair, the way they smile or grimace, their posture and dress. There are less obvious but equally effective ways to use certain tools. Photographing a historical plaque might save you the trouble of copying down a long notation and, more importantly, it might free you to pay better attention to your surroundings or the person you are interviewing.

MAPPING THE ACTION

Remember that a setting is a stage of action, not just window dressing. It's the stage on which actors—real or invented—will move through their encounters with each other. When you go to write the story, whatever it is, you'll want to block out the action, just as if you were directing a theatrical play or a movie, and this spatial sense will be critical to making the scene clear and real. This is apparent on, say, a battlefield, but no less important in a living room where a husband physically abused his wife: Where was the furniture? What could she duck behind for protection? Where were her avenues of escape? Where was the child (you?) watching from?

Even the inside of a small space like the back of a truck has its own geography. In order to portray the artists of deception who broadcast bogus high-fidelity sound effects of tanks to panic German listening posts in World War II, I needed to re-create what they actually did: What did they touch? How did they manipulate the equipment? And so on. I routinely called one of my sources, who had ridden for months in the back of a half-track—which had front tires and rear tracks like a tank—operating the equipment on the night battlefields of Europe. He had to be able to do it all in pitch-darkness. I would phone him and say, "Close your eyes—now reach left. What's there? Tell me what you are doing with your hands? Which way are you facing? Where are the other guys sitting? What do you hear?" And he would oblige, going away in his imagination to that little steel space he occupied sixty-odd years ago and walking me through every movement, every detail, he could recall—using both intellectual memory and muscle memory.

Space can be captured visually in images and also in maps. Think of existing spatial representations as tools in your research kit, and also consider making some of your own. The first thing I do when I arrive anywhere new on a research project is to grab all the local maps I can find, including and especially the hand-drawn amateur kind. I often invite interviewees to draw maps to illustrate the stories they tell me—who was standing where, next to whom, where the intruder entered from, and so on. Sometimes the map will reveal that the story they are telling is physically impossible—it simply couldn't have happened the way they claim. Other times it will reveal resonant details that weren't in the narrative of the story.

The World War II soldiers of deception routinely drafted maps of their "shows" in advance of an operation, then drew other maps afterward as part of their debriefing. Many of these men were professional artists, so their maps are astonishing not just for their accuracy but also for their beauty. They presented me with a large hand-printed color map they created after the war detailing their entire campaign from D-day to the end of the fighting—a gorgeous graphic outline of their collective story.

Before beginning my paddle of the Cape Fear River, I "ran" the whole 200-mile course many times on Google Earth Maps, scouting rapids and landings, noting county lines and intersecting roadways, memorizing bridges and other landmarks, and in general educating myself about the relationship of the river to the countryside, towns, and cities it passes through—much of which is invisible from the river behind thick foliage or high banks.

Diane Sorensen, in researching her ancestors who settled in what was then the frontier of Nebraska, pored over maps of counties and the sections into which they were divided. She wanted her novel to be firmly—and accurately—rooted in the land they farmed. Then she marked where each of her family members had settled on that map—the sons and daughters and grandchildren of the original settlers. She discovered an astonishing fact: if she drew a circle around any homestead with a radius of seven miles, she could connect all the intermarriages. Seven miles turned out to be the limit for easy social contact by horse and buggy, so a boy or girl was likely to find a mate somewhere inside that circle. The evidence—their story—was quite literally mapped onto the land—and onto those paper plat maps gathering dust in the local historical society.

Remember, a map is not a neutral object—it always displays a value system, a way of foregrounding what is important. So highway maps rarely even name any but the largest waterways, just as nautical charts do not concern themselves with roadways on shore. Topographical maps offer detailed information about natural features and the contours of the terrain, but they also will ignore most human-made features, just as a subway map will usually note only those surface streets that intersect with stops.

So maps have an agenda, even down to the naming of places and features they contain, and studying maps can often help you make sense of why things happened where, when, and how they did. A review of antique maps of the Cape Fear River, for instance, revealed that its name changed based on who was politically ascendant: Rio Jordan (Spanish), Clarendon and Charles (English), and at last Cape Fear (United States). In Alaska, Mount McKinley has disappeared from contemporary maps, replaced by Denali, the name used by Native Americans. Perusing maps of the same place over time can yield insight into political power, cultural values, and the growth of knowledge itself—as can be readily seen by comparing early maps of colonial harbors with those generated by the National Oceanic and Atmospheric Administration.

You can also create your own spatial representations of your story's setting. Sometimes, for example, it's useful to shoot photos or video panoramically, in a 360-degree circle around a given vantage point, so you have an exact sense of the physical or geographical relationship of landmarks in a setting. And a map can be a great tool for writing a memoir. Draw a map of your own past during the time covered by the memoir, ignoring scale and with no intention of being complete. Place your home in the center and then create the matrix of the physical world you inhabited: the high school where you played in the marching band, the movie theater where you had your first kiss, the skateboard park where you found out the hard way about drugs, your friend's apartment hangout across town, the corner where your dad wrecked the car, and so on. You'll quickly understand the priority all these places hold in your story, the relationship they bear to each other, along a timeline or sequence.

Such a map may be as small as the inside of your house—your parents' bedroom on the ground floor, your stepsisters' bedrooms on the second floor, your own small bedroom down in the basement next to the laundry room, the dining room where you were not allowed to play (the table was always set with linen and crystal), the kitchen where you always ate standing up at the counter. You can tell by the features on my imaginary map what kind of story might live in that house, what a memoir might be attempting to resolve.

Later, when the time comes to write, one way to outline is to draw a map of the action, with time or date codes. You can do this on a whiteboard or bulletin board—actual or digital—numbering scenes in sequence: 1, 2, 3, and so on. You can link notes and photos to each locale or scene, much like the "murder wall" that TV detectives use to keep track of connections between victims and suspects. Any story is all about connections. Such graphic representation gives you the advantage of seeing the story all at once, as a unified picture, rather than as a linear narrative unfolding in parts. And the intentional collage you create might become its own work of art.

A SOUND BREAKTHROUGH

A digital recording can preserve crucial ambient sound—birds, the racket of traffic, machine noise, another conversation across the room—not just the accurate transcript of what is being said. All of these details may prove valuable when it comes time to write. One of my students, a seasoned reporter named Liz Granger, showed up in class one day with an amazing gadget—a pen. But not just any pen: this one was a smartpen, made by Livescribe. In a special notebook imprinted with a digital command bar across the bottom, she could write and record audio at the same time. Then, by tapping the tip of the pen onto the words or symbols on the page, she could play back the portion of audio that occurred while she was transcribing those words.

I came home raving about this remarkable pen to my wife, Jill, and within a few days I received one for my birthday. Almost immediately, I put it to work recording several long interviews. Unlike so many high-tech gizmos, this one turned out to be easy to install and use, even for a non-techie like me—a matter of just a few minutes. And as soon as I was done recording, I could sync the whole interview to Evernote, a free online data organizing tool (you may want to pay the modest fee to get the premium version, useful if you intend to upload lots of video and graphics).

Evernote displays not just my audio file, so that I can play it and move back and forth inside the recording by simply manipulating the progress bar, but also a graphic facsimile of my notebook pages. So I can also reference my handwritten notes while I listen to the interview. The page numbers of the notebook appear under the audio file, so there's no problem figuring out from the audio where to locate the notes—just as the notes link instantaneously to the audio recorded at the moment of writing. Perhaps a new device will show up tomorrow that will make this one old hat. But I mention it because it breaks new ground, linking audio and handwriting, then automatically organizing the material into a usable and searchable format. This is a quantum leap from "old school." Thus it points to a future in which writers will have at their fingertips—quite literally—tools that combine what used to be separate, discrete, and usually time-intensive functions.

These tools are no substitute for attentive listening or smart questions or the practical intuition of how to connect the dots of information gathered. Any tool that relies on a battery charge is prone to malfunction, usually, it seems, at the most inopportune time (the reason I religiously charge all my rechargeable devices just before going into the field, change out old batteries for new in other devices, and pack spare batteries along just in case). But they can liberate the writer to pay attention to other things, to be a more effective researcher. The smartpen has changed the way I transcribe interviews. Since I know at a glance where everything is on the audio, it's not necessary to transcribe every moment of the interview—always a time sink. I can go to select portions and use it, knowing that if I need other portions, they're waiting and easily retrieved. It changes the way I take notes, as well—since I don't have to write whole sentences or phrases. I can jot down a keyword, even make a crude symbol of a house or car or whatever to indicate that at the moment the interviewee was discussing those subjects. I can still use my old system of one to three stars to remind me of especially revealing or useful moments of conversation that I know I want to include as soon as I hear them spoken—the number of stars indicating just how wonderful the moment was, with three stars being pure gold.

LOW-TECH CAN BE HIGH-TECH

But sometimes there are good reasons not to use a recorder at all. Even though most people nowadays are almost too media savvy, completely unfazed by audio and even video recording, there are still some people who prefer you don't record them. An old moonshiner I was interviewing spoke in a rich mountain dialect, employing turns of phrase I'd never heard, punctuated liberally by profanity that was downright eloquent. I repeatedly asked to be allowed to record his stories, but he just as repeatedly said no. He gave me two good reasons: One, he didn't know me well enough to decide if he wanted to trust me; and two, he was afraid that a transcript of the recording would contain too much profanity and make him look ignorant. He was counting on me to cast his words in a way that would do him credit, but of course I missed almost all of those wonderful turns of phrase—I just couldn't write fast enough to keep up.

Thomas French, who specialized for years in writing long-form narratives for the *St. Petersburg Times* and turned several of them into books—most recently *Zoo Story: Life in the Garden of Captives*—has other reasons for relying on notes and memory rather than a recorder. Though in *Zoo Story* his subjects were mainly the community of adult zookeepers, in much of his work he finds himself interviewing teenagers—as he did for *South of Heaven: Welcome to High School*

at the End of the Twentieth Century, the chronicle of a year spent immersed at Largo High School. He explains, "I don't use a tape recorder
because a lot of time I'm shifting from an interview to a scene—I'll be
in the car with somebody where we'll have two minutes when they're
driving and I'll ask a couple questions, and then a few minutes later
they're going to be running across the football field. So for a lot of my
reporting a tape recorder wouldn't help."

But French has a secret weapon of sorts: he is fluent in shorthand—
that lost art that once defined both a good beat reporter and a cracker-
jack stenographer in the days before word processing. Most of us
develop some kind of personal shorthand, but the nettling challenge
is being able to read stale notes made weeks or months before and de-
cipher our own handwriting. Formal shorthand is beyond old school.
French was allowed much greater latitude than the typical reporter,
working for months on a single long story, and transcribing so many
hours of tape would have added weeks to the process—weeks he
didn't have. He goes on, "I also felt pretty confident that I could get
down what people were saying very accurately because I had taken
shorthand in high school to become a reporter. . . . The other thing
that's really great is that because they can't read what I'm writing,
they very quickly stop trying to read what I'm writing." He makes a
valid point. If the subject becomes too self-conscious that his or her
words are being recorded for posterity, they can start to become rehearsed, sound less candid. "That can be a problem—people say, 'Oh,
you thought that was interesting!'" French says. "With me, they give
up. They laugh about it for a second—you can read those chicken
scratches? And so I read back to them what they just said. Then they
relax; they just forget I'm taking notes." So for him, shorthand becomes a way of making the interview process invisible, less obtrusive.

Low-tech tools have intrinsic value of their own and sometimes
serve multiple functions. That pen you're using might function as a
measuring gauge in some contexts. Binoculars might not only mag-
nify but also focus your field of vision. A magnifying glass turns out
to be useful for both practical and aesthetic reasons. On the practical
side, it does exactly what its name says: it magnifies. If you ever want

to read a trove of handwritten letters, especially old letters with ink or pencil marks that have faded with time, you need this tool. I recommend the kind that has a large rectangular lens inset with a small circular super-magnifying lens. Except for the inconvenience of carrying it around, the bigger the better. Faded or scribbled penmanship that seems, at first blush, completely illegible often magically becomes legible when enlarged—as do tics such as "devil's teardrops" dotting the letter "i." A magnifying glass might also reveal the almost geographic texture of old handwriting, not just the actual words on the page. With a magnifying glass, you can discern what might otherwise be invisible: watermarks on paper; sun-faded labels on old medicine bottles; engravings on personal jewelry; the texture of paper and clothing; maker's marks on jewelry, locks, moonshine jugs, and other handmade items; and serial numbers on almost anything—which can often be traced with astonishing accuracy through the manufacturer, a museum professional, or on the Internet. Simple magnification can lead to a wealth of information about the provenance of the object— who made it, when, who bought it, where, and how it was used—and can lead to a more figurative magnification of its meaning.

Beyond physical tools, there are the tools of a trained intellect and temperament: humility, open-mindedness, alertness, diligent attention, good listening, perseverance, and resourcefulness. A vivid imagination may be the most crucial tool of all, allowing you to connect the dots of disparate facts from widely divergent sources into a scenario that makes sense—the way a good detective or archaeologist forms a theory of the action based on evidence.

One critical tool is any credential that can gain you access—which is often easier than you think. Again, sometimes low-tech works best. One method is as old as the human tribe: word of mouth. Once you have gained the trust of one informant, he or she becomes your reference for others, the one who vouches for your character, so that they let you enter their lives. But high-tech can work hand in hand with word of mouth. A thoughtfully designed website or Facebook page can introduce your work to a prospective source, establishing your bona fides. A link to some of your writing, or better yet a posted excerpt, can be extremely helpful in showing that you treat your interview subjects with respect and empathy and don't make them look like fools. (The low-tech version of this is to carry some copies of your work that you can hand over to a prospective subject who wants to check you out and doesn't go online.) Think of such a site not as self-promotion but as a kind of publicly available background check, and use it accordingly. Don't plaster it with intimate personal details about your love life or your meals, or make it a billboard for your politics. It's a professional reference. You will, if you are lucky, enjoy the opportunity of interviewing people from many professions, religious and cultural backgrounds, political persuasions, and so on. Your job is not to challenge or judge but to listen and understand, to approach every encounter with empathy and an open mind—and that's the persona who should inhabit your Internet presence.

Finally, any "official" credential can be helpful in certain circumstances. I carry business cards with my university letterhead embossed on them. If you are a student visiting a university library or special collection, an e-mail or letter from a teacher can vouch for you—and even if not required, can elicit a greater level of professional courtesy. A letter or e-mail from an editor interested in seeing the finished work, whether as an assignment or on spec (they will buy it if they like it) can help in other situations.

YOUR PRESENCE ON THE SCENE

Although it may seem odd in the context of writing, think about what you wear as a tool of sorts. This is not an important consideration if you are simply going to spend a long day at the library—just dress as comfortably as you can. But if you plan to interview someone, give a little thought to your appearance. Coat and tie, for instance, can either be a gesture of respect for the person and the circumstances (a memorial service for a cancer victim, say)—or it can be off-putting (the shop floor of an auto plant). Whenever I rode along with cops, I always wore a coat and tie—for one thing, they required it, and for another, it helped me blend in. Citizens and criminals alike all just assumed I was a detective and paid me no mind. (Once, on a particularly hectic day at a state police troop, I actually was asked to escort a murder suspect to the desk of the booking sergeant, which I did.)

My informal rule is to try to dress in a way that puts my subject at ease and allows me to blend in with my surroundings. To interview moonshiners, I might wear jeans and a flannel shirt. For a country club luncheon, I'll call ahead and find out if there is a dress code, or perhaps slacks and a golf shirt will suffice. "Business attire" means coat and tie (but not a suit) for men and either a dress, pantsuit, or slacks and top for women—what you would wear to an office job. The particulars will vary, but the important point is to actually think about the impression you will be making. You're not there to be a distraction. You're not the star of the story. In fact, if you're doing your job right, most people will hardly notice your presence.

Clothing becomes more of a tool if you plan to be out in the field for any extended period. Good walking shoes, for instance, or some kind of rain gear. A hat to keep off the sun. I like pockets—so I can stuff my tools unobtrusively into places where I can reach them (and not have to carry a pack or bag of any kind)—and they also live in the same pockets of my Carrhartts or my vest so I can reach for them in the dark or while paying attention to something else and always find them. Bob Reiss often travels to third world countries in sub-Saharan Africa or the Amazon rain forest to research his stories. He packs old jeans, T-shirts, and sweatshirts, planning to leave them behind. Sometimes he trades them for souvenirs, and other times he just gives them away to helpful locals who are grateful for the clothing. He returns with a light duffel and without any hitchhiking foreign microbes.

Ted Conover went basic to research his first book, *Rolling Nowhere*—he pretty much traveled with the clothes on his back, a small notebook and pen, and a plastic milk jug for water. He was young and resilient, and he rode the rails through all kinds of weather, hanging out with real-life hoboes for weeks at a time, every so often coming up for air, getting off the road for a brief respite. In 2014, long married and with a grown son who wanted to follow in his father's footsteps,

Conover re-created a portion of this journey carrying a change of clothes and a smartphone—using its digital maps function to locate not just railyards but also motels where the two could hole up and ride out bad weather or just get some welcome rest.

MAKING SURE YOU CAN FIND IT

The last matter to pay attention to is using tools to organize your research. Here is the only commandment that matters: *If you can't find it, you don't have it*. We all have attics and basements and garages full of wonderful stuff that we know we have but just can't find—so it's sometimes easier just to buy a new one than to excavate the old one. Warning: this is the basic dynamic of hoarding. As a researcher, you're not a hoarder. True, you want to cast a wide net and be open to all sorts of material, searching for it in the most unlikely places, but you also want to be both efficient and effective. Time and energy are precious and, ultimately, if you can't bring a piece of research to bear on your writing because you can't find it, what good is it?

Finding your material again begins with how you store it in the first place. Here we can invoke what I call the "Outward Bound" rule. Outward Bound is famous for taking people to their physical and emotional limits in wilderness situations—hiking through the desert, snowshoeing through the winter wilderness, or paddling through the Everglades. And at the end of each trek, when the adventurers have finally arrived at their destination—usually exhausted, ravenous, thirsty, mosquito-bitten, or clapping frost off their mittens, ready to wolf down a hot meal and a cold beer and enjoy a hot shower and a soft bed—they are given one more last, crucial, spirit-crushing task: cleaning and stowing all the gear. Obviously, this is the last thing any of them wants to do—hump their canoes to the rack and hose them off. Or unpack tents and sleeping bags, clean them, and repack them. Or any of the other myriad maintenance chores. But it's the essential last step of their adventure. And it's exactly what you, the researcher must do.

After a long day of trekking around some unfamiliar town on the prairie, say, or traveling six hours in a car with some crab-pickers on their way back from a festival and listening to their stories, or spending a sunless day in a special collections room bent over old documents, or even making the rounds of a family reunion talking to long-lost relatives, you must put your gear in order. This can be as simple as Wi-Fi syncing your tablet so that all of your notes are now stored redundantly on Evernote or a similar program. But before you do that, make sure you have labeled the notes with date and place and subject heading, so among the many files you store, you can find this one again with a keyword search. And maybe you also have to jot down some additional notes, explaining why you took the notes you did, clarifying connections in the material. You will not remember this later. We all believe we have wonderful memories, but memory is tricky and unreliable, and the smart researcher backs up the hard drive in her head.

While you were in the archive, you were on the clock—making the most of your time, writing without a whole lot of editorial oversight. You were raiding the archive of any useful loot, gathering it as quickly and efficiently as you could. Now's the time to clean up your notes a little, make sure they actually make sense to you when you come back to them—because that may be weeks or even months in the future, and our memories are simply not that good. If you've taken handwritten notes, browse them and make sure that you can read your handwriting and that what you wrote makes sense. I don't trust my own penmanship—it seems to erode into nonsense after only a few days, so I try to type the scribble into notes as soon as is practicable—in the process, of course, adding other notes that expand upon or clarify my original notes.

As Sorensen writes of her research experience, "One major lesson I learned was to write as many field notes as possible during the day, or at least write for a while at the end of the day. It's terrible how fast nuances are lost." And she's right. You are likely to remember the gist of the experience, the broad strokes, but each hour that passes will blur the finer points, erasing small but crucial details, wiping out intuitive observations you made on the scene but didn't write down in the moment.

I do *not* immediately transcribe my interviews. Typically this is done at my home office, at leisure, when I am fresher, in batches. But I do spot-check the recording to make sure the recorder was working, and if it was not, it's time to make as many notes as memory allows. And if possible to sync the audio with Evernote (or your favorite program)—or to download the audio from the device to a computer or thumb drive as soon as possible. If I have any papers or other materials, I organize them and put them together in a folder or envelope and label the outside of the packet. When I'm back at my office, I'll file it in the appropriate box with other materials I've gathered for the project. If I have come into possession of an artifact—an actual object of some kind that bears on my project—I will makes notes about what it is, who gave it to me or where I found it, and what it means; find a safe container for it; and keep the notes with the object. I may also photograph it, just in case.

Since your research may find its way to you in many forms, including both digital and hard copy, it's useful at the start of a project to set up both a digital "file cabinet" and an actual one. Even if you use a cloud-based organizing tool such as Evernote or iCloud, it's prudent to back up your files some other way. One simple way is just to create a clearly labeled project folder on your computer, then add subfiles—again clearly labeled (interview D. Smith; map of living room; list of players 1952). I also advise keeping a dedicated thumb drive for each project—they're a cheap and portable backstop.

Set up a system that makes sense to you. Simpler is better, because you will be more likely use it than a system that is brilliant but complicated. At the end of that fatiguing day of field research, you'll want to be able to do the least work necessary to keep your material in good order. So you'll notice above, for example, that in my list of subfolders, each begins with a research area: interview, map, list. Thus I can add other "map" or "interview" or "list" folders, and they'll all immediately (and automatically) be grouped together, and within that group, they'll all be alphabetized—also automatically, which means I don't have to do anything extra. This will help me find what I need easily. Another writer might put the proper name first as a finding aid, so he or she can find all the notes that pertain to that individual at a glance. It doesn't matter what your system is, only that it works for you.

The same process applies to an actual file that will hold paper. I prefer some kind of file box to a large cabinet, since a box is more portable—I can haul it to another work space if need be. It is also focused on one particular project. If I start another project, I start another file box. When I am finished, I can then store the whole box in my closet in case I need to check the notes or sources during the process of publication—after which the box will either be discarded—if its contents do not include valuable documents but only copies of what I have stored digitally—or purged of copies or material that turned out to be irrelevant and removed to the attic, in case I need it in the future.

Research-based writing requires storage of one kind or another. Storing your material in a sensible manner right from the start will save you hours of frustrated searching later in the writing process. Whenever you need something, you'll find it—and therefore you will have it. This sounds like advice for dummies, but time and again I find myself reminding myself to do it. It takes discipline and ultimately becomes professional habit. And good habits are just as hard to break as bad habits, because they are automatic, requiring no thought or decision. You just do it that way.

Figuring out which tools work best for the kind of writing you want to do is worth your consideration, because ultimately the tools you use will play a large role in determining not just the success of your research but also both how you conduct it and the nature of the creative work it inspires. But in the end, a tool is a tool—meant to help make possible both the research and the creative project at the end of that research. There's no need to become such a gearhead that your infatuation with tools interferes with your larger purpose. Use only what you need. Different projects will often require different tools. When I paddled and boated two hundred miles of the Cape Fear River with a guide, a biologist, a river keeper, a photographer and birder, and a boat captain, using a recorder was simply not practical, but my little notebooks, even drenched, served me just fine. At the end of the journey, I hung them on a clothesline in the garage and they dried out beautifully, the tannin-stained pages redolent with the aroma of the river itself.

There's a telling anecdote from the space program that serves the researching writer with a useful reminder. Apparently at the dawn of manned space flight, NASA spent a lot of time and money trying to develop a pen that would write upside down in zero gravity. Because of excessive cost, NASA eventually scrapped the project and—like our Russian space rivals—simply gave its astronauts pencils. If a tool isn't working, discard it for a better one. Sometimes low-tech is high-tech.

Prompt #5: "Tools of the Trade." Make a list of five essential tools for the kind of writing you want to do. For each tool, list at least three unconventional uses. For example, I like to make notes in durable little notebooks bound by a rubber band—a conventional use. But since I know my notebooks are 5½ by 3½ inches, I can use them to measure items in the field that I later want to describe; I also allow subjects to draw illustrations or maps in them for my later reference; and if I want to show the scale of an object, I can place a notebook in the frame of the photograph.

Prompt #6: "Mastering the Machine." Obtain a digital recording device or smartphone app, and practice using it by conducting a mock interview with a friend or family member.

4 ARCHIVES: WHAT THEY ARE, WHERE THEY ARE, AND HOW TO BEST USE THEM

One of the things that has stuck with me is the idea that
the writer should have the most complete archive of her project
in existence. —Heather Hammerbeck, nonfiction writer

I don't believe in the terror of the blank page or writer's block. The reason is simple: the writer never starts from nothing. There is always the world—always the stuff of the world: facts, impressions, documents, people's stories, geography, nature, science, history, places, public events, private dramas, lived experience, and imagined yearnings. So there is always something to write about, once the writer has acquired the habit of research—a sense of moving through this world with eyes and ears wide open, alert to movement and sound and experience. The archives are everywhere around us: not just in libraries and special collections, but in out-of-the-way places, the stories people tell, memories, old shoe boxes full of photographs, letters and diaries of loved ones and strangers, and a thousand other repositories. Those archives are full of both mysteries and the keys to unlocking those mysteries, revelations that shock and delight, insight that enlarges the writer's understanding of his or her personal story and challenges the writer to push craft to the limit in service of complex truth and beauty.

In the broadest sense of the term, at least seven kinds of archives present themselves for creative research, ranging from documentary repositories to knowledge gained through lived experience. This chapter and the ones that follow discuss these various types of resources and how you might use them in your projects. Following is a list of seven archival categories, each with examples of resources within that category. The list is by no means exhaustive, and a different writer might group them in different categories. Items may overlap from one category to another—for instance, maps are often printed paper archives containing much written information, but they also contain an invaluable visual element. But the point is that for our purposes "archives" are more than just repositories of documents: they constitute a wide-ranging and exciting trove of raw material for creative work.

So treat the categories for what they are—a convenient way to keep track of opportunities—rather than as gospel. It's useful to remember that such resources can be used in different ways, depending on the needs of your project. Sometimes reading the text of an old document online is fine, but other times you want to hold the original in your hand, to feel the fragile weight of history or personal suffering or joy that comes through the authentic thing itself.

The main point is not to be limited in your research to what is available on the Internet or in the library, where all too many researchers begin and end their quests. And if you are going to the library, understand how many different "libraries" there are within the whole. William Madison Randall Library at my university, for instance, contains more than merely thousands of books and periodicals; it also is home to a partial Government Documents Repository; music, video, and recorded word libraries; a map room; a Special Collection of manuscripts, books, screenplays, and other papers; art and artifacts; an Interlibrary Loan service linking it to libraries around the world; and a vast electronic database set that lets you to search a host of general and specialized resources. So keep an open mind and explore.

As you explore, remember Aristotle's famous dictum: *Know thyself*. But think of it now in a different way—not as an admonition to examine your life and motives, though that can be valuable, but as a warning *to know a thing firsthand*, to know it from your own best evidence, experience, and judgment. Remember how we began our discussion of research in chapter 1: Always seek out *primary sources* wherever and whenever possible, rather than relying on second- or third-hand accounts. They will get you as close as possible through that Zone of Noise and to the Actuality.

SEVEN KINDS OF ARCHIVES

1. Paper Archives (discussed in this chapter). Note that many of these may also be now available in electronic format but have historically been kept on paper first or primarily—and bear in mind that despite frantic ongoing efforts at digitalization, millions of paper records remain just that. And just as some electronic archives can offer more "information"—for example, enhanced coloration, capability to zoom, enhanced definition of faded script—many paper archives can offer what electronic archives of the same material cannot: texture, a sense of actual size, and the ineffable weight of the past in your hands. Paper archives include the following:

- Libraries
- Special collections
- Private papers
- Letters
- Diaries, journals, field notes, etc.
- Business ledgers
- Government documents
- Parish records
- Trial transcripts
- Books and monographs
- Periodicals
- Phone book/Yellow Pages/business directories

- Atlas/maps/charts
- Bibliographies
- Unpublished manuscripts
- Literature of the period
- Medical records
- Technical manuals

2. Electronic Archives (discussed in chapter 5):

- Search engines and general websites on the Internet
- Interactive sites—including People Finder, MapQuest, etc.
- Blogs and social networking sites
- E-mail
- Text messages
- Tweets
- Online and digital databases (see your library's homepage for a complete list)
- Data from electronic instruments, e.g., Global Positioning System (GPS), radar, medical monitoring instruments, weather arrays, seismic readouts

3. Living Archives (discussed in chapters 6 and 7):

- Live presentations, e.g., lectures, readings, broadcast appearances
- Personal interviews, recorded or noted, directed or oral history style
- Observation of living persons, e.g., watching a wooden boat builder at work
- Expert consultations, e.g., having a nuclear scientist explain to you how fission works

4. Visual Archives (discussed throughout the book):

- Photographs
- Film and video
- Online video sites, e.g., YouTube

- Art, e.g., drawings, sketches, paintings, frescoes, icons, statuary, sculpture, illustrations
- Blueprints/floor plans
- Maps/charts/atlas
- X-rays and other images generated by technology
- Graphs/charts/diagrams
- Symbols
- Mathematical proofs
- Artifacts
- Museum dioramas and displays
- Inscriptions/mottoes/logos, etc.
- Signage

5. Audio Archives (in new and old media, such as cassette tape or 78 rpm records):

- Music
- Audiobooks
- Speeches/public addresses
- Literary readings
- News recordings
- Radio broadcasts
- Interviews
- Cockpit voice recordings/radio transmissions/911 calls, etc.
- Natural sound
- Manufactured sound
- Sound effects
- Online MIDI, MP3, and other format files
- Personal recordings

6. Archives of Memory and Imagination (discussed in chapter 6):

- Discovering connections among disparate elements of research.
- Extrapolating from known facts to create plausible scenarios and fill in "missing" scenes

- Using logic to weigh evidence and testimony to determine the likeliest truth
- Using intuition the same way
- Daydreaming your way inside other people's lives, other periods in history, etc.
- Using some point of common ground to find empathy for people who are utterly different based on their times, places, actions, circumstances, religion, social status, etc.
- Reconciling conflicting or contradictory testimony and evidence
- Interrogating your own memories and triggering new ones
- Comparing your memory against other evidence, e.g., someone else's memory of the same incident, photographs or video, etc.

7. Experiential Archives (discussed in chapter 8):

- "Walking the ground," i.e., going to a place and experiencing it firsthand
- Reenactment
- Tactile impressions
- Performing an activity
- "Ride-along"
- Actual participation in an event
- Immersion, i.e., long-term participation
- Undercover participation
- Handling artifacts
- Buildings, monuments, ruins, and other parts of the built environment

CONVENTIONAL INSTITUTIONAL PAPER ARCHIVES

We traditionally tend to think of "archives" as formal repositories of paper documents, curated and maintained by professional gatekeepers. The origin of the word itself comes from the Latin *archium*, or *archivum* derived from the Greek *archeion*—a word for both the chambers of government and the repository of state papers. Of course there are many such archives, beginning with the National Archives and including presidential libraries, university special collections, documents held in private nonprofit and corporate collections, regional and local museums and historical societies, and so on. As the list indicates, there are other types of archives, but let's start with the kind traditionally meant by the term.

When planning your archival research, start by browsing the National Archives website (www.archives.gov), which presents all sorts of useful information about what kinds of records are held at which site that are available and in what format—digital or hard copy—and how to enlist the aid of either a NARA archivist or a freelance researcher whom you can hire to locate specific material if you can't go in person. It also provides guidance on copyright, reproduction of images, the protocols for visiting in person, and an online *Freedom of Information Act (FOIA) Reference Guide* (http://www.archives.gov/foia/) laying out the specific procedures you must follow to obtain government records.

A web search using keywords such as "archives guide" will turn up a variety of other helpful sites, advising the researcher how to access records in diverse archives in the United States and abroad. There's an etiquette to accessing special collections and other repositories— whether at your own institution or someplace else—and it's important to know it and make use of it.

First, you'll want to make arrangements in advance. This can typically be done by e-mail or phone. Contact information is usually available at the website for the archive you wish to consult. Remember that archivists are busy and you can't expect them to respond immediately to your request. Some specify a response time, but many do not. So plan well ahead of time—certainly days, even weeks, if possible. While hours of access are generally available online, such a schedule may be interrupted by holidays, special events, or the personal schedules of key personnel who may be off to a conference, on sick leave, or on vacation. Smaller archives, while housing perfectly wonderful collections, may be staffed by volunteers—or even a single volunteer—and open only upon request. Other times, the website just doesn't get updated in a timely way and the schedule of operation is out-of-date. The last thing you want to do is drive three hundred miles to an archive, only to find out it is closed early for the weekend.

Larger institutional archives generally have an online catalog of holdings, accessible to anyone. So, for instance, you can access the main website for the Louis Round Wilson Library Special Collections at the University of North Carolina at Chapel Hill, then choose among options such as "Southern Folklife Collection" or "North Carolina Collection" and click the tab for "Search & Find" and choose "Catalog" if you already know what item you are looking for. If you don't, you can browse the holdings by clicking on the "Collections" tab, which brings up an alphabetized list of names and titles. Clicking on any of them will tell you the nature of the holding—document, book, photo, audio recording, et cetera—and what it contains. And it will yield the crucial accession or collection number—the code by which the physical item can be located in the collection—then break the collection into series and folders, again including a description. Other tabs will give you helpful advice about how to navigate the collection and how to use finding aids.

The Library of Congress website—also useful as a general introduction to the process—advises:

Finding aids provide a gateway to this wealth of Library treasures, helping you discover and navigate through the thousands of boxes and folders that house each collection. These guides provide comprehensive overviews of unique Library resources. Progressively detailed descriptions of a collection's component parts summarize the overall scope of the content, convey details about the individuals and organizations involved, and list box and folder headings. Special service conditions are noted, including terms under which the collection may be accessed or copied. Links are provided to digitized content, when available.

Most reputable archival websites tend to be pretty user-friendly, and if you're used to Google searches, the whole process is a familiar exercise of point and click, search by keywords, clicking to open an abstract or full electronic document in pdf or other format. As I've noted, most archives have digitized only a small portion—often the most frequently accessed part—of their collection, and the rest is still there in boxes tucked away. Luckily, the finding aid is usually online, and that tells you what is in all those un-digitized boxes.

The idea is to find what the archive has that you need; if possible access it remotely; if not, know how to locate it when you get to the physical location; then spend your precious time in the archive raiding it for whatever may prove to be of use. I typically employ two strategies that have proven very useful. First, I enlist the aid of one of the archivists—in advance of my visit, if possible. I brief that person on what I am trying to find out and why and the nature of my project as it is forming, and show the archivist a printout of some of the items that appear useful. In describing any project, I paint with a broad brush, make it clear that the project is still forming itself so as not to close out information that might prove useful, even if I myself don't know about it yet. I can always discard an avenue of research that turns out to be irrelevant. Almost always, the archivist will recommend other documents or collections that I should consult—usually better stuff than I could have found on my own, often cataloged under less obvious terms.

Second, I won't spend my time inside the archives reading comprehensively. I will read enough to determine whether the item is useful. To the extent I can, I will arrange for photocopies of the documents that look promising. This is not always possible, and in that case I do read intently, making notes on my iPad or notebook computer, if allowed (and so far I've never been denied) or with pencil and paper, typically provided at the archive. You will be required to park your pens and other belongings in a locker for the duration of your visit—too many miscreants before you have ransacked or vandalized the collections, so this is an unfortunate but necessary precaution.

You may or may not be allowed to scan or photograph the holdings—check with the archivist or the rules spelled out on the archive's website. Many older documents are light-sensitive and can be degraded by flash photography or photocopying. Others are protected by copyright or other proprietary interests. The many and varied archives I've accessed over the years always have some sort of arrangement by which you can obtain a photocopy or a scan, if the condition of the document and copyright allow it. Charges vary widely, so make sure you know up front what you are paying for and getting and what the timeline will be for delivery.

As noted in the discussion of research tools, before being allowed to access the archive, you may be asked for an academic or professional affiliation, so if you don't have one, it can be useful to recruit one in advance—a publication willing to look at your work on spec (meaning that they will look at your finished piece and publish it only if they like it), or a professor who can provide you a reference on university letterhead vouching for your status. Bear in mind that, like any organization, an archive needs to justify its budget by showing that it is useful. Thus it keeps careful track of who uses the archive and to what purpose, as well as what other institutions provide clients. Except in the rare cases of private holdings, the people who run the archives generally want you to visit and take advantage of the resource they have spent their careers building.

At any of the sites administered by the National Archives and Records Administration (NARA), as at some other prestigious collections, you will spend the first hour or so being vetted for an ID and issued a card, as well as undergoing other security precautions. Such procedures tend to change from time to time, so find out as much as possible about current procedures at the archive you intend to visit to make the most of your time there—and to be sure you are not denied access because you lack the proper ID. A standard photo ID will suffice: a current driver's license or passport.

On site, you may be allowed to handle rare documents only with linen gloves, which are provided—or not at all. Rare books or monographs may be placed on reading stands, to be moved only by the archivist.

SLEUTHING FOR HIDDEN CLUES

In consulting archives, you want to be alert for what is not obvious. Cathy Day—author of *The Circus in Winter*, a fictional history of her hometown, and *Comeback Season: How I Learned to Play the Game of*

Love—has for some years been hard at work on a book about Linda Lee Thomas Porter, best known to contemporary readers as the wife of Cole Porter, the Broadway composer (whose many famous tunes include "Begin the Beguine" and "I've Got You Under My Skin"). Day has blogged about the fascinating progress of her research on *The Big Thing*, and in an e-mail she explained how helpful some of the newly digitized archives have been, in particular the searchable digital archive of the *New York Times*, inclusive to 1923, and the Google Books project, which has amassed a huge digital database of works in the public domain, including many volumes of the Social Register and college yearbooks.

"This is how I came to realize that in her time Linda was the celebrity, not Cole Porter," she writes. "She married her first husband, a very rich man, at a time when there were no movie stars; the wealthy—the Astors, the Vanderbilts, the 400—were our celebrities." Linda Porter's first husband was E. R. "Ned" Thomas, "the bad-boy son of a robber baron." Thomas was a colorful character indeed, as Day explains: "Ned ran a brokerage with Edwin Post, husband of Emily Post, who published quite a few commercial novels before she wrote *Etiquette*. Ned also owned a newspaper whose most popular columnist was Bat Masterson." Masterson was a noted Western sheriff. "Ned's sister bought the Newport mansion of Mr. and Mrs. Edward R. Wharton. Edith Wharton's house." Day goes on, "In fact, when Linda married Cole, the headline in the *New York Times* read: 'Mrs. Lee Thomas to wed.' And then below in smaller font: 'Kentuckian to marry Cole Porter in Paris today.'" So the key to finding archival material about her subject lay in searching not for "Mrs. Cole Porter" but for "Linda Lee Thomas" and "Mrs. E. R. Thomas." As Day puts it, "I didn't look for her through a Cole-centric lens."

The best material about your subject is sometimes found in a box with a different label. Special collections items tend to be named for the person or family that donated the material, who are usually featured prominently in it through their correspondence, business records, diaries, and other documents (e.g., "The B. D. Witherspoon Family Papers 1860–1912"). But all too often the name on the collection is misleading, one step removed from the person or event you may be researching. In my university library special collections, for instance, is one box labeled "John F. Schrank Letters"—containing original handwritten letters. Who in the world was John F. Schrank? Well, it turns out he was the guy who tried to assassinate Theodore Roosevelt with a pistol in 1912. Shot once point-blank in the chest, Roosevelt famously gave a windy speech anyhow, before consenting to receive medical treatment.

Schrank wound up in an asylum in Wisconsin, where he wrote spirited letters to his former doctor, Adin Sherman. Five years after the assassination attempt, he writes, in neat cursive, "Dear Doctor, my final release as a sane man can only be a credit to you. . . . [Y]our people have treated me well and have helped me to a better and saner mind, if at times that treatment has perhaps not been as pleasant as it might have been." He pleads for the doctor to accept his recovery as sincere, writing (with a bit of manipulative flattery, perhaps?), "I have caused you perhaps unnecessary unpleasant hours and sur-prises these years, which may well have justified your doubt as to my sincerity, allow me to say that you are a shrewd experienced man in your line of business and a rogue will hardly ever escape your vigi-lance. . . ." Schrank praises the system of "expert testimony," presum-ably the doctor's, that got him committed, even though he himself, of course, no longer needs confinement, and ends his letter, ". . . you well know that my deed in 1912 was not inspired by a desire for noto-riety and far be it from me to embarrass or injure men who have done but good to me."

Thus a key piece of original psychological context of a historical deed resides in a collection of letters by the would-be assassin to his doctor, housed in a university far from any presidential library. So be alert that the stuff you need may not always be conveniently la-beled. Collections of letters, for instance, too often contain only one side of the correspondence, so they may reside in the archive of the individual who received them, not the author. This can work to your advantage at times, especially if you are trying to recover the lives of individuals who were not famous and never held the public eye.

If, for example, you want to find letters from a semi-literate Piedmont farmwife, widowed and made destitute by the Civil War, the papers of Governor Zebulon Vance in the North Carolina State Archives contain not just the amazing number of letters he wrote (in a big furious slanted longhand that paid no attention to the ruled lines on the page) but those he received—not just from historical figures such as Jefferson Davis (who wrote in a painfully miniature, crabbed, excessively neat hand) but also from hundreds of farmwives, soldiers, shopkeepers, and other ordinary citizens.

If you're lucky, the person you want to write about was a compulsive keeper—of records, letters, business papers, public speeches, even his or her own medical records. Finding a private archive might be as simple as consulting another author's bibliography or doing an online search, or it may require a little sleuthing, backtracking from an organization that person may have been affiliated with or cold-calling the lawyer who represents the estate. Maybe an old newspaper article holds a clue—a mention of a surviving relative. Casting your net on social networks might yield results—"I'm working on a piece about so-and-so and am interested in finding any documents about her, or anyone who might have such documents."

Here is where your attitude can play a key role. If you come off as a know-it-all or are reluctant to reveal your own ignorance, archivists and others in a position to assist you may assume that you don't need their help. So be candid about your own inexperience. Enlist their expertise. Ask for their help and advice, and follow it. And don't abuse their time or patience—realize they have other duties besides helping you on your quest.

Of course whenever you're embarked on a project, the universe conspires to bring you what you need. When I was researching that top-secret band of artists who fought in World War II, I was at a loss for photographic evidence: they were, after all, top secret. One day the phone rang and an intelligence analyst from Fort Belvoir wanted to know if I had any photos of the men I was writing about. (How had he even heard about my project?) I told him I had very little to go on. Well, he told me, his stepfather was the unit photographer and had kept all the original plates after the war, and did I want any of them for the book? He had heard about the project through the grapevine of veterans I had been interviewing.

Another time, I happened to serve on an arts council hiring committee with the executive director of the Surry County (NC) Arts Council, Tanya Jones, who just happens to be the great-great-granddaughter of Eng Bunker, one of the original Siamese Twins. She proved a wonderful source of information as I wrote about the eldest sons of Chang and Eng riding off to fight in the Civil War. She even arranged a visit to the house where Chang and his large family lived (each twin kept his own house, a mile apart, and they rotated three days at each residence; wives and children stayed put in their respective homes; Eng's house no longer stands)—complete with extra-wide doorways and staircase and low banister rails, since the twins were short and wide, forced by their connection always to move in tandem, side by side.

VIVID PAPER LIVES

If you can find that trove and be granted access to it, then immerse yourself in it. You may share the experience of Susan Orlean as she was researching *Rin Tin Tin: The Life and the Legend*—a book that is by turns inspiring and heartbreaking. Orlean immersed herself in the private archive of Lee Duncan, the original trainer of the famous movie dog Rin Tin Tin. She writes:

I had finished reading through almost all of Lee's papers at the Riverside Museum, starting every morning before the sun became so punishing that the shades had to be drawn and the parking lot pavement got tacky. I began noticing letters that Eva [Duncan's wife] had sent canceling some of Lee's travel plans, and notes from Wauhillau LaHay and Screen Gems executives asking after Lee's health. Then I came across letters Eva had written to people who owed money for their puppies, asking, with a new urgency, when they were going to pay. I knew that I was edging toward the inevitable. My perspective was one that the people involved could never have had: a bird's-eye view of a road and its end point that a traveler on that road could never have seen.

For Orlean, the experience of learning about a man's life from a paper archive is anything but flat or dull. "This was the first time I had ever spent so much time learning about one person's life, and it was a new experience for me to fall so deeply into it, and strangest of all, to feel, as I did sometimes, that I knew more about Lee than he might have known about himself, and more than I would have known if I had met him and talked to him and learned about him in that more usual way," she writes with candid fascination for the process of discovery.

The thing about a box of collected papers that is different from an autobiography or even an edited collection of letters is that it contains not just the triumphs and public moments that the subject wishes to share with an audience but also a lot of mundane material never intended to be read by strangers. Private, personal, perhaps unflattering at times, at other times simply boring. But offering unalloyed insight into the person's daily life and also the arc of that life through time and circumstance. Orlean continues:

Before I spent these hours in Bert's storage room and Lee's file boxes in Riverside, I had never realized how crackling and alive someone's papers could be. I always assumed that archives would be as dull as an accountant's ledger. But instead, they made me feel as though I had drilled my way inside a still-humming life. It was all there—the details and the ordinariness, the asides and incidentals, and even the misfires and failures that might otherwise have gone unnoticed. These are the things that make up an actual existence, the things a person wouldn't think to share because they seemed inconsequential, or wouldn't be willing to share because they seemed too intimate, but they are at the heart of who we are.

Eudora Welty was another writer who discovered an archive languishing in a trunk in the attic, when she opened and read the letters her mother and father had exchanged as sweethearts and newlyweds. Her father, an insurance man, traveled frequently and would write his wife from the train, posting the letter in the mail car. In *One Writer's Beginnings*, she writes, "I didn't in the end feel like a trespasser when I came to open the letters: they brought my parents before me for the first time as young, as inexperienced, consumed with the strength of their hopes and desires, as living on these letters." Through her father's breathless words and her mother's expressions of love, Welty could envision them both in a new way, existing beyond the role of mother and father to her. They were daring and youthful, embarking on their own great adventure. We tend to know our parents and grandparents only in the present tense of our own lives, but in glimpsing their intimate past, Welty discovered a whole new dimension to her parents, one that only deepened her love and admiration for them—and turned them into distinct individuals with lives beyond her own.

Sometimes paper is not just paper but a doorway to the past, living words that take shape as human actors before our very eyes.

Prompt #7: "Search the Archive." Locate an archive that holds primary documents relevant to your project. Visit the archive and discover some provocative fact that leads you in a creative direction.

Prompt #8: "Living Letters." Locate a trove of letters to or from an individual about whom you wish to write. First, *before you have read the letters*, write a paragraph describing the person; Next, *after reading the letters*, write another descriptive paragraph, based on what you learn and hear in the voice of the letters.

5 IT MUST BE TRUE—
I SAW IT ON
THE INTERNET

I must confess that I've never trusted the Web. I've always seen
it as a coward's tool. Where does it live? How do you hold it
personally responsible? —Stephen Colbert, comedian

We've all seen those silly commercials in which a hopelessly naive
young woman believes anything she finds on the Internet—including
her blind date, a chubby, beret-wearing American dolt who claims to
be a French model. That's the curse of the Internet: everything appears to carry equal authority. Anybody can make a website and post
the most outrageous claims to truth, enhancing those claims with
Photoshopped pictures, artfully edited video and audio, and a host
of other tricks to con the unwary into accepting for true the most
outlandish falsehoods, conspiracy theories, and racist, sexist, or homophobic drivel. So how does the conscientious researcher determine which sites to trust in the "Wild West" of the Internet? Start by
treating an electronic source as a *source*, first and foremost. Remember that you are navigating through the Zone of Noise, approaching
the Actuality. Apply the same tests you would to any source:

- Who is the author or authors and what are their credentials?
- Does the site provide a transparent list of its sources and their
  provenance—that is, where did this author get his or her information?

- Does the information presented jibe with that provided by other sources that have proven reputable—that is, can you independently verify it?
- How close is the authorial source to the material being presented? And what is the author's relation to it: Eyewitness? Victim? Perpetrator? Disinterested observer? Scholar or professional researcher in the discipline? Hobbyist?

The Internet is a great place to conduct some early foundational research, survey the subject, find out what's out there, track down ancestors, locate sites on a map. And there's one big caveat: Electronic sources typically provide only a beginning, a foundation; they can help you figure out where else to go, but they are no substitute for other kinds of necessary research.

Wikipedia may be convenient but it also tends to be fraught with errors. This is in the nature of the enterprise, which invites virtually anyone to weigh in on any subject. Sometimes the information will be accurate and useful, but other times misleading or just plain wrong. From time to time, I spot-check entries on a range of subjects that I have researched in depth only to find that the Wikipedia entries repeat discredited accounts of history, compound errors by repeating an error from a popular source, or simply render interpretations that are widely off the mark of professional scholarship. At best, Wikipedia articles include sources cited, and these sources might get the researcher closer to the facts in question than the article itself—which may have been written by a seasoned professional or an interested amateur. So if you use Wikipedia, use it only as a starting point—then drill down through better sources. There are markers for trustworthy websites, rules of thumb that can keep a writer from embarrassment while taking advantage of the tremendous engine of knowledge it allows us to access. You can trust a site such as the Massachusetts Historical Society, university sites, even many corporate sites, for facts—and there are reliable indicators in their web addresses to help you sort this out.

Every internet site has a URL—uniform resource locator—that serves as its electronic address. There are technical reasons why the system is set up with a protocol identifier, such as "http" or "https" and associated files or web pages. All you need to know is how to read a web address to determine its reliability as a source. The most obvious telltales are the name of the site (e.g., nps for National Park Service) and the suffix—the part that comes after the dot:

- .com for a commercial site
- .edu for a college or university or other educational institution
- .gov for a government site
- .museum for worldwide museums
- .net for Internet administrative site
- .nom for personal site
- .org for a nonprofit
- .pro for professional site (lawyers, doctors, etc.)
- .store for retail business site
- .tel for Internet communications services
- .travel for travel-related sites
- .web for Internet site about the World Wide Web

There also are country codes—uk for the United Kingdom, for example.

This is changing fast. In 2014 the Internet Corporation for Assigned Names and Numbers (ICANN) at last received permission to add 1,000 new suffixes—some of them location specific, others generic words such as .tattoo, .hello, and .clothing, as well some others that are brand specific, such as .nike and .cadillac. One reason for the expansion is simple volume—some 100 million websites already end in .com, and there aren't enough available names for new businesses. By far the most common suffixes are .com, .edu, .gov, and .org.

PURPOSE AND RELIABILITY

As with any source, you need to know why you are consulting it. So if you are looking for verified scientific information, for instance, an .edu is likely to be more reliable than a .com site, since the latter has a commercial interest in whatever it presents. But beware: an .edu site might also just be a sophomore college student's term paper. The information at the bottom of the home page (usually) should disclose who authors and maintains the site.

Likewise, .org sites hosting archives and museums are likely to have better information on historical, cultural, or artistic matters. But sites with political agendas can also end in .org. The John Locke Foundation, for instance, regularly posts information on history, and it may be perfectly accurate. But it's important to remember that the foundation exists to advance a Libertarian agenda and is likely to interpret historical events in that light. This is not readily apparent, since the JLF, like other political organizations across the political spectrum, has mastered the cagey rhetoric of appearing to be nonpartisan. Its website proclaims, "The John Locke Foundation was created in 1990 as an independent, nonprofit think tank that would work 'for truth, for freedom, and for the future of North Carolina.' The Foundation is named for John Locke (1632–1704), an English philosopher whose writings inspired Thomas Jefferson and the other Founders." Well, who can be against "truth," "freedom," and "the future of North Carolina"? I certainly hope my home state has a future, and I'm all for truth and freedom. And Jefferson was a great American, albeit a slave owner. If you click through the "About JLF" menu you actually find a heading that reads, "Is the John Locke Foundation conservative?" And if you click on that question, you get a really twisty answer:

Some people ask us: Is the John Locke Foundation a Republican group? No, the John Locke Foundation is nonpartisan.

Others ask: Is the John Locke Foundation conservative? The answer to this question is not as simple.

The John Locke Foundation believes in free markets, limited constitutional government, and personal responsibility. In the modern American political context, those principles are labeled conservative. Historically, and in most other countries today, those have been considered liberal or "classical liberal" principles. Some observers also consider those principles libertarian.

If someone asks whether the John Locke Foundation is conservative, (classically) liberal, or libertarian, the appropriate answer is "yes."

So it is all these things at once—"classically" liberal, libertarian, and conservative. Since at least 2009, libertarian is a label associated with the Tea Party, which is firmly, if not always happily, rooted in the Republican Party, and the values espoused above have no connection to contemporary liberalism, except as opposites, or to an agenda Thomas Jefferson would sign on for. So the character of the organization becomes apparent in its tortuous lawyerly explanation of its own values.

Liberal sites, too, will spin facts and statistics to bolster their positions, for their mission is not really to *educate* but to *advocate*. And their very names and the language with which they express their missions tend to camouflage their political agenda. The banner for the Center for American Progress, for example, features the motto: "Progressive ideas for a strong, just, and free America." Once again, who can be against justice and freedom? Common Cause works for "open, honest, accountable government." Does anyone really want dishonest and unaccountable government? You get the picture.

So if you are looking for unbiased factual information online, look to organizations that have no political agenda. This goes even for organizations that advocate for causes in which you believe—a clean environment, say, or medical research. The best sites reveal their sources, and you can check the validity of a scientific study or a historical synopsis or demographic statistics by vetting the source.

So the U.S. Census Bureau's population statistics are going to be about as solid as you can get—factoring again all the imperfections of the process. Statistics on gun violence, on the other hand, are going to be trickier—since the U.S. Centers for Disease Control and Prevention has been barred by Congress from collecting such data. So the National Rifle Association is likely to provide one set of numbers, and the Brady Campaign to Prevent Gun Violence another, and you'll have to do some further digging into their sources and even their sources' sources to determine who is spinning what numbers how.

Ask yourself, what does this organization stand to gain by providing this information? On a commercial site (I love the Martin Guitar site, for instance), the goal is to promote products. If you want to know about their products, happy browsing. If you want to compare one guitar with another, you probably need a disinterested third party who does not stand to gain, whichever instrument you buy. A version of *Consumer Reports*, not funded by advertising or sponsored by commercial entities.

Remember, too, that just because an organization has an agenda doesn't mean it is not telling the truth. I serve on the board of the Cape Fear River Watch, and our whole reason for being is to protect the quality of water in the Cape Fear River, a laudable goal. We often find ourselves in political battles against heavy industrial developers or state lawmakers, but like many organizations, we craft policy based on facts. The scientists on our board make sure of that. So if you want to know the sources of any of our facts or statistics, they're cited openly, as are the credentials of board, staff, and researchers. You'll find out not just where the statistics were generated, but also by what logic they were combined or compared. You can look them up and decide for yourself whether they are reliable.

Transparency, the provenance of information and the credentials of those who supply it, allows you to judge for yourself, to dispute any of the facts with better sources, to argue with any of the logic. Many reputable sites urge you to do just that and to bring to the host's attention any information that feels erroneous so corrections can be made. That still doesn't mean you take any statements at face value—track them back to the source and make sure the source is reputable. But if the River Watch site takes a stand against, say, a multinational company that wants to locate a limestone mine and cement plant on the river (a real case), with millions of dollars in potential profits in the balance, it's fair to ask what's in it for River Watch? Not money, since there's no equivalent commercial opportunity. That still doesn't mean it's immune from challenge, but it does take the profit motive out of the equation.

So if the pharmaceutical industry, say, sponsors a study, that is likely not to have the presumed level of integrity of a study funded through a National Science Foundation grant and conducted by university researchers publishing in peer-reviewed journals, where their findings are open to enthusiastic critique by the rest of the profession. The pharmaceutical industry isn't in business to promote health but to make a profit for its shareholders by selling health-related drugs—a perfectly legitimate aim. But the two are very different motivations. Certainly the university researchers are after prestige, perhaps tenure, perhaps more grant money to keep their laboratories funded, but they also publish under the scrutiny of peers who can make *their* reputations by debunking flawed science—a huge built-in check on fraudulent or just plain sloppy research.

Remember what I said earlier about knowing *why* you are consulting a web source. If you want to know what the National Rifle Association stands for, as in the example above, its website is clearly an authoritative source. If you want to find out what the libertarian arguments are for or against a given government policy, the John Locke Foundation will provide you exactly that. Likewise the website of MoveOn.org will provide an excellent tutorial in liberal social policy. The website is actually a tool for political action through the launching of online petitions to sway lawmakers, ironically founded during the impeachment of President Bill Clinton with a petition to "Censure President Clinton and Move On to Pressing Issues Facing the Nation." And as for commercial sites, if you're researching motorcycles, cosmetics, real estate, appliances, jewelry, luggage, quarter horses, or any other commodity, commercial sites can provide you chapter and verse on what products are available and where, the company history, contacts within the industry, manufacturer's specs, even owner's manuals, and other facets of the commodity in question. But don't look to the company that makes a product to give you a credible comparison with competitors' products—that's not its job.

In addition to URL suffixes, other telltales can clue you in about the reliability of a site. Some of the obvious red flags include the following:

- The site is named for an individual. Public figures, including authors, usually have such a site, and it may be perfectly factual; nonetheless it's likely also to be a promotional tool—your own included; social media sites are curated to highlight a person's virtues and accomplishments.
- When you click to the site, you're greeted with a barrage of music and video animation.
- The site is clumsily and unprofessionally designed, full of mismatched fonts, over-the-top graphics, and busy background "wallpaper."
- The text is full of grammatical and spelling errors, laid out in a manner that makes it hard to read.
- The author(s) of the site and any sources for the information it contains are hard to uncover in the foliage of special effects and text that obscures rather than reveals.
- The site immediately confronts the viewer with racist, sexist, homophobic, or aggressively violent patriotic or jingoistic language.
- The site hasn't been updated for a very long time.

In other words, reliable sites tend to be professionally designed, regularly maintained, transparent in their authorship and sources, and connected to bona fide organizations or individuals who can be vetted through another source. There are always exceptions, such as the mom-and-pop museum that may house valuable artifacts but has an amateurish website, the great-great-grandson's tribute site to his Civil War ancestor that may present documents (letters, a diary) unavailable anywhere else, a quirky individual who collects old folksongs and shares them via the Internet.

PROS AND CONS

For some time now, of course, YouTube and similar sites have provided a priceless real-time video archive. The trouble is—and will be for the foreseeable future—Big Data. Every minute, another 100 hours of video is uploaded onto YouTube, according to YouTube's own statistics (http://www.youtube.com/yt/press/statistics.html)—a decade of music, cute pets, and zany antics every day. Each month, viewers watch more than six billion hours of video. Put into perspective (as YouTube helpfully does), that's about an hour of viewing for every inhabitant of the planet. YouTube now contains thousands of *years* of video. It's searchable, to an extent, but there's just so much out there, as with many other kinds of online data. In order not to be overwhelmed, the researcher has to narrow his or her search as sharply as possible, and this of course runs counter to the creative process of research, which starts with a large aperture and narrows only later.

On the upside, it's obvious to digital natives that Facebook and other social networks turn out to be handy way to contact potential sources and subjects, as well as to put out the call for help in locating what you need to find. Smartphones are ubiquitous and indispensable. If, like me, you are a so-called digital immigrant, the pace of electronic innovation can make your head spin. But it's here to stay, and savvy researchers will make the most of it, adapting our methods to take advantage of what are, after all, just new and more efficient ways to do time-honored work. A young writer I know was doing his best to track down a young woman making a name for herself on the dirt-track stock car circuit. He called her manager, her home, her cell phone, texted her—nothing worked. As soon as he left a message on Facebook, she messaged him right back. And of course e-mail, which seems almost archaic now, can be a great way to stay in ongoing contact with a source—even to do a text interview, which, while not ideal, may be the best realistic option in some cases (see chapter 7 for more on interviewing). I used e-mail to reach out to some of the writers quoted in this book, who preferred being able to marshal their thoughts and express them in writing, knowing they would be used as a reference, rather than to speak more informally about their craft.

The advantage of the text interview, on whatever platform, is accuracy and finished thought—a text that is literally rendered in black and white. Very handy when consulting a technical expert or seeking an unambiguous, definitive pronouncement. The disadvantage, of course, is that the answers are rehearsed and polished—exactly what you probably don't want in an interview aimed at discovering the personality of the subject—and unlikely to surprise you with spontaneous answers that lead the conversation into uncharted, fascinating territory.

So electronic communication is your ally. And the Internet is one marketplace of sources, with all the virtues and flaws of any other source, amplified, magnified, and speeded up. And remember, it's just the starting point in researching your project: look beyond whatever you find there, track it back to its source, then use it to broaden and deepen your research.

Prompt #9: "Virtual Reliability." Browse the Internet and find three sites that you deem reliable for informing your current project, and list the reasons why (e.g., institutional affiliation, transparency and quality of quoted sources, etc.). Find three others that seem distinctly unreliable, and again list the qualities (or faults) that make them so. And ask one further question: Under what circumstances might one of the "unreliable" sites prove to be a reliable source?

Prompt #10: "Movies of Life." Search a video archive such as YouTube for video of a person or event at least a hundred years old (the Vitagraph Company was actually recording footage of the Spanish-American War in 1898). Obviously such "video" began life in another format—probably as hand-cranked motion pictures or kinescopes. Watch the action as it appears on YouTube and describe it in at least a paragraph that captures not just visual detail but texture, mood, and tone (i.e., the attitude of the filmmaker toward the subject—e.g., neutral, admiring, bemused, etc.).

6 THE ARCHIVES OF MEMORY, IMAGINATION, AND PERSONAL EXPERTISE

It isn't so astonishing, the number of things that I can remember, as
the number of things I can remember that aren't so. —Mark Twain

Memoir, properly understood, is not a pleasant stroll down memory
lane, a kind of highlight reel of your life's best or worst moments. At
its most powerful, it is driven by the heartfelt desire to come to a reckoning about some matter that disturbs you, keeps you up at night,
baffles you. You want to get to the bottom of it. Or maybe you just
want to spin memories into a fictional piece or a poem that captures
some essence of your earlier self as a way of better understanding that
self—revealing yourself *to* yourself.

Either way, remembering is not a passive activity of simply re-
trieving stored files from your brainpan: memory begets memory.
There are wonderful mnemonic devices that can help spur the act of
remembering. Here's a simple one: write down the names of each of
the kids you remember from grammar school. Now write everything
you remember about each of them: hair color, attitude, habits, how
they dressed, whether they were funny or likable or standoffish. For

each, try to recall an actual scene, a moment of action, an event in which they took part. A context.

As you conjure each one, more details will come flooding back, until soon you have an unruly cast of real characters from long ago. Test your memory against photographs and home videos, against the memories of relatives and old friends, and cross-reference your personal story with what you find in old newspapers, magazines, and yearbooks of the time. If you reference a book, song, movie, or TV show, read or watch or listen to it again and compare the new experience with your memory of it (another advantage of the Internet— almost everything is out there now, a click away).

Carolyn Forché found herself in the middle of a covert war in El Salvador in the late 1970s and gave her testimony of death squads and torture rooms in *The Country Between Us*, a powerful book of poems that became a literary touchstone for a generation of writers. Decades later, preparing to write a prose memoir about those days and what they meant, she revisited that country, once more walking the ground where she had experienced such fear and horror, as well as deep friendships and a sense of humane purpose. Her working title came from the first line of one of the most memorable poems in the collection, "The Colonel": *What You Have Heard Is True.*

Of her first sojourn in that once-embattled country, which ambushed her with its government-sanctioned violence against innocent citizens, she says, "I did not know where I was going, or that I would not return as the woman I had been." She recognizes it quite clearly as the intersection of her personal experience with history— the place where many of the most interesting stories live. In her memoir, she was not interested in laying out the basic public events of that history. Instead, she wanted to write from inside history, trusting in the authenticity of her stance of personal witness. She worked from fifty boxes of notes, reports, leaflets, white papers, letters, even airplane boarding passes. But her real archive was and remains her memory. "Memory is not a reservoir of your storied past," she says. "It is more protean and complicated." And when she was deep in the writing, when her mind and memory had transported her back to those days, she found that memory begets memory with a clarity that is almost cinematic, each frame tugging along the next, all the images and voices and feelings flooding through her onto the page.

To write *American Band: Music, Dreams, and Coming of Age in the Heartland*, Kristen Laine moved back to her home state of Indiana and immersed herself in a high school marching band similar to the one in which she herself had performed. She did exhaustive interviews, true, but she also awakened her own rich seam of memory. Molly Walling prodded relatives to fill in the dark missing pieces of her family story to write *Death in the Delta: Uncovering a Mississippi Family Secret*—a true tale of a racially motivated murder that forced her to rewind her childhood memories and reexamine them in light of what she was learning from archives and interviews. Researching and writing a book about a loved one committing murder required of her a reliable sense of integrity: she confronted not only the motives of those who had killed and covered up the crime, but her own motives in wanting to know and tell the story. This examination of conscience lends the book a deep credibility and anchors the reader's faith in the author to tell the truth.

THE ACTIVE IMAGINATION

Imagination works in a similar way. It's not just a matter of sitting quietly under a tree and waiting to be inspired. Rather, accessing your imagination means actively daydreaming, using your facts as a reference. For example, I once wrote a fictional scene in which Teddy Roosevelt was preparing to leave with the Rough Riders for Cuba during the Spanish-American War. I knew from many sources that he suffered from terrible myopia and could hardly function without his thick spectacles. So common sense told me that he would take extra pairs. He was going into a battle zone, where he could expect any piece of equipment—especially something as fragile as pince-nez eyeglasses—to be damaged. But they had to be handy in the field. Where would he keep them? In its way, it's a trivial question, but stories—and history itself—live or die based on such mundane details. Had he lost his spectacles and become effectively blind, he never would have led his troops up San Juan Hill, so he never would have become governor of New York and vice president and then president, so good-bye, Panama Canal and national parks, and on and on. Anyone I know who needs to wear glass or contacts to function in the world is conscientious, sometimes to the point of obsessiveness, about them, and TR of all people was ambitious, hugely aware of his public persona, and determined to act heroically—which meant he must be able to see what was happening around him.

I studied a photo of TR in uniform and imagined where I would secrete spare glasses. I put on a jacket similar to the one he wore and slapped my pockets. Same with trousers. Not in his pockets, where they might too easily be crushed. I had an old slouch hat like his and put it on. At once the answer was obvious—in his hat. In the nineteenth century, when all men wore hats, they kept all manner of items stored there: money, playing cards, even weapons. Lincoln famously kept his "office" in his voluminous stovepipe hat. Now that I thought I knew where to look, I was able to consult sources for the firm that had tailored his uniforms—and sure enough, these confirmed that he had special pockets sewn inside his hatband to hold spare glasses. So imagination is both a questing tool and a repository of knowledge you don't know you have until you engage that tool.

In *One Writer's Beginnings*, Eudora Welty explains how travel beyond her safe, known world of childhood inspired a greater understanding of memory and its role in the creative act, which for her turned out to be an act of yearning. She writes:

But it was not until I began to write, as I seriously did only when I reached my twenties, that I found the world out there revealing, because . . . memory had become attached to seeing, love had added itself to discovery, and because I recognized in my own longing to keep going, the need I carried inside myself to know—the apprehension, first, then the passion, to connect myself to it. Through travel I became aware of the outside world; it was through travel that I found my own introspective way into becoming a part of it.

Memory: discovery, connection, pattern, the retrospective rondure that a life takes on once we have seen how choice leads to consequence.

Near the end of her memoir, after quoting a passage from her novel *The Optimist's Daughter* in which her character dreams of crossing a bridge over the confluence between the Mississippi and Ohio Rivers on a train—a dream inspired by a beautiful memory—Welty writes:

Of course the greatest confluence of all is that which makes up human memory—the individual human memory. My own is the treasure most dearly regarded by me, in my life and in my work as a writer. Here, time, also, is subject to confluence. The memory is a living thing—it too is in transit. But during its moment, all that is remembered joins, and lives—the old and the young, the past and the present, the living and the dead.

Memory—a confluence of experience and a treasure, the creative instinct that transcends time and brings together moments far removed along the arc of a lifetime to comment upon one another.

MEMORY IS FICKLE

We also know from the work of researchers like Daniel L. Schacter (*Searching for Memory*) and others that memory is a fickle phenomenon. The act of remembering is complex, relying on several different systems for accessing different kinds of "information," be it factual or emotional. Our brain is not simply a hard drive of stored impressions to be called forth by the right code.

It matters a lot, for instance, how strong our emotions were running when we experienced the thing that becomes memory. Some scientists make a compelling case that most of what we experience in life is not remembered at all in the first place, so it can't be recovered—that only those events linked to some high emotion we were experiencing at the time of the event find their way into our memory, encoded along with the emotion that accompanied them.

What we "remember" of the rest may be constructed from other sources, tricking us into believing the scenes and conversations and events that trace the paths of our lives. This, they argue, accounts for why most of us have far more vivid memories of childhood and young adulthood than of experiences that occurred later in life. When you do a thing for the first time—first day at school, first kiss, first trip abroad, first death in the family—it comes freighted with much higher emotion than all subsequent occasions. Many things become routine and therefore, quite literally, unmemorable. This is also why the music that so moves us is usually the music we listened to as adolescents, when our brains were still forming, when our lives were roller coasters of hormone-driven emotional highs and lows and the act of listening to music was itself a new experience.

Just as profoundly, Schacter and his colleagues have successfully implanted false memories into their subjects—caused them to "remember" vividly events that never happened—and could be proved to never have happened: a broken arm in childhood, say, when an X-ray clearly shows a bone that has never been broken. So memory is incomplete, and sometimes it lies, and it can be manipulated without the one remembering even knowing. This doesn't mean it loses any of its allure as a writer's archive—on the contrary, the very unreliable nature of memory makes it all the more fascinating.

When I was a kid, probably seven or eight years old, my two older brothers decided to build a tree house in a sturdy tree that stood in the vacant lot adjacent to our house. I have a vivid memory of that day. I was standing on the ground, maybe ten feet from the tree. One brother was perched in the tree on a limb holding a hammer, and the other was climbing the trunk to join him. Something distracted me, so I was looking away from the tree at the moment when the brother in the tree dropped the hammer. The hammer landed directly on the head of the brother climbing the tree, who fell to the ground, knocked momentarily unconscious. Now here's the strange part. We all agree that I was standing on the ground and took no part in the action. But for decades my other two brothers argued over which one had dropped the hammer and which one had been clobbered by it. *Both* claimed to have been the victim of the falling hammer. For each, the memory was vivid and real. But clearly one of them was misremembering. Finally, following my father's funeral, some forty years after the incident, we gathered at our boyhood home and reenacted the event. Only then did we all agree—at least provisionally—who had dropped the hammer on whose head. I have always loved the discrepancy (in fact, I felt a little sad that we finally agreed) because I found it psychologically very interesting that both brothers should insist on having been the victim—in effect, to hold the moral high ground. And it seemed to me no accident that the fog of memory at last cleared only on an occasion drenched in strong emotions of loss and grief.

So don't paper over discrepancies—use them to your advantage. The way we misremember an event supplies a wealth of information: emotional, psychological, cultural, based in our character and experience. It just may not be the best or even the only archive from which to determine the actual facts of an event. Imagination plays a crucial role in understanding and interpreting facts—and casting them into a plausible fiction. So any writer who wants to create a *What if?* scenario that transcends household reality uses the factual world as a starting point—but only as a starting point.

DREAMS AND PLAUSIBILITY

In an earlier chapter, I mentioned Bob Reiss's research for his novel *Salt Maker*, based on a fictional scenario in which the president of the United States is tried for treason for failing to launch a nuclear strike at the Soviet Union. Once Reiss had found experts to verify that indeed such a scenario was *possible*, he had to make it *plausible*. He had to begin in the world of real facts: How does the early warning system alert us to an incoming Soviet missile? How much time would a president have to react? What could cause a false alarm that seemed very real? What is the actual law governing treasonable acts, and who enforces it? Who would prosecute the president under what theory of the crime? How would a defense attorney defend him? Who would be president in the meantime? And on and on.

Such works of fiction traffic in subjects that a lot of people know a lot about, and so before you can launch your flight of fancy, you have to lay solid groundwork. You have to really know your stuff. Imagination works both with and beyond the facts. And when you do, the fiction can become all too plausible. In 1979 a motion picture called *The China Syndrome* posited a scenario in which a nuclear power plant suffers a potentially disastrous accident, which is filmed by a television crew. The dogged crew—played by Jane Fonda and Michael Douglas—tries to expose the lapses in safety procedures that caused the accident, but is thwarted by a major cover-up, until the plant supervisor, played by Jack Lemmon, takes drastic action to avert catastrophe. Twelve days after the movie's release, a partial meltdown of the plant at the Three Mile Island nuclear reactor in Pennsylvania unfolded in a way that was uncannily similar to the plot of the film, the worst nuclear accident in U.S. history. The imagination can thus prefigure reality, and it can also speak to us in other ways.

Jason Mott's blockbuster first novel, *The Returned*, brings together memory and imagination. The novel begins when the long-dead son of an elderly couple shows up at their front door, looking exactly as he did on his eighth birthday—the day he drowned in a nearby river. We soon learn that this phenomenon—*returning*—is happening inexplicably all over the world. In a note to the reader at the end of the book, Mott talks about how the story began with a dream he had about his mother near the anniversary of her death. He writes, "We shared something that, for me, is only possible within the dreamscape: a conversation between a mother and a son." In the following months, as hard as he tried to re-create that dream, he could not. He confided all this one day to a friend. He continues, "Sometime later in our lunch, as conversation was running low, my friend asked, 'Can you imagine if she really did come back, just for one night? And what if it wasn't just her? What if it happened to other people, too?' *The Returned* was born that day."

It doesn't take an armchair psychologist to realize that we all process the people and events of our lives through our dreams, random as they may seem. Whatever is lingering in the subconscious eventually finds expression somehow, some way. Whatever triggered Mott's vivid and emotionally compelling dream—grief, love, longing, a sense of unfinished business—was profound enough to compel him to express it in words—his art. "*The Returned* became more than just a manuscript for me; it was also an opportunity," he writes. "An opportunity for me to sit with my mother again. An opportunity to see her smile, to hear her voice, a chance to stay with her in those last days of her life, rather than hide from her the way I did in the real world." This sounds a lot like the same kind of compulsion that fuels memoir, meditating on what is past and gone in order to create a vessel for meaning.

In wrestling with all the emotions unleashed by the writing of it, Mott came to another epiphany. "I eventually realized what I wanted the novel to be—what it *could* be," he says. "I wanted *The Returned* to be an opportunity for my readers to feel what I felt in that dream back in 2010, to find their own stories here. I wanted it to be a place where—through methods and magic unknown even to me—the hard, uncaring rules of life and death do not exist and people can be with those they loved once more." So a night dream inspires reflection and conversation, and the dynamic of the dream takes root in the writer's imagination, flowering into a story that is, finally, all about the reader.

We all have an archive of memories—however vague, imperfect, incomplete, and elusive. Mining that archive can require both a habit of reflection and some ingenuity in prompting it with photos, smells, words, voices, even other people's memories, to jar loose some of the precious images and sensory experiences that have gotten stuck in some recess of our mind. And we all have an imagination, a tool that can be sharpened with use. To be a good writer, you must be an accomplished daydreamer. And even when you are not actively thinking about a project, your subconscious mind is. Pay attention to your dreams, for we dream obliquely, sneaking up on our preoccupations slantwise. Listen to your intuition as it connects the dots while you are not looking. Our idling imagination is good at assembling into patterns the facts and impressions we have discovered, connecting ideas and images that, rationally, don't seem at all connected. Our imaginations sometimes work metaphorically, connecting things on a figurative rather than a literal level.

It is often in the act of looking away that we catch the most valuable insight out of the corner of our eye. Insights, ideas, images, connections, even the words to express them, often come tumbling out of our imagination unbidden in the morning shower, on a long car trip, during a lazy ramble through the park. Memories and ideas alike can be triggered by a noise, a word, a scrap of a tune, a billboard, a stray remark by a friend at lunch. Close your eyes and listen.

WHEN YOU ARE THE EXPERT

We often call upon experts to help explicate technical or complex projects. But sometimes you the writer are the expert: your experience qualifies you to help the reader to discover the subject. This may be because you actually went to the place or did the thing about which you are writing, or your ethnicity, gender, race, or occupation lends you a valuable perspective. Rather than let this realization make you smug or arrogant, let it humble you and lead you to remember just how you got your expertise so you can re-create the process for your reader.

An ER doc named Paul Austin wrote a terrific episodic first-person account of tending to gunshot victims, attempted suicides, hypochondriacs, burn victims, injured ballplayers, and all the rest, while trying to maintain a sane family life and retain his sense of hope and humor (*Something for the Pain: Compassion and Burnout in the ER*). In another moving book, *Beautiful Eyes: A Father Transformed*, he writes from a different identity, as the father of a girl born with Down syndrome, addressing how this remarkable child has taught him wonderful and humbling lessons about fatherhood. He doesn't stop being a doctor, but that role is relegated to the background, and now he draws on his expertise as father and husband. Susan Kushner Resnick—a seasoned reporter experienced in writing about *other* people's dramas—wrote an absolutely gripping account of conquering a near-fatal bout with postpartum depression—*Sleepless Days: One Woman's Journey through Postpartum Depression*)—because she was the one who survived it. Both Austin and Resnick were careful to consult many other sources to provide context and even greater authority to their own hard-won expertise.

It isn't just nonfiction writers who take on the mantle of expert. Both Tim O'Brien and Bruce Weigl have drawn deeply from their experience as combat infantrymen in Vietnam—O'Brien in such works of fiction as *Going After Cacciato* and *The Things They Carried*; Weigl— a Bronze Star awardee—in poetry collections such as *Song of Napalm*. For both writers, the experience of combat was transformative in their development as artists. Weigl testifies to this process in his memoir, *The Circle of Hanh*: "The paradox of my life as a writer is that the war ruined my life and in return gave me my voice."

In his masterful long poem "I Have Seen Black Hands," Richard Wright, the son of an illiterate black sharecropper, draws on his "expertise" as an African American man struggling to succeed in a racist era—"I am black and I have seen black hands / Raised in fists of revolt, side by side with the white fists of white workers. . . ." And, of course, he is best known for *Native Son*, based in the Chicago he knew so well. John Irving, a champion collegiate wrestler, was able to cast T. S. Garp, the hero of his novel *The World According to Garp*, as a wrestler and later a wrestling coach. He knew the physical demands of the sport as well as the psychology of competitiveness firsthand from many hard years of experience.

Such expertise isn't reserved for professional writers. Indeed, if you are a novice, recognizing your own credentials to write with authority about an important subject is a big step toward finding your confidence. We all have many identities, based on age, gender, ethnicity, background, sexuality, where we live, our profession, our abilities, our life experiences, and so on. Some of these identities change as we grow older and take on different experiences and roles. If you're stuck, spinning your wheels, unable to engage in some meaningful project, take half an hour to inventory your multiple identities: husband, mother, ex-football player, amputee, only child, cancer survivor, firefighter, native Chicagoan, actor, gay man, military veteran, oboe player, news junkie, gardener, Christian, Asian American, shade-tree mechanic, singer in the church choir, aspiring chef. Each of these identities yields clues about our passions, the matters that fill our hearts, engage our minds, challenge our convictions, fuel our creativity, and occupy our time and energy.

Each is likely at the center of at least one memorable personal anecdote that can be exploded into a larger story. And each has imparted to us important *knowledge*—practical, emotional, visceral, intellectual, moral. So a transgendered woman in an undergraduate composition class writes a moving account of just how difficult her life is on campus. Another woman writes of losing her marine husband to an IED and finding herself a widow at twenty-three. An un-athletic gay man writes of his decision to take up competitive running at the age of forty-eight—having been diagnosed as HIV-positive—and, for the first time in his life, enjoying the camaraderie of a supportive network of straight male friends. A twin daughter of a mother who is also a twin interviews her sister and writes of the challenge of creating a unique identity in a culture that automatically pairs the two of them as if they are a matched set, not two very different individuals. People tend to assume that whenever she looks at her sister, she sees herself—yet unlike everyone else, she *never* sees herself and her sister together except in photographs. And it turns out (so the psychologists tell us) that the self we see in photographs is not the self who is most familiar; that self is the inverse image we recognize from looking in the mirror. All the above are true examples, and the writers deserve to tell their own stories in full.

THE "INSCAPE" AND TERMS OF ART

Nomi Stone, who earned her PhD in anthropology at Columbia University and is a well-regarded poet, uses research to ground her poems. "Yet poems of course are never mere information," she reminds us. "Poems are about affect and color and the poet's particular seeing.

They are what happens when you dunk the world into the inscape, and return the world to the world, differently." That "inscape"—our interior self—includes all that we know, our life expertise.

One way we mine our expertise is through language—the specific jargon or technical terms we master in order to participate in a group, profession, or activity. Some of it is quite formal, a way of describing with precision a procedure or item or responsibility: terms of art. But a lot of the most interesting language we all know is insider slang, often laced with dark humor or irony. Thus Paul Austin, the ER doc, talks about "moving the meat"—treating patients quickly and then either "streeting" them or admitting them. Like many insider terms, it sounds crude, yet actually describes a humane efficiency in direct, if ironic, shorthand. The goal is to keep things moving, get the patients treated as quickly as possible, and either send them home or put them under more comprehensive care. Rock climbers refer ironically to having a "high gravity day"—that is, a day during which they fall a lot. Thomas French (*Zoo Story*) listens closely to both kinds of language:

I love the way people speak. I love the jargon. . . . If you hang out in a NICU (neonatal intensive care unit) with the nurses, they have a whole jargon that I just fell in love with. So, for instance, they will refer to "Well, I've got a bad baby here." Or "I've got this baby who's not behaving." That's the jargon they use. And what they mean by that is not that the baby is actually a brat. They're so little, they're not making conscious decisions about anything. What they mean is there's something going wrong with that baby—so keep an extra close eye on them.

Again, such banter reveals a deep sense of concern and care. French was not simply idly hanging out in the NICU hoping for a story. He was attending his own premature daughter through the touch-and-go months after her birth—and only when she made it to the other side of that dangerous limbo, would he write about her amazing will to beat the odds. So his first experience with the jargon of the nurses was as an anxious parent, not a reporter—attuned to every nuance of what they were saying, listening not just for information but for hope. At that fraught moment, that was his expertise.

In creating an inventory of your identities—and therefore of areas in which you might be an expert—write down the lexicon, both the formal terms and the slang. Some of this is bound to be crude, even off-color, but in doing so you will remind yourself of how much you know and how evocative is the language of your expertise. The words and phrases themselves can suggest avenues for research and writing, call up imagery, suggest storylines. Writing begins with words, and in each of your identities resides a colorful secret language.

Prompt #11: "Dreaming into Words." Keep a pad and pen beside your bed. The next time you have a vivid dream, write down all you can remember of it, even if your recollection upon waking is fragmentary and hazy, as is often the case. Take some time out of the day when you are fully awake and alert to reflect on the dream, to read what you have written and add any details or observations that occur to you. Then seek out someone who knows you well, a friend or loved one, and discuss the dream. Go back to your written account, reflect on the conversation, and come up with the first line of a story or poem inspired by the dream.

Prompt #12: "Memory Test." As succinctly as you can, write down your memory of a significant event that you witnessed or took part in. Now test the reliability of your version by finding at least three sources that confirm or refute some part of your memory of the event. For instance, I have a vivid boyhood memory of standing in the rain alongside the Penn Central railroad tracks with my parents to watch the funeral train of Robert F. Kennedy pass. I recently found the blurry black-and-white photo I took of the train with my Brownie camera. But the photo is lit by bright sunshine.

Prompt #13: "Your Expert Identities." Inventory your several identities and list them according to your family, ethnic, and religious background; your age and gender; your life experience; your politics and ethics; your professional experience; and any other activities in which you participate. Write a brief anecdote related to one of them. Does it suggest a larger story?

Prompt #14: "The Language of the Craft." For two of the above, create a lexicon: terms of art, formal jargon, and insider slang. For each term, write a line that describes suggested areas of inquiry, story lines, ideas, and insights.

7 THE WARM ART OF THE INTERVIEW

Listening to my tapes, I learned that I often interrupted people just before they were about to tell me something I never would have suspected, so now I tried to let the subject guide the interview and to encourage the interviewee's anecdotes. —Honor Moore, author of *The White Blackbird: A Life of the Painter Margarett Sargent by Her Granddaughter*

The ability to conduct a good interview is one of the most useful skills a writer can learn. We tend to think of it primarily as a tool for journalists or biographers, but really a good interview is nothing more than a lively conversation in which you—the interviewer—learn information you probably could not discover any other way. Thus it can be the perfect way for a novelist to understand certain kinds of people he or she wants to write about. They might not be the primary characters in a story or novel, but their actions, their motivations, and especially their voices must ring true to the reader. Spending time among police detectives, cannery workers, ER nurses and doctors, refugees, battered women, immigrants, orphans, business executives, teachers, construction workers—pretty much any class of people defined by their occupation, their leisure interests, their location, their ethnicity, their religion, whatever matters to the project—means talking to them and especially *listening* to them. Hearing not just what they talk about or their opinions but also the cadence of their speech, their idiom, their humor, the full range of their expression. It's no accident that John Steinbeck captures the speech of the Dust Bowl refugees in *The Grapes of Wrath* with such lyrical precision—the novel began as a documentary project, and Steinbeck interviewed scores of such people in squalid camps in California.

For a poet, the ability to capture voice on the page and make it sound true to the reader's ear is crucial, and, again, listening to those voices in the world is key. When we make it a point to talk to interesting strangers, they usually tell us interesting things. They give us fresh ideas. They set off flashbulbs in our imaginations. They upset our preconceptions. They challenge our settled views on politics, race, religion, matters of social justice—usually by complicating them. And complication is good for the writer, leaving room to unravel the tangled skein of competing truths, to negotiate the excruciating nuances, to find the choices that matter. They jolt us out of our lives, and in so doing teach us about ourselves. And of course for the nonfiction writer, the interviewee becomes a prized source of expert knowledge who can offer a tutorial on the chosen subject and guide us toward a deeper understanding of that subject.

Despite conventional wisdom, an interview is not necessarily a series of questions and answers. If I could, I would banish the term *interview* altogether, since it conjures for too many of us a stressful, even adversarial meeting in which there are good questions and bad, right answers and wrong. Think of the police "interviewing" a witness or suspect, or the classic job "interview." In both cases, the interviewer is manipulating the subject, however subtly, to reveal what the subject may wish to keep confidential—either because it's incriminating or because it would cast him or her in a less than flattering light—in order to get a clear and accurate picture of who the person is and how much to trust him or her. We're not talking about that agenda-driven kind of conversation, at least not usually. Rather what we are really talking about is a warm human encounter, fraught with possibility and challenge. It requires preparation and proceeds according to a certain etiquette that preserves the dignity of all parties in a nuanced transaction, more pas de deux than interrogation.

I rarely bring a long list of questions to an interview. Usually there is one big thing I want the subject to speak about. I may be curious about other things, but knowing what lies at the heart of my curiosity helps center me and allows me to listen to all the other things the person says. Not long ago I interviewed an old blues musician named Ironing Board Sam. He had been helped by the Music Maker Relief Foundation—a brilliantly effective nonprofit that rescues musicians who have fallen on hard times, often because they get off the road in old age without a pension. They were never superstars but men and women who created and kept alive the American traditions of folk, blues, jazz, old-time, bluegrass, and all the rest. In addition to helping these players pay rent, get their teeth fixed, see a doctor, buy a new instrument—whatever they need—Music Maker also professionally records them so their work is available for sale, recordings that constitute a rich archive of music that would otherwise be lost.

For the able-bodied players, Music Maker finds them gigs. Ironing Board Sam, who had come home from the road flat busted after more than four decades of performing, now had a regular weekly gig, a new record, and festival dates to look forward to. His life had been turned around, the bleak prospects of a lonely old age transformed into an active artistic and social life with purpose. He was reaching a brand-new audience of young listeners, and the main thing I wanted to ask him was what that meant to him: what came over him when he was onstage, performing for a live crowd? After a long afternoon conversation, it was the very last thing I asked him. He smiled and in his eyes went back to some faraway place deep inside and maybe a long time ago. He said softly, "It's my life. It heals me." His simple metaphor—"heals"—cuts to the heart of the sense of rescue and resuscitation, of saving these aging artists both physically and artistically, making them whole again. It's not a word that ever would have occurred to me.

I have a whole notebook of quotes from that interview I didn't use. For one thing, the piece was assigned at fewer than a thousand words. So, for example, Sam told me he knew when he had reached a certain level of mastery: "When you can look around the room and play, you're a piano player." Sam also told me the story of how he got his name, a long rambling account. So I didn't include that but summarized it as succinctly as I could: "He mounted his first portable organ on an actual ironing board for a gig in Miami in the 1950s—and was tagged with the moniker 'Ironing Board Sam.'" And even though I knew I'd be writing a short piece, before I talked to Sam, I interviewed Tim and Denise Duffy, founders of Music Maker. They said smart, compassionate, illuminating things, which I included in my early draft:

The rewards come daily. Tim says, "Just seeing Ironing Board Sam this morning pop out of his house and jump into his car and go do something. When we met him, he didn't have anything. . . . But now he has local gigs, he's going to go make a new record with a big record company, he's going to the Jazzfest."

But, Denise points out, there is an emotional cost to working with musicians in their eighties and even nineties: "We spend so much time with these artists over the years that they become like family—and all too often you have to say goodbye. That's the hardest part of the job.

"And then the other hard part is that the well of poverty is so deep, we can't fund-raise our way out of all these people's poverty," Denise says. But they end their isolation—too often the fate of elderly people—by incorporating them into the Music Maker family.

"If they feel like they've passed it on, they're like, 'Debt paid!'"

And then cut all of the above.

In the final draft, I gave each of them just one quote that I hoped would define them and leave the emphasis on Sam. Tim Duffy: "In the beginning, poor working-class people invented the greatest, most valuable export of our nation—blues, jazz. It defines who we are as a people—how we talk, the religious ways, the folkways." I cut all the references to Sam's second chance, because it was already covered. Denise Duffy: "The senior artists, their musical heritage was given to them by uncles and fathers and mothers at the beginning of the last century, and they carried it with them, and they all feel a tremendous responsibility to pass it on. They love working with younger musicians, where they can teach them the different styles—on the back porch, the same way they learned."

Cutting the part about how hard it is to say good-bye to the ones who die, and how large a need is still going unfilled, was difficult. Both seemed like important matters. But the point of the piece was to celebrate an altruistic act of redemption, perhaps to inspire readers to also pitch in, which meant offering hope instead of resignation. And you'll note that the quotes I cut were awfully good ones. As in all revisions, it's easiest to cut the obvious clunkers, but you're not really revising till you're cutting good passages that somehow just don't fit the project. For a book-length treatment, I undoubtedly would make different choices, explore that exquisite grief and the larger plight of the elderly artists who finish their lives lonely and forgotten. That emotional one-two punch would have overwhelmed such a short piece.

Another writer might have made different choices. But it goes back to the notion of knowing why you are interviewing a subject, what insight and meaning you are after. I have three standard questions, two of which I ask near the end of an interview: "What haven't we talked about that I need to know?" And "May I contact you again to follow up on what we're talked about today, and how best should I do that—telephone, e-mail, snail mail, et cetera?" Many times I have another question—the "show me" request. I ask to see something related to what we're talking about. As I traveled the country interviewing those artists who had served in that secret deception force during World War II, whenever possible I interviewed them in their homes or studios. At some point in our conversation, I would always ask, "Did you bring anything back with you?" One guy bounded upstairs and I heard him rustling around, and a few minutes later he reappeared wearing his Class A army uniform from 1945. "It still fits!" he said, beaming. Another hauled out an ammo box full of belts of live Spandau machine-gun rounds—and insisted I take one. Bill Blass had pieces of art he had bought and sent home. Others had drawings, sketches, notebooks, old letters, handmade Christmas cards. All of it made their stories more real and tangible, while inspiring other memories.

FINDING GOOD SOURCES

So just how does a writer locate outside sources both as interview subjects and also expert consultants? This can be a systematic process sometimes—as when a writer searches out experts by reviewing the faculty roster on a university website, which typically includes areas of specialization and often links to publications in the field. So for a recent documentary film project, while seeking out experts to explain what a barrier island is and how it is formed, I was able to locate not only several geologists and coastal ecologists but also links to their scholarly papers and PowerPoint slide shows they created to illustrate their theories. I would have done the same thing if I was aiming for a cycle of poems about how wind and water sculpt the island, or a short story featuring a main character who does field research on a barrier island.

This technique also works for government offices, corporations, clubs, benevolent organizations, trade associations, nonprofit groups, sports teams, medical practices, and so on. Check out who is on their roster—usually available online or in their printed literature—and find them on social media or through Google. Dogpile.com or other sites can often yield contact information. Or simply make a phone call and ask to talk to the person. It may take several tries, one person handing you off to another, but gentle persistence pays off. Reaching out to sources is also a matter of the grapevine—that is, finding a friend of a friend of a friend. A colleague of mine had interviewed a coastal geology expert for a project, and through him I got contact information and an e-mail introduction, so that when I contacted the expert, he was expecting to hear from me and eager to talk.

Sometimes when configuring a long project, the writer essentially screens candidates to find the most promising subjects for the story, as when Walt Harrington tracked down artisans for his book *Acts of Creation: America's Finest Hand Craftsmen at Work.* When

Thomas French began his research for 13, a long newspaper series on middle schoolers in Tampa, he first contacted schools and explained his project to principals and teachers, who recommended students who might be interested. After lots of preliminary interviews, he settled on the ones he would follow, based on a variety of factors: how open they were, their level of expressiveness, the depth and breadth of cooperation their parents were willing to allow, and the intangible virtue of just seeming *interesting*. In that pre-interview stage for such a project, the writer is essentially trying to suss out which candidate is likely to deliver the most compelling, entertaining, meaningful story.

Another tactic is simply to go where the kind of person you're looking for is likely to be. In search of a present-day moonshiner, I called the Appalachian Heritage Center and found out about a fellow they actually hired to demonstrate the process of distilling whiskey as a tool to preserve folkways. He was an old lumberman who often participated in folk fairs. So at the next Mountain Heritage Festival, I located him at his craft station, where he was actually demonstrating how to use an old-fashioned crosscut saw. But what he talked to me about was making moonshine whiskey. People congregate according to their interests—at sporting events, jazz clubs, gun shows, music fairs, Civil War reenactments, community meetings, church services, yoga centers, gaming rooms, and so on. It's a simple truth but a useful one: seek them out in their native habitats. Often my last question to any interviewee for any project is "Can you suggest anybody else I should talk to?" That question usually leads to an even more interesting source.

Also, don't discount your own personal network. Remember that game "Six Degrees of Kevin Bacon" in which players compete to prove that they are linked to the actor by the fewest personal connections? All of us have family, friends, work colleagues, and acquaintances who in turn have their own networks of people. We frequent health clubs and coffee shops, go to church and the dog park. All these places are full of interesting people who might be exactly the person we need to talk to—either for their own contribution to our project or because they can lead us to a friend or sister-in-law or acquaintance who is. All of them are only a casual conversation away.

In my experience, writers are usually their own worst obstacles to access. While it may be true that under certain circumstances an organization will require some bona fides to grant access, it's also true that simply asking politely can open lots of doors. And sometimes being a writer is beside the point. Many communities have ride-along programs with police, for instance—any citizen can ask to participate. Any citizen can sit in a courtroom and listen to a trial. Historic sites, factories, ports, even some military bases offer tours. Celebrities may guard their privacy, but when a famous person is giving a public talk, anybody can step up during the Q&A and ask a question, and you can quote the answer. Almost every organization of any size has someone whose job it is to interact with media and the public, and that person can introduce you to others in the organization and get you in the door. There is no magic credential required. Of course, it's true that any person or organization can deny access, but, honestly, in my experience very few have ever asked me for references or a faculty ID or a résumé of published work—and certainly not a press pass. Very often the writer is worrying about this far more than the potential interview subject.

SAVING WHAT YOU HEAR

One thing you can't avoid about interviewing is the work required to somehow record and recall it. Do you literally record it on some device to be played back later, or do you "record" it with pen and paper? As I noted in chapter 3, I prefer whenever possible to record the interview electronically, especially if I am working on a book that may take months or even years to complete. I like the accuracy and completeness such a recording offers. When using a recorder, you should ask the subject to identify himself or herself by name and title. This is usually sufficient to establish that the subject has agreed to the interview and is aware of your project. Some media outlets require that you actually ask the subject if he or she agrees to the interview on the record, to forestall any issues later, if an interviewee has second thoughts. In any case, you always want to declare yourself as a writer and make sure the person understands you are interviewing for publication or broadcast. Some book publishers and magazines will require a written release, especially if you are dealing with a controversial subject or you plan to extensively write about a non-public figure's private life.

The ones I have used are simple documents of a few sentences that include the subject's name, title, address, contact phone and e-mail, and any other information pertinent to the project. Then follows a brief, clear paragraph, for example: "By signing this form, I grant my permission to use my comments, audio and video recordings, and any other materials I may provide to be published and/or broadcast in all media for this project. By doing so I do not give up any copyrights or other rights I may hold to such materials." The name of the project is included on the form, which is dated and signed by both the subject and you. Some publishers will have their own specific forms. Forms tailored to all sorts of projects can be found on the Internet. The goal is simply to have a clear understanding with your subject that his or her words might become part of a published or broadcast work. "Other materials" may include photos, artwork, or recordings they themselves have made that are relevant to the story. But most of the time simply declaring your intention, taking good notes, and/or recording the conversation is fine.

The primary consideration is to ensure that the interviewee feels comfortable, that the encounter does not feel strained and artificial and self-conscious. In such a case, a notebook may be the best option. And if the "interview" is really a long-term encounter, hanging out with a subject for a week on the road or revisiting him or her frequently in the course of months, there may be many times when you simply listen and take no notes, simply pay attention. There may also be subjects you can reach only by telephone or computer on FaceTime, Skype, e-mail, or by trading social media messages. You can easily record with FaceTime and Skype with the subject's permission—and the recording will have no impact on the tenor of the interview. Again, ask the subject up front for permission to re-cord the interview. The second two, e-mail or social media, provide a written transcript. An advantage of a written interview, such as one conducted through e-mail, is that the subject can furnish thoughtful answers and you know that your quotes are accurate. What may be sacrificed is spontaneity, candor, or colorful, informal turns of phrase that may get edited out.

So sometimes technological aids become crucial. Other times, ethical and legal issues come to the fore. Or simply matters of per-sonal comfort and preference. What is the best way for you to record and organize your result? If you can't find what you've discovered or figure out why you thought it useful to know, it's hard to use it creatively. Do you simply scribble diligently while someone else is talking, or do you rely on some kind of recording device? Do you transcribe the whole interview yourself, or do you hire someone to do it, or do you transcribe only certain passages? I've revealed some of my working method in chapter 3. Here I'll say only that when I decide to transcribe an interview, I always do it myself—otherwise I miss tone of voice, ambient background sound, laughter, pauses—all the things that lend dimension to the conversation. When I hear the actual voice, I am often reminded of the speaker's posture and man-ner, her facial expression, her halting manner of speech. I can hear if a line is delivered straight or with irony. If I rely on notes only, at the earliest opportunity—before my scribbling becomes an illegible cipher even to me—I type a transcript and add whatever else I can recall from the interview—both what was said and details about the place, the person, the circumstances, the weather, whatever seems pertinent.

How do you make use of the interview in a creative piece as a foun-dation for dialogue? You want to know not only whom to interview but what you hope—or need—for the encounter to succeed. Start by realizing that an interview is a kind of date. Ordinarily, the subject is a stranger who may or may not have any experience being interviewed. Most private people don't. You can't just barge into their world, stick a recorder in their face, and hurl questions at them, expecting they will immediately reveal their most intimate truths to you, a stranger, to use for your own purposes. You need to create a sense of trust—and it has to be genuine. It's not a con job. You really must *be* a person they can trust with their story. This takes time—maybe just a few minutes of small talk, maybe months of coaxing via letters or telephone. And often it's clear in the course of an interview that trust has either been established or eroded.

I wanted to interview the late Ellsworth Kelly, the painter, about his wartime experiences after D-day in Europe, but at first he wouldn't talk to me. By gentle persistence, through a series of telephone calls over the course of months, I finally was able to get him to grant me an interview. It turned out he had been recently interviewed by a journalist who then did a hatchet job on him in print, and he was understandably wary. Very nervous, I arrived at the small town where he lived about fifteen minutes early and pulled to the curb outside the local church to consult my notes and settle my nerves. Almost at once, a man came out the church, approached my car, and asked if he could help me—I think he was a sexton. I explained why I was in town and that I was early. I knew Mr. Kelly lived nearby and didn't want to be rude by showing up before my appointment time. He went back inside, and within a couple of minutes a dark SUV rolled up next to my car and the tinted window slid open. A man in sunglasses said, "Mr. Kelly will see you now." I followed the SUV around the corner and down the road a ways to Mr. Kelly's farmhouse.

We met in a very formal space. Mr. Kelly turned out to be a soft-spoken, unassuming man, gracious as he could be, and I liked him immediately. He had a humility about him, a thoughtfulness, that belied his celebrity in the international art world. We talked about some of the Asian artwork in the room—not his own—and, as he began to trust me, we proceeded into more intimate territory, both figuratively and literally. He invited me to walk outside with him, and we talked as we ambled down the lane, ending up at his painting studio. He ushered me inside, and there in the high-walled studio stood giant panels that he was preparing for an installation in Berlin. But the treasure was a folio of wartime drawings he had done at the front in the awful winter of 1944–45—during the snowy cataclysm of the Battle of the Bulge. One by one, he took them out of the folio and told me the heartbreaking story behind each drawing or painting.

Even so, he was not comfortable with my recording our conversation and never gave me permission to use my digital recorder, so I listened hard, took furious notes, rushed back to the cabin where I was staying, and spent the next four hours writing down everything I could recall about our encounter and what he had told me. Ultimately he gave me permission to use some of his wartime art in the book—to my knowledge the first time it had ever been seen by the public—and it was a huge testament to his trust. Because I was after accuracy above all, I allowed him to review how I quoted him prior to publication. He graciously suggested only a couple of corrections—one of them the name of a bird I had heard wrong, for he was a practiced bird-watcher whose art was profoundly inspired by the paintings of John James Audubon.

THE ART OF LISTENING

Nomi Stone writes, "For the past ten years, I have sought to heed Carolyn Forché's call to comprehend the impress of the social on the poetic imagination, conducting ethnographic fieldwork and writing poems first on an island off the coast of Tunisia and then in mock Middle Eastern villages across the United States." In the latter project, Stone faced serious ethical and practical challenges as she interviewed soldiers during war games in the desert of the western United States designed to train American troops for combat in Iraq. She recalls, "I came from a theater of war to war as theater." She was very much interested in the "role players"—Iraqis playing the role of the enemy to the U.S. soldiers. Most had come from Iraq after helping American forces as translators or guides, and they or their families back in Iraq might be put at risk. It was not enough to earn their trust; she also had to make sure that she guarded their identities in anything she would write about them. "Fieldwork is really important, and at its best it is collaborative," she says. She relies on her interlocutors to guide her through the cultural and political realities of their situation, and the interviews are crucial in the process—to both her anthropology and her poetry. For Stone, those she interviews become in effect part of a creative team, of which she is also part. She says, "My training as an anthropologist has attuned me to some ways of getting it right, and being a poet has summoned other attunements."

Thomas French is one of the best interviewers I've ever seen—not because he is a charismatic genius, but, on the contrary, because he is humble and soft-spoken, very respectful of his subjects. He likes listening to people talk. He has both empathy for those he interviews and a highly trained sense of what to listen for. He often conducts interviewing clinics for reporters and creative writers, calling on a volunteer and then simply talking to that person as he would any subject in the field. I once watched him conduct such an interview in a room full of about eighty writers. The subject was a woman who worked as a college administrator. After only a few minutes into the interview, we were all hanging on every word. Recounting the mundane details of an ordinary day, the woman revealed fascinating insights about her life.

French's technique is simple but, like many simple things, requires practice and patience. "So I just tried to give her as much opportunity as possible to feel safe," he says. "But ultimately it's the other person's option. And I get journalists who ask, 'Well, how do you trick somebody? What's the trick to get somebody to open up?' And my answer is 'There's no trick. If you're tricking, then you're not doing it right.'" French hits upon a crucial truth here: it doesn't matter how smart or clever you are if the other person shies away from talking to you. Ultimately the subject has much more control over the encounter than we do. French explains:

There are some people who are very adamant about being aggressive in an interview. I'm not a fan of that at all. I think you can bluster somebody into giving you one answer. You know, yes or no to whether they stole $40,000 from the glee club. But I think if what you really want to do is learn something about them, you can't trick or force that. You've got to give them enough information so they can decide if they feel safe. So that's what I try to do in that circumstance, that's what I always try to do.

Again, remember that when you begin an interview, you start a relationship with another person. It might remain very formal—a mayor or senator, say, briefing you on a policy matter. Or it might quickly become intimate, a non-public person revealing a guarded memory of some formative experience. As humans, we crave a personal audience, someone who will listen with interest to our troubles, our ideas, the details of how we spent our day. And often it is easier to reveal startling, intimate truths to an interviewer—a relative stranger—than to a friend or loved one. I've frequently had the experience of someone telling me something very private and shocking, only to add that they've never told anyone this before.

The challenge is to practice a *listening silence*—alert, attentive, yet restrained. French says, "What happens when you interview for a story is you're essentially interviewing for *meaning*." In his exercise—as in his real research—he often starts with the simplest kind of prompt: "Walk me through your day so far from the time you woke up. Describe your bedroom. What did you have for breakfast? When you opened the refrigerator to get milk, what was taped on the door? Who else was in the house?" And so on. The smallest details—the picture of the child on the fridge, the husband sleeping in as the wife rises to go to work in the dark, and so on—create a vivid experience of a life—and the drama of that life, the meaning of words and actions.

THE DRAMA OF THE ORDINARY

It can be the ordinary elements of a life—not the one moment of tragedy or melodrama or heroism—that turn out to offer the most meaning, because they happen over and over again, forming the person. French explains:

There are events that happen to us that are singular—they happen once—and they really change things for us. But an awful lot of our life's deeper context is embedded in our everyday routines. And so that exercise, those props, are just ways to show that. To show that if you start asking some questions about everyday things, then the deepest parts of that person's life can come to the surface, if they want it to, if they're willing to do that.

It's a matter of listening for meaning in the ordinary, he says. In our ordinary lives, we reveal our concerns, our prejudices, our beliefs, the things we stand for, the things we fear. Writers trained to focus on the sensational, the extraordinary moment, the once-in-a-lifetime event, can resist this simple truth. "I do that exercise with journalists a lot, and they're more surprised by it than other kinds of writers I've worked with," French observes, "because as journalists we're trained to believe that the everyday is *not* interesting."

The thing is, you never know what people will say, if you can get them talking, if they trust you enough to reveal themselves. French continues:

The other thing that happens, and it happens with a prompt like that one, is that people can catch you off guard with their willingness to go more deeply than you had expected. I've seen some journalists, some writers, who that actually freaks them out and they back away when their subject does that. That's actually a bigger problem. . . . Sometimes it's *our* resistance to being willing to go where the answer is truly going to lead you.

French tells the following story to illustrate a truth that I've learned over and over again: the best interviews surprise us. In the context of an ordinary conversation, a person reveals some truly startling fact, some extraordinary experience. He was conducting a clinic with a cadre of reporters and editors from the *American Statesman* in Austin, Texas, and as usual asked for a volunteer. He didn't know the guy who volunteered to be the subject. He started interviewing him with that same prompt: What happened to him that morning from the moment he woke up.

What he said was that he had actually woken up at, like, 3:30 or so, and his wife was not in his bed, and he went down to their son's room to see if she was there, because sometimes when he would wake up in the night she would comfort him and lie with him. And he went down the hall to the son's room, and the son wasn't there either. And the dog, who was normally puttering around at his feet, if he woke up in the middle of the night, wasn't around either.

So suddenly he feels like he's in an empty house. And the thought that he had, in this sort of half-awake fugue state, was that he'd died and that this was the afterlife—and that he was alone. Now how could you anticipate that answer?

The answer, of course, is that you can't—and moreover, you shouldn't. (The wife, son, and dog were actually safe in another room.) Anticipating an answer in an interview is like an actor on stage reaching to pick up a telephone before it has rung because his script has told him what to expect next. But the interview is a live moment, and you can never know the next words to come out of anyone's mouth. That's the excitement of it. French concludes: "So a lot of it is just being willing to listen." And if we're *not* willing to listen, we can be our own worst enemy.

As someone who has mentored many writers, French sees too many fledgling writers commit one essential mistake:

They hurry. They're in too much of a hurry. Someone is giving them something great—and they hurry past it. They hear it, and some part of them thinks it might be interesting, but they've got this list of questions, and they think they have to get through those questions, that list, with military precision, and they hurry past the good stuff . . . because whatever the good thing is that's popped up unexpectedly, it doesn't fit their preconceived notion of what they're going to get, what they think they're going to write. They don't even know that they have an agenda, but they do.

French is always looking for what he calls *points of human contact*—small, everyday details that make a person real to a reader. These details are what give great novels, poems, and nonfiction narratives their sense of being alive and real.

I once interviewed an artist who showed me a model train layout he had constructed of the town where he grew up—exactly as he recalled it from childhood. It was a kind of three-dimensional act of nostalgia for boyhood and love for his deceased parents. The detail was irrelevant in a literal sense to the story, but it spoke volumes about who and what had formed his values. He and his wife were elderly, but he kept a photo of his wife as a young woman in his study—she had been a magazine model—and when he showed it to me, his eyes misted with a fierce love: she had never ceased to be that beautiful ingenue to him.

An old soldier once confided to me that after being mustered out of the army, he was so shocked and bewildered by what he had been through that on his way home, he bought a civilian suit and, in the train station restroom, stripped off his uniform, donned his civvies, and simply left his old uniform on a bench. I was able to incorporate this gesture in a novel about a sailor who has undergone the trauma of recovering his best friend's bloated corpse from a sealed, flooded compartment after a U-boat attack. Both men were literally trying to strip away the violence and pain of war.

Mark Cox, in his poem "Things My Grandfather Must Have Said," brings the deceased to life with all sorts of ordinary details recalling moments of rural family life, including his one: "I want to be wearing the State of Missouri / string tie that no one else liked . . ." Whenever I read that, I know exactly who this guy is—old-fashioned and not stylish but fiercely loyal to some idea of himself and how he looks to the world. It is exactly the kind of detail you would have noticed in an interview, and asking about it gently would have provoked a story about where he got the tie and when, and why he likes to wear it—and all the times that his wife probably told him to take it off. There's something boyish about the detail, even—maybe especially—assigned to an old man.

French found such a point of human contact while doing his long-form newspaper series on seventh-graders. He was interviewing their math teacher and recounts:

She was one of the teachers that the students just loved, which meant that they opened up to her—which meant she was really important for me to get to know. The girls especially liked her, because among many other things, she was helpful to them when their period would arrive unexpectedly or when some female emergency would come up. She actually had a drawer in her desk full of emergency supplies—tampons, sanitary napkins, and stuff. And for a girl to go to her desk and discreetly open the drawer and take something out, she didn't have to ask permission in front of the class—all she had to do was quietly say a code phrase to the teacher. And the code phrase was "The *Eagle* has landed."

When he tells me this story, I lose all semblance of professional interviewing demeanor and burst out laughing. We keep repeating the phrase to each other and laughing even harder. "I love that! I love that—it makes me laugh, like it makes *you* laugh!" he says. "For just a split second, it makes me imagine being a girl in that position, being embarrassed, and how great it would be to find a teacher who would help you through that moment of embarrassment in such a sweet way. And I really admire in that detail and in many, many others, the creativity that people use to get through every day."

French is almost always seeking the answer to a basic question: "How do we navigate through a day?" The answer matters, because it gets to the mysterious and genuine core of who we are, what we value, how we do our work, how we honor or betray those who count on us. Spoken words start to uncover *meaning*.

WHOM, WHERE, AND WHY WE INTERVIEW

We tend to interview people for one of four reasons:

1. They are fascinating in their own right for who they are and what they have accomplished—e.g., a celebrity or politician or inventor.
2. They figure as players in a public or private drama—e.g., a murder case or our own memoir of single motherhood.
3. They are an exemplar of a group we want to explore—e.g., astronauts, artists, battered women, middle-schoolers, orphans.
4. They are experts in some field relevant to our research—e.g., scientists, businesspeople, lawyers, doctors, detectives, etc.

Clearly in the first two cases, access to a particular individual is critical for telling your story. But in the latter two cases, if one individual isn't available or won't talk, you can move on to another exemplar or expert.

To research her first novel, Michelle Boyajian shadowed a district attorney through a lengthy trial in order to be able to capture authentically on the page the fictional trial of her mentally handicapped protagonist in *Lies of the Heart*. Her "interview" lasted months, supplemented by e-mails and phone conversations. In another instance, a young writer I know located an old classmate from an abusive disciplinary school. The woman was now in prison, an accessory to a horrific murder, and through thoughtfully composed letters, this writer carefully laid the groundwork for what turned out to be—as she expected—a very emotional face-to-face interview. The writer wants to figure out how she managed to come through her adolescence to "normal" adulthood while her old best friend spiraled into using drugs, prostitution, and ultimately committing murder.

Whatever the motive behind the interview, ordinarily you'll want to prepare for the meeting. These days an Internet search can usually produce a basic résumé, and the more public the person is, the more you'll find. Not just their vital statistics—where they were born, where they live, how old they are, where they work, what their biggest achievements are. If they've written a book or given speeches, find the texts and do some reading. Even many private individuals now post extensive personal résumés on social media sites: favorite books, music, and movies; best vacations; personal and family milestones, and so on. It is a curated profile—meaning that the person is crafting a specific identity that can be unrealistically flattering and impressive—but it is useful nonetheless.

Give some thought to *where*, ideally, the interview will take place. I much prefer to meet a person on his or her own ground—either at home, literally, or in some other rich environment, especially one in which he or she can actually be *doing* something. If she's a research scientist, I want to see her in action in her lab. If he's a forest ranger, I want to hike up into the bush with him to check out the wilderness campsites. I want to be able to describe the way they move, how they handle the tools of their trade, how they react to what's going on around them. And at home and at their workplaces, people usually are surrounded by the evidence of who they are. This ranges from the doctor who hangs her degrees on the wall of her office to the foster mother whose living-room wall is a gallery of portraits of the children she has cared for, or the metal sculptor whose garage is piled with misshapen hunks of iron and steel and redolent with the smells of scorched metal.

In such locales, the people we are interviewing have at hand souvenirs, props, copies of relevant documents, as well as all the furniture of their life. The interview location is not just a real-life meeting place. It's likely also to function as a stage of action, a place that helps your subject's personality come to life. And you can use it as such a stage if you write a version of the interview as a scene, either factual or fictional. A wonderful expression of this is found in Walt Harrington's inspiring book *Acts of Creation: America's Finest Hand Craftsmen at Work*. Harrington wanted to learn what drives a man or woman to pursue a life in making *things*—working with their hands, doing hard and demanding physical labor in service of an ideal. It would not be enough just to meet a fine furniture maker or stonemason for coffee at the local diner. The research staff of *This Old House*, the magazine that commissioned the pieces that eventually came together as a book, would locate potential subjects—"nominations." Harrington recounts, "I would call them on the phone, talk to them for twenty minutes or half an hour, and in that time I could tell. Are they smart? Are they open? Are they thoughtful? Are they talkative? Are they excited about doing the project? And once they passed that, then it was—and again I was teaching full-time and doing all this other stuff—then it was, well, next Thursday, Friday, and Saturday are you going to be working on something?" If the answer to all those questions was an enthusiastic "yes," he proceeded to the next stage.

"Well, do you have a project"—I would start with—"that you can finish while I'm there?" Almost never could they finish. But the floor guy could say, "I

can lay the floor that Friday night that you're here." I would basically negotiate with them to make sure there was *real action* happening while I was
there—it was natural action, but I can't say I just walked in the door and they
did whatever they did. I made sure they were doing something that was relevant to what I was doing. And so I'd arrive on Thursday afternoon. I would
go over there. They would usually show me around their workshop. Then
I'd sit down and interview them for several hours, do the whole background
thing: "Who are you and how'd you come to this?"

Harrington had already set the stage for a narrative that would
include real action, dialogue taken from the interview, and "found"
dialogue, that is, whatever happened to be said by the craftsman or
anyone else in the course of working on the project, not just to him
but to anyone else in the shop or workplace, from which he selected
the most telling or resonant exchanges—in other words, all the elements of a dramatic scene he could observe and reconstruct on the
page, with added context from outside research. And what he discovered was a whole new and complex layer to the story. He continues,
"So when I would sit down, it was really a pleasure. Once I realized
that every single one of them had a secret story about the mysteries of
creativity that they almost never talked about, because when you're a
craftsperson, you hang out with other craftspeople and, as the blacksmith said, people are not talkative and articulate about this because
that's not where the craft happens. The craft happens between *hand*
and *head*. And so they're not talkative about it. They're not *used* to
talking about it."

Harrington spent hours in each workshop, watching the craftsman at work. But it was not a passive exercise—it was also a very active and painstaking interviewing process. He explains:

I took scores of photographs of course and I tape-recorded and I took notes.
And I had to do a lot of, "Now what are you doing there? Why are you
moving your hand that way?" Because I knew I wanted it to reflect what
craft is, which is this remarkable collection of precise actions with complete
attention to detail. And I knew the stories had to mimic that precision and

attention to detail. Their words alone couldn't describe what they do, because what they do is not verbal. It's this relationship between the way their brain works and the way their hands work and the way the brain of their creativity works.

Tapping into the secret of how their hands worked with their brains required being in the workshop or on the job site, which was not just the *setting* for the story but also, and more importantly, the *stage* on which they played out the drama of their vocations. Their words were only meaningful in the literal context of what they did with their hands: fitting a tight dovetail joint; guiding a massive boulder into place on a custom-built hearth as it dangles in a sling under a crane; shaping an ornamental sculpture that will adorn the façade of an historic building.

PREPARING FOR THE ENCOUNTER

People are not always the only—or even the best—experts on themselves and what they do. Another way to find out a lot about someone is to talk to other people who know them. When Tom Wolfe came back to North Carolina looking for Robert Glenn "Junior" Johnson—the famous bootlegger and stock car racer—to write about him for *Esquire* ("The Last American Hero Is Junior Johnson. Yes!" March 1965), Johnson advised him to talk to his friends and neighbors—they would tell Wolfe the truth, he said. He wasn't about to brag on himself. And it turned out that Junior Johnson's friends and neighbors had a lot to say, much of it tinged with admiration, affection, even awe, and Wolfe created his legendary story.

But think this through. If you start asking neighbors and friends and family members about a person before he or she knows you're doing a story about them, you might just spook them. A public figure is more likely used to such attention. It may be more appropriate to make such inquiries after you've talked to your subject—but every case is different. The main thing is not to waste your subject's time by asking for basic information that you should already know. Katie

O'Reilly, a nonfiction writer who has also produced stories for public radio—including one about a local politician who inspired an ongoing old-fashioned street protest—says:

I tried to do a significant amount of prep before each interview, and have questions written out, but also to exercise flexibility and follow conversational rabbit trails. Being willing to think on my feet and come up with new questions on the spot resulted in some of my piece's more interesting fodder. I think it's important to go into interviews without many expectations, and instead approach them as open-ended adventures. I also landed on some of my best story ideas while transcribing the interviews. Listening to a source's story for a second or third time is always a good way to mine for more nuanced points to address.

In addition to following an actual murder trial at the elbow of the prosecutor, Michelle Boyajian interviewed other experts, including a speech pathologist: "I like the fact—I love the fact—that at some point during the interview, you get just that one little spark, you can feel it in the interview, and mark it with a star and you've scribbled something and you can't read it, but at some point you remember, ah—that was the moment!" Boyajian was looking for a dramatic device for her novel that would bring various characters together in an intimate environment that was also fraught with tension. "I did not know how to get the group dynamic," she says—that is, how to create a plausible scenario in which her various characters would interact—but the answer came from an interview. "I remember Jeanie, the speech therapist, said one part of speech pathology is to have group therapy. Which was a great device in the end." Thus the characters could sit around together revealing their deepest feelings in an authentic scenario that moved the story forward, without seeming contrived.

Boyajian was new to the whole process of conducting an interview, so she prepared carefully for her first interview with the speech pathologist, intending to record the conversation and transcribe it so she would capture all the technical information as accurately as possible. "That was my first bad interview," she says. She was aware the ambient noise of a loud environment could interfere with recording. "But I knew Jeanie from class and it seemed like such a quiet restaurant! I was blown away that there's a recorder on the table in front of us, but what I can hear is people in the kitchen! Things dropping! And I'm like, how did it pick *that* up when we're sitting over the recorder." That's a strange artifact of microphones—they tend to pick up all sorts of things louder and more clearly than the human voice: the clatter of utensils, the sloshing of a drink, air-conditioning fans. And sometimes background voices come through loud and clear (in this case the waitress and cooks), but the softer voice nearby gets muffled. The good news is that a little practice can help you master the technical problems, which may be as simple as making sure you're sitting or standing close enough together to talk comfortably, or as complicated as using a clip-on or lavalier mic or recording a voice over the telephone.

Harrington talks about the importance of practicing your craft until it is second nature—and the interview is part of that craft. "Michael Seward, the furniture maker, told me at first, 'I had to just think about cutting dovetails, because if I didn't, I'd screw it up. But after thousands of dovetails, I got to the point where I could do it without thinking about it.'" It's like practicing scales on the piano until your fingers find them through muscle memory alone. Harrington develops the point: "And he said, 'It's not that it made my job easier. What it did was it allowed me to spend that time thinking about what I was doing in design and form and art. It freed me up.'" The discipline of conscientious practice brings artistic freedom. "You learn to walk through the craft part of it," Harrington says. You conduct interviews, take notes, take pictures, report the scene with all five senses. "And when you can do it without thinking about it, then you can think about what does it all mean? How does it all hang together? If you don't get past that point, I really don't think you can ever put this together at a pretty high level, because it will always have that wooden, formulaic feel to it."

Harrington felt a great sense of privilege in being allowed inside these artisans' workshops—and inside their personal stories. They were different—unlike him, they worked with their hands—but he also experienced a profound connection between what they were doing and what he—and the rest of us writers—try our best to do. He says, "It was a weirdly, almost mystical, kind of thing to be able to do these stories. I felt like I was going inside this little secret world that people like myself had very little appreciation for. I felt like I was unlocking this for people like us."

EMOTIONAL AND ETHICAL CONCERNS

Just as challenging for most of us is navigating the emotional and ethical boundaries, handling the deeper questions that can arise suddenly without warning during an interview. Kirsten Holmstedt often encountered such moments while interviewing women soldiers for her first book, *Band of Sisters*, and expresses the challenge in one word:

Responsibility—I didn't realize this when I started *Band of Sisters*, but oftentimes I was the first person that the service men or women confided in. I say service *men* because I'm thinking of a situation where I was talking to a navy corpsman whose girlfriend (a soldier) I was featuring in the book. She was blown up by an IED [improvised explosive device].

He was in Iraq but in another location when the explosion occurred. He talked about when he heard the report that she had been wounded and being in the ambulance that retrieved her. I don't want to say I was cavalier about the interviews when I started out. Let's just say I didn't have the sensitivity and awareness that I have now.

The more time I spent with each woman on her story, the more aware I became of the treasures that were their stories, their memories. I always felt honored to be the one to share their stories with the public.

If anyone talks to you long enough, he or she will say something they never intended, never expected to reveal, maybe never even remembered until that moment. This is not a trick to exploit the subject—just the opposite. It means the interview is getting real, that you've passed the rehearsed narrative and are in fresh territory, punching through the shallow floor of polite conversation to the deeper shadow place where the real story lives. Unless you're trying to persuade a criminal into confessing, it's not about gulling the subject into self-incrimination. More likely the subject will reveal thoughts or feelings or experiences that deepen the encounter, show him or her in a more vivid and human light. Time and again, I've conducted interviews that finish with the subject in tears—recalling a loved one, a traumatic event, a moment of utter happiness. And others have ended in the raucous laughter of relief and recognition. This is usually a good thing—people are often grateful to be brought to that emotional place in memory.

Of course, most interviews are likely to far less emotionally evocative, but keep in mind that even the seasoned interviewer can't help but get caught up in the emotion of the subject. If he is in tears, you probably will be too. If she laughs—well, laughter is infectious. And you may well go home gratified by the interview—and emotionally spent.

The other truth about interviewing is that most people bring to the encounter a native decency conditioned by cultural expectations. Polite people are uncomfortable with silence—it seems rude, especially if we are the host. So let the pause, the hanging beat of silence, be your ally. Teachers and cops know this. Let the silence hang long enough—and usually a few seconds seems like an hour—and the subject will say something, just to be courteous, which leads to saying something else, until a conversation is happening. Sometimes it sputters into life only after some excruciatingly awkward moments, but other times it revs to life at once, and after five minutes you feel as if you've known each other for years. And at least initially, it doesn't really matter what you talk about—only *that* you talk. The star of the interview is not you, of course, but whomever you are talking to. That person wants you to put yourself out there, to engage, not merely "pump" them for information. They usually want—and need—to know something about you so they can decide what kind of person you are and, thus, whether and how much to trust you. So relax. Find some common ground and make small talk—about the weather, baseball, how lovely the view is from their balcony, whatever. Do not declare strident political positions or religious convictions—this isn't the time or place. This is about what *they*—not *you*—have to say. Remember, it is a date—likely a first date. You don't start off discussing marriage plans but rather trading anecdotes about where you're from or what sorts of things you're interested in.

TRUST AND VERIFY

Holmstedt talks about the relationship of the interviewer to her subject:

Trust was/is huge. If you don't have trust, you don't have anything. You gain it by being yourself, being honest, listening, and really hearing what the other person is saying. I was surprised when a female Cobra pilot told me that she had failed a flight exam. These pilots are extremely confident and don't like admitting their mistakes. I like to think that she told me this story because she knew I wouldn't make it the focus of her story but a part of her story. She trusted me.

Holmstedt also learned something else, that sometimes the researcher must be a little bit of a pest, worrying out the necessary facts, even if those facts are awkward or unflattering. There is no substitute for dogged persistence. She says, "When I write these profiles about women in combat, I go back to them countless times. I would tell myself that I couldn't call that person one more time, but I had to. If I were going to get it right, I had to make that one last call. Or five more calls. I didn't want to be a pest, but far worse than being a nuisance is getting it wrong." And at times that means asking difficult, even taboo questions:

My job was to ask the hard questions. It's not cool to ask a soldier if he shot someone, but I needed to know if my women shot anyone. That would be important to the story, because I would want to know how she handled it. On occasion, when I didn't want to ask the hard questions, I relied on my editor to force my hand. And I was always glad he did. And I always blamed him when I asked the soldier the question. One woman shot at an Afghan boy. I didn't ask her if she hit him. Frankly, I didn't want to know. But I needed to know. The day she deployed for the second time to Afghanistan, I called her and asked her if she shot the boy. She told me she missed. And then she elaborated on what the consequences were of missing and what she would do the next time she was in that situation.

Imagine the level of trust such a conversation requires—to ask the hard question and get an honest answer.

Which brings up one last issue about interviewing. What do you do if your subject is lying to you, and you suspect it, maybe even know it for sure? I have to admit, I haven't encountered this often. Usually if a subject gets something wrong, it's an honest mistake—he or she simply misremembers or has misspoken, or maybe never knew the whole truth in the first place. Often you can check a fact or a date or a place with an objective record of some kind and make the needed correction, or at least acknowledge the discrepancy. The error tends to be small and easily fixed: the event in question happened on a Friday, not a Tuesday; the locale was not this bar that other one; I was eleven years old when it happened, not ten.

But if someone is deliberately fabricating a version of events that is false, for whatever motive, the best advice I ever heard came from a retired police detective. When confronted with a suspect whose story just seemed fishy, she would ask him to tell it in reverse. Where were you at one a.m. on Friday night when the burglary occurred? How about at midnight? And just before that? And so on. She discovered through long practice that people are very bad at lying in reverse—in fact, they're bad at telling stories in reverse order period, unless they practice very hard at it. Sooner or later she would catch her suspect in a glaring discrepancy, the timeline of his story would unravel, and the truth would come out.

In nonfiction if the liar persists, you can just present his or her version alongside contradictory evidence and let the reader judge the truthfulness of the account. For the poet and fiction writer, the lie is just as revealing of character as the truth—maybe more so. The reason for the lie—to avoid confronting an unpleasant truth, to deflect guilt or shame or embarrassment, to protect reputation, for simple gain, from long habit, or just for the sake of manipulating or controlling the story—might open a whole new area for scrutiny. Many of the great works of literature are built on lies and secrets that are outed—from *The Great Gatsby* on back to *Macbeth*. Remember, narrative itself is just a complex and nuanced vehicle for revealing information—factual, dramatic, emotional—in an order calculated to maximize interest and meaning. It is opening a box of secrets and letting them out one at a time. It includes misdirection and false leads.

Deception, deliberate or inadvertent, is the currency of many great memoirs and poems. This is because it reveals us at our most human, desiring somehow to make the facts fit the movie we envision of our lives. Think of the case of Brian Williams, the world-renowned TV journalist and network news anchor. He enjoyed an aura of credibility and integrity shared only, perhaps, by a few precursors considered by many to be the giants of journalism: Edward R. Murrow, Walter Cronkite, Peter Jennings. Then we learned that he embellished or invented stories that made him seem even more heroic: surviving an air attack in a Blackhawk helicopter in Iraq, fending off marauding gangs in post-Katrina New Orleans. Now his career is the stuff of tragedy, a study, perhaps, in the unrelenting demands of celebrity, of what happens when the writer becomes too much the star of the story and gives in to the human temptation to embellish, to enlarge, to ramp up the danger while firmly casting himself as the star of the matinee. This can be a handy instinct for a fiction writer or poet, but lethal for a nonfiction writer. Williams's case is almost a literal metaphor: the writer belongs behind the camera, the subject of the interview out in front of it. He was required to be in both places, with unfortunate but in some sense predictable results. I have great empathy for him—and great respect for his reporting. We all embellish our private stories as we rehearse them over and over again, but his personal stories were also public.

A related challenge is how to interview a celebrity or well-known public figure—an actor or sports star who brings to the interview rehearsed sound bites, or a politician who has a ready, canned answer he or she wants to give no matter what the question is. This can include even local celebrities such as high school football stars and business leaders. How do you penetrate the public persona and get such people to truly reveal themselves in a fresh way? Again the object is not to somehow goad them into saying something embarrassing but rather to engage them beyond the superficial, to have a truly interesting conversation.

One strategy is simple: spend time with the person, as much time as you reasonably can. It takes a lot of effort to be "on," and most people eventually tire of keeping up their guard. In those unguarded moments—when they're tired, away from distractions, doing something just for fun, relaxing after a couple of beers, whatever the case—they will tend to forget the public script and speak more spontaneously. Again, this bespeaks a level of trust that you should honor.

Another strategy is to come up with a question or subject that no one has ever asked about before. In other words, if you don't want a typical answer, don't ask a typical question. You can learn much about a politician's character by talking about fly-fishing or movies or cooking—some shared passion or pastime—and any such subject might be a back door into a more direct discussion of policy or governing philosophy. In fiction it's axiomatic that a character is defined by his or her desires and fears—what they want and what they are afraid of. Real people are characters too, and the same insight applies.

Finally, here's one of my favorite questions to ask of almost anybody in any context: Who are your heroes? Sometimes the answer is predicable—a baseball player is inspired by Willie Mays or a politician by Teddy Roosevelt. But sometimes not. When I asked the famous clothing designer Bill Blass whom he admired, he immediately started talking about Ernest Hemingway, how Hemingway exuded an irresistible personal style, how style itself could be a statement of character. He was talking not just about the author's prose style but also about how he dressed and comported himself in public and in private, and in the process revealed a great deal of his own ethos, a very deep integrity about how he defined himself and his work.

So interviewing begins with a decision about whom to interview, why, where, and using what tools. It requires preparation and a respect for the process, as well as both a disarming humility and the habit of listening. French explains:

There is the interviewing, and there is the simply being quiet and observing them, but at a certain point, the two morph into the same thing, where it's all just learning more about how this person gets through the day in the world. And I've learned sort of when to be quiet, when to *not* ask questions and let things unfold in front of me, and times when it's more likely for somebody to open up and talk about what just happened twenty minutes ago or an hour ago.

You can't rush the process, be constantly glancing at your watch, trying to hurry the process along. A lot of the conversation may lead nowhere. The interviewer must operate by the fiction that he has all the time in the world. French says, " A lot of it is just *patience*. And when you find a subject that you just have to understand because there's something about them compelling to you. That's the key. Your curiosity and attention span are really key." It all begins with curiosity. French says, with some puzzlement, "There are people out there, unfortunately—some writers—who aren't very curious about perspectives other than their own."

I share his puzzlement. Writing is all about empathy, and that begins in understanding what it's like to go through another person's day. And the expert on that subject is, of course, that other person. Interviewing is a social act at once primitive and enlightened, and it can lead us to amazing stories.

Prompt #15: "Interviewing for Meaning." Find an interesting person and interview him or her for at least half an hour on a recorder, then transcribe the conversation (I warn you, this is time-consuming, though not very intellectually demanding, so plan accordingly). Write the following:

- A dated transcript of interview—be sure at the top to identify the subject and where the interview took place, or if it is a telephone interview; be sure also to obtain the permission of the subject before recording.
- An edited—and much shorter—version of the interview, arranged with any necessary scene-setting, description, or narration in such a way as to provide a vivid profile of the subject.

Prompt #16: "Gaining Access." Assign yourself—or if you are a teacher, your students—to gain access to a variety of people and organizations and report on the level of success.

8 WALKING THE GROUND AND HANDLING THE THING ITSELF

My mother gave me a cigar box after my brother
was born. Inside it a tiny filly so smooth the plastic
had the feel of water or green velvet on a girl's dress.
Because of my mother's honesty, I regard the moment
as a sort of exchange: this horse for this new boy.
—Charlotte Hilary Matthews, "The Feel of Water"

There is just no substitute for being there—wherever *there* is for your project. Some of my *theres* have included a mansion in Stratford-on-Avon where secret special troops trained during World War II; a legal distillery run by an old-time bootlegger in the North Carolina Piedmont and a not-so-legal still site run by another; a clothing factory in China where workers happily stitched into sweaters and T-shirts labels that read "made in U.S.A."; a country churchyard in North Carolina where lies buried a rural schoolmaster who died claiming to be a Napoleonic field marshal; the heaving hull of a container ship in open water as I scrambled aboard via a rope Jacob's ladder; the basement holding cell of a police station; a canoe overturning in whitewater on the upper Cape Fear River.

The writer is often in motion, and there are useful things to know about travel and working in the field, including how to cope with the unexpected. Above all, *being there* confers the unmistakable authority of *presence*: the narrative resounds with the authority of firsthand experience. Lavonne J. Adams infuses her poetry with such an authentic sense of place. *Through the Glorieta Pass*, poems of women on the westward migration, called her to the West to reprise many miles of their rugged journey. For a collection about Georgia O'Keeffe, she visited O'Keeffe's studio and sojourned in the painter's landscape. Time and again, John Jeremiah Sullivan (*Pulphead*) travels to locales off the beaten track to write about a Christian rock festival in Lake of the Ozarks, the Future of Humanity Institute at Oxford University, a maze of caves in Mississippi, or the Rastafarian scene in Jamaica.

Diane Sorensen made several trips to research her novel in progress about her Danish immigrant ancestors, who came by way of New York and traveled by covered wagon to Nebraska. She fastened early on the dual themes of "immigration" and "homesteading," planning to choose a main character from among her forebears and build a compelling storyline around his or her adventures in America. Initially, she found the idea of a research trip daunting and confined herself to Internet searches and the like. She writes:

When it came time for the "Walking the Ground" assignment, my first impulse was to go to Nebraska. But it felt too soon. I was not prepared enough to enter the heartland of my story. And it was February! Nebraska had a couple of feet of snow on the ground. So I decided to turn my attention to the second theme that had emerged: immigration. Again, I focused on one person. My grandfather, Jens Sorensen, came alone to this country when he was about twenty, searching for adventure and his father who'd disappeared into the U.S. ten years before.

Retracing his steps, she went to New York. She remembers, "This first research field trip triggered a burst of excitement for my book project. Until then, it had been largely an interesting intellectual exercise. But once we flew to New York and I walked the grounds of the Statue of Liberty, Ellis Island, and Castle Garden, I became so much more emotionally invested in the project."

That emotional investment is crucial. To that point, a project can seem academic, removed from the writer, not quite urgent or fully real. Being there can bridge that emotional distance, and the place itself can—and usually does—offer useful surprises, bonuses for the effort you took to get there. Sorensen explains:

Aside from acquiring two nice volumes of historical photos, the sensory and visceral experience was invaluable. The ferry took us on the same route my grandfather and great-grandfather followed, with the Statue of Liberty towering over us. We toured Ellis Island, and I walked through the bowels of the baggage room and then up the stairs where Jens must have waited for hours before finally entering the Great Hall. I sat in this light-drenched cavernous hall, feeling how small and vulnerable he must have felt, just one of the masses trying to immigrate. I journaled some of my observations.

It is this emotional connection that can really launch a project into orbit, and literally putting yourself in the place of the ones you are writing about can be the spur that provides that ineffable spine-tingling connection. It allows you to inhabit their experience in an immediate and visceral way—seeing what they saw, smelling what they smelled, feeling the same hard floor under your feet. And in this case, having actually taken the blustery boat ride across the wind-chopped harbor and stood inside the Great Hall on Ellis Island, Sorenson could write scenes of her grandfather's arrival in the New World with the authority of personal experience, extrapolating from her firsthand impressions to envision the same scene a hundred years earlier, the place teeming with Old World families conversing in a score of different languages.

As so often happens, the research trip added its own bit of serendipity, as Sorenson relates: "We also had the good timing to visit the city during a showing of the 1910 Armory Art Exhibit, presented by the New York City Historical Society. Originally staged at the New York Armory, this collection of American and European works represented the 'state of the art' in art in 1910, just a few years after my grandfather landed." Every good writer I know can tell similar uncanny stories about how he or she accidentally stumbled onto an event or person or place or opportunity that was totally extra, not counted upon in advance, a lucky surprise. But the truth is no mystery: Not only does luck favor the prepared mind, but it favors the writer with the prepared mind who is in the right place at the right time. And for that to happen, you have to go somewhere.

When Sorensen made it to Nebraska later that spring, more unexpected discoveries were waiting, including one that turned out to be crucial in understanding the nexus of social relations in late nineteenth-century Nebraska. She writes, "One of the key revelations from the trip was the seven-mile radius rule"—which I alluded to in chapter 3.

For the early settlers, fourteen miles was about the maximum distance a person could comfortably travel in a single day—seven miles there, seven miles back—and still allow enough time to do morning chores before leaving, and evening chores upon returning. Their school, church, and choice of mates, all fell within that seven-mile radius. In my family, for example, there is a tight cluster of homesteads all owned by the Arp family and the families they married into. The school was within two miles; the church was within seven; their main town, Mason City, was five miles away. Vivian Arp's mother was a Cady; they owned the property directly adjacent to Peter Arp's homestead. When one family member moved outside that seven-mile radius, another cluster formed.

Now she had not just the geographic stage for her novel but the dynamic of that geography—the exact equation that governed who met and married whom. A simple truth, but one invisible until you're walking the ground.

Research for a novel about Paul Revere took me to Boston, Lexington, and Concord, Massachusetts. One autumn morning, as I walked the Battle Road outside Lexington, retracing the path the British regulars marched on the morning of April 19, 1775, mounting their surprise raid, I felt the miles in my legs—the long twisty climbs and descents, around every corner a perfect spot for an ambush. I walked for only five or six miles, but those troops had walked all night after being on duty the entire day before. It dawned on me just how tired and out of sorts they must have been by the time they reached Lexington—footsore and blistered in their stiff square shoes, their too-tight clothes rubbing rashes onto skin wet from crossing swamps and creeks. They would have arrived at Lexington Green hungry and thirsty and in a foul mood, resenting mightily the farmer militia that had caused them to be sent on this tortuous march.

I rounded one bend and all at once there stood the Hartwell Tavern, looking exactly as it had on that long-ago day. And in the rail-fenced yard, British regulars loitered around a cook fire, their muskets stacked nearby. Reenactors, of course, but for one disorienting moment I was back in 1775, smelling the wood smoke and listening to the banter of soldiers. These troops, of course, were harmless, but the ones who had come up that road at dawn on April 19, 1775, represented the state of the art in lethal firepower. In writing about Paul Revere and the terrible running battles at Lexington and Concord in 1775 after he roused the militias in the countryside to stand fast against the British regulars, I needed to understand the weapons of the day—among other things.

CONNECTING THROUGH OBJECTS

A friend invited a Revolutionary War reenactor to his farm so he could teach me to load and fire a musket. This weapon always seemed quaint to me, a kind of toy version of the modern firepower wielded by soldiers and cops—AK-47s, M16s, Mac-10s, and Uzis. Sure, they made noise, but they were clumsy and, we were always taught in school, not very accurate. And they fired exactly one inaccurate shot before needing to be reloaded. We stood in a farmer's field in the early morning mist, and he fired at a target—an old highway sign affixed to a broad tree—fifty yards away. Then it was my turn. He coached me through the loading drill. Then I cocked the hammer, lifted the heavy musket to my shoulder, and squeezed off a shot. The hammer dropped, the powder popped in the flash pan, the thick wooden stock slammed back into my shoulder, and a long flame flared out the barrel—and on my first try I nailed the target dead. The metal sign was pierced by a hole the size of my thumb. The one-ounce lead ball was imbedded deep in the trunk of the tree.

This was no toy. To load, level, and fire it required strength in the arms and torso, and it kicked the shoulder with unexpected force. And when he affixed the long nasty bayonet—with its blood-gutters and sharp tip—I had in my hands a terrifying weapon indeed. The British battle tactic called for one volley shot, then a walking bayonet charge with unloaded muskets. Watch a line of men coming across the field at you with that in their hands and you would dissolve in a puddle of jelly and run for your life. But, in fact, at dawn on April 19, 1775, the farmers and tradesmen on the Lexington Green stood fast. They were not professional soldiers, just citizens with strong convictions. Handling the weapon changes how you think of those men, the nature of their stubborn courage, because you realize that you probably could not do what they did. Handling the thing itself makes you understand just how remarkable those men were—and that moment in history—and all the ways it could have turned out differently.

Reenactment helps to put you in the mind-set that a writer must have to accurately capture the truth of the past—uncertainty about what will happen, who will win. You must write from the moment forward, not in settled hindsight. Those citizen soldiers didn't know what would happen next, how it would all turn out, how many of them would lie dead by day's end. We tend to think of history as sort of inevitable—it happened, and so the fact that it happened blots out all the other futures that were possible in the moment of its happening. Yet any given moment could have turned out differently, with a range of consequences.

Also as part of my research I read the autopsy of Crispus Attucks, an African American stevedore killed in the Boston Massacre (and immortalized by Paul Revere in a popular woodcut). The autopsy was conducted by Dr. Benjamin Church, who later was arrested for treason—against the Patriots. Crispus Attucks had fallen on snow. A stout cudgel lay just beyond one outstretched hand. His body lay sprawled on its back, blood already coagulating in a thick black pool under the back and neck, the chest torn open by two musket balls fired point-blank and from a little above, as if he were already on his knees when he died. One ball had ripped open his chest, broken the second rib an inch from his breastbone, blasted downward through his diaphragm, blew his liver and gallbladder to pieces, severed the aorta descendens just above the iliacs, then exited through his spine. He was probably dead before he hit the ground. The second ball was incidental but bloody, another rib shot.

So those hot-headed Patriots in their quaint tricorn hats and those British regular soldiers in their colorful lyric-opera uniforms were engaged in a deadly business after all. And because I had fired the kind of musket that had felled Crispus Attucks, felt its mule kick in my shoulder, put my finger into the hole it made in a metal sign, felt the visceral power of such a killing piece, the words of the autopsy were not abstract. In my imagination I could see that man face the British muskets on that snowy night and then be surprised by the powerful punch of the bullet as it knocked him down hard, and the last thing he heard on earth was the close report that bucked his eardrums. I, too, had heard that muzzle blast up close.

Handling the thing itself can close the distance between then and now, between history as quaint and picturesque, and history as a living present full of human passion, struggle, emotion, uncertainty, and lethal danger. It can put you right inside the scene, seeing, hearing, and feeling the tension of the moment.

In researching *Zoo Story*, Thomas French spent large parts of six years at the Lowry Park Zoo in Tampa, getting to know not just the names and habits of the animals but also the complex social hierarchy of the keepers. While he relied on scores of extended interviews and other sources, time and again in his endnotes about some of the most dramatic material, he is able to write "the author witnessed" the event. These moments were neither planned nor predictable—because he was on site so often for such long stretches of time, he put himself into a position to take advantage of happy accidents, remarkable interchanges between animals and humans, stray conversations among keepers that reveal startling information, as well as the actions of visitors.

Also, French was *game*—willing to follow the keepers anywhere on their rounds, to accompany them on field trips as far away as Panama, and to work alongside them shoveling animal waste, cleaning enclosures, toting and hauling. And so he found the sudden and wonderful rewards of close encounters with animals that most of us see only on video or behind bars. In one scene, he describes how the assistant general curator, a man named Ged Craddick, is feeding a young tiger cub named Enshalla by cradling her on his lap and squirting gruel into her mouth from a syringe. He observes:

Holding a baby tiger is nothing like holding a housecat. When you hold a tiger cub, it's impossible to forget even for a second that very soon this stunning creature now nuzzling your arm will be capable of hunting and killing you. The tension between those opposites—the adorability of the fluffy cub, the menace of the apex predator waiting to emerge—is electric.

And lest we think he is merely being fanciful, in an endnote to the scene, he tells us exactly how he knows this: "This description is based on the author's firsthand experience at the home of Don Woodman, a veterinarian who worked with Enshalla as a young tiger. At the time of our interview, his family was foster caring for a litter of ten-week-old tiger cubs orphaned after they were confiscated from a facility where they were being neglected. During our interview, one of those cubs kept climbing onto my lap and trying to gnaw at my notebook." So the tooth marks on his notebook are a vivid reminder of the encounter.

THE VALUE OF BEING THERE

Walking the ground of your subject matter can entail also handling the props in that world and giving yourself over to the experience of being in that situation. I have a vivid memory, as a young reporter, of allowing cops to book me as they would a suspect: fingerprinting me, standing me up for mug shots, then handcuffing me and leading me away to a basement lock-up cell that was nothing like the jail cells in movies. No bars, just a solid steel door with a slit window, solid walls, and floor. The cop who escorted me to it—my older brother—reminded me that it was Friday, and they could hold me for seventy-two hours without charging me, which meant I'd have no access to a telephone or chance to plead for bail with a magistrate until Monday. No one else would know where I was. Meantime I'd be alone in a soundproof underground steel box. If I were a real criminal, he said, and smiled.

On another occasion I voluntarily submitted to being stunned with a Taser gun—brand-new technology in those days. These Tasers didn't shoot the darts on wires but simply issued a strong jolt of electricity into the victim. Each cop was required to undergo a bout of being Tased before being allowed to carry the weapon, just to make sure they really understood its power. If they could do that, then I as a reporter could do it, too. Should do it. So I braced, and the charge stung me hard, buckled my knees, and I turned to jelly on the floor. I've never felt such a sense of absolute powerlessness, being unable to control my muscles. Oddly, after a moment or so, I was fine again. All of these experiences combined to give me a whole new empathy for those arrested and detained, whether innocent or guilty. Reading or writing about them, I can still feel the sharp tingling jolt of that Taser and the deep sense of utter abandonment of that basement holding cell.

DARING TO DO IT

Sometimes the experiential world of our subject seems foreign, quite removed from anything familiar to us in our routine lives, and it can take a bit of moxie to cross over into that territory, where our story lives. Sometimes the most vexing limitations are self-imposed. Kirsten Holmstedt faced a daunting challenge in pursuing the stories of women warriors: finding the right women veterans who would open up to her. She recalls:

When I started *Band of Sisters*, I set my own limits. I began with a lot of "I can'ts" because I was dealing with the military, and the whole structure just seemed larger than life and somewhat intimidating. I never doubted that I could get an interview with a female soldier. I had developed a good rapport with the different branches of the armed services. But there were other things that I didn't think I'd be able to do that I did. For instance, I was interviewing a female sailor on an aircraft carrier while it was in port in Norfolk, Virginia. Her boss said that if I really wanted to know what it was like to work on an aircraft carrier, I needed to fly to it when it was at sea. He told me how to put in a request to fly in a military-operated turbo prop to the carrier. I started the process but didn't think I'd get a flight. I just thought, what do I have to lose?

That's a good lesson—sometimes you just have to go for it. Writers get told "no" a lot, but all it takes is one crucial "yes" and we're in business. Holmstedt continues:

Next thing I knew, I was doing the arrested cable landing and spending the night on the carrier. The next morning, we did a catapult take off, where the aircraft goes from zero to 150 mph in three seconds. Those were some of the highlights, but the important fact, as it relates to interviewing, is that I was able to see and feel firsthand the conditions of a carrier at sea. Working on a carrier during wartime is considered one of the most challenging jobs there is—and now I know why. I don't have to rely on someone describing it to me. Any time you can take out that step and experience something for yourself, do it! Don't limit yourself.

When Holmstedt starting working on the article, her journalism experience was limited to articles for a small town newspaper. It so happened that there was a military base nearby, but she had no special access or connections before she began the project beyond some casual acquaintances there. She was utterly convinced that there was no way she had either the resources or the talent to make the project work. So she basically had to rise to the occasion, put her ingenuity to work, and find some faith in herself as a writer. One contact led to another, and each interview led to a further conversation to clarify and expand on what was learned in the first—the questions she forgot to ask, the elements that, upon reflection still weren't clear. She just kept going, always learning from her mistakes. The book was a product not just of special talent or long experience but of passion and sheer determination to do it, no matter what.

This is not a call to try daredevil adventures purely to prove a point. Always calculate risk as best you can and listen to that little voice in the back of your brain that will warn you when you are about to do something foolish. But that said, you must dare a little. For each of us, that threshold is different. It may be as mundane as helping to muck out a zoo enclosure, or as daring as strapping behind the pilot of a supersonic jet about to be catapulted off an aircraft carrier to a place far over the horizon.

One such moment for me came on a mild summer evening as I was shadowing a docking pilot on the Cape Fear River. It had all begun a week or so earlier when I dropped in at the pilots' office and explained to the man in charge what I wanted to do. I played with his friendly Australian shepherd and told him about myself. I was prepared for him to tell me that what I wanted to do was out of the question, to lecture me about liability issues, and I had all my counter-arguments ready. But I didn't need them—the playful dog broke the ice. I had an Aussie at home. After a few minutes, he told me he would call when the next ship was due. I would have to be ready on short notice, and they would not wait for me, and when the call came a few days later, I dropped what I was doing and went.

The pilot who took me in tow was one of a small elite band of men who board incoming ships while they are still in the rough ocean fairway approaching the river mouth, then take command of the vessel and steer it up the narrow twisting channel to a safe berth at the Port of Wilmington. We sledded out to sea aboard a battered black and red tugboat to the *Hanjin Los Angeles*, a 950-foot-long container ship—67 feet longer than the *Titanic*. Somewhere near the sea buoy marking the entrance to the river fairway, the dark gray sea scalloped with wind-chop, we turned and fell in close beside the gargantuan ship, matching its speed exactly, with only a dark narrow gap of water between the tugboat's rail and the towering steel side of the ship. The pilot casually mounted the lurching rail, gauged the pitch and roll of the vessel, then lightly stepped across the gap of water onto the lowest rung of a rope Jacob's ladder dangling down the side of the ship. He scrambled up and disappeared inside a hatchway, several stories above.

For me it was a moment of truth—I had not expected that tonight's trip would require any bravery on my part. I had only a second to make up my mind. I mounted the rail, then took that big dangerous step across the chasm to the dangling ladder. I can still feel the intense heat radiating from that great black hull as I climbed toward the opening, which seemed to be miles above. In fact, it took only a few seconds of steady climbing and I was inside, the rough cylinder of the rope permanently stored in the muscle memory of my hands—and my heart still pounding.

It was the thrill of that climb, the sensation of the hot steel against my body as I ascended, the towering height that became all too real as I dangled on the outside of a moving ship twenty feet above the churning water, the surging momentum of that great black machine thrumming as if alive, its vibration entering my body—all of that was the blood of the story, and all that happened next: entry into the air-conditioned interior, a quick ride up an elevator to the bridge, opening like a great glass-enclosed veranda on which stood a compact seaman steering the ship with a solid steel wheel the size of a dinner plate, the vista that opened for miles out the windows on all sides of the river and the wetlands beyond it. All the details I needed were right there at hand—people doing interesting things on a massive moving stage against a dramatic backdrop. All I had to do was pay attention.

You just can't get that stuff from books.

Hands-on experience can be essential to your being able to present your story with implicit authority and plausibility. But there are dangers as well as opportunities in this approach. A writer I know, victimized by a gun-wielding robber, researched her own experience by putting herself on the other end of it: learning to fire a handgun at a shooting range. She discovered the lure of handling all that power, the seductive confidence that could quickly give way to lethal arrogance. Handling the pistol deepened her experience of something that had already happened. It made it even more disturbing to her in retrospect, made the danger she had been in feel more immediate as she relived the terrible moment all over again.

HANDS-ON RESEARCH

An entire subspecialty in anthropology has grown up among researchers who try to emulate the practices of our Stone Age ancestors: chipping flint arrowheads, hunting with stone-tipped spears, making fire from flint or friction. They are essentially putting themselves in the places of humans who lived far beyond the pale of recorded history, trying to understand their lives by doing the same things that they did to survive.

In a similar fashion, Lavonne J. Adams tells of her quest to learn and write the truth of the role played by the frontier scout Kit Carson in the forced internment of the Navajo at Bosque Redondo, New Mexico. As a Helen Wurlitzer Fellow at Taos, she scoured the local library for any books or documents that might inform her body of poems. Adams recalls:

When scanning the shelves of books that referenced Native American Tribes, I pulled a book about Navajo rug weaving, took it back to my casita to read. The author of this book discusses her relationship with a Navajo woman who she clearly admires, Tiana Bighorse, who taught her how to weave. As the book progress, the reader learns that Bighorse's father was one of those interned at Redondo, and that the author encouraged Tiana to write her family's story. That rather inconspicuous reference led me to the book *Bighorse the Warrior*, important to me as one of the few texts I located that recounted the story from the Navajo perspective.

Bosque Redondo was a forty-square-mile camp established near Fort Sumner, New Mexico, in 1862. The U.S. Army rounded up Navajos from their native lands in New Mexico and Arizona and sent them on the infamous Long Walk to internment there. Too many did not survive the journey. Adams continues:

Most of this project relies on actual artifacts, and the belief that the objects we own, the objects we use and value, reflect the stories of our lives. As a result of this philosophy, I wandered museums across New Mexico and Arizona, twice visited the National Museum of the American Indian in Washington, D.C., sketched silver necklaces and mourning jewelry, ink and medicine bottles, took notes in my journal that described saddles and rifles, tobacco pouches. Every object evoked an emotional or intellectual response, provided the impetus to write. When I wasn't traveling, I read books that contained photographs of Sibley stoves, of ceremonial headdresses and pipes, of Kit Carson and his wife, Josefa. To encourage further inspiration, I gathered postcards featuring the faces of the Navajo—of women weaving, of men tending the sheep.

Necklaces, medicine bottles, saddles, rifles, tobacco pouches, postcards—the ordinary, magical stuff of life.

Recently I had the chance to handle a different kind of artifact—for a story about the North Carolina shad boat, the state watercraft. It's always possible to write about such a subject from historical documents, but what if I could actually find one of those old boats, which were built from the 1880s into the early decades of the twentieth century? I did find some—in a maritime museum collection, rotted and unseaworthy. I ran my hands over the rough old wood, the scabbing paint. But I also located a replica built by volunteers with the help of museum professionals and arranged to sail on it out of Manteo harbor on Roanoke Island, where such boats were once ubiquitous—built from local white cedar, called juniper by the islanders, a wood that resists rot and doesn't warp as it dries. The builder who came up with the design—George Washington Creef—was a gentle soul with a flowing gray beard and large expressive hands. The locals called him Uncle Wash. He always built in pairs, keeling two boats from a single cedar log.

Once aboard the shallow, broad-bottomed open fishing boat, the skipper let me take the helm. For an hour and a half or so, I was able to tack and jibe the craft across Shallowbag Bay, feeling the genius of its design in the easy power of the tiller, sensing through my fingers the moment when the centerboard bit as if locking into gear and the hull cocked over and lurched forward in a sudden rush of acceleration. I could write about the exhilaration of silent speed, a sensation like free fall. Putting the boat through maneuvers, I understood implicitly why fishermen so loved the design that they used it for many generations. Even loaded, it handles as easily as steering a car. It isn't tender or tippy, so it would have made a great working platform. And it can be handled by two or even one man.

One archival detail that, for me, brought the story home emotionally was that when Creef's wife became ill, he split a cedar log and made two coffins. He buried her in one and went to his own grave in its twin twenty-four years later, snug in his last "boat." Having sailed his creation, I know in my heart why he built those coffins as if they were boats. They were works of grace and speed, crafted to carry his friends and family across dangerous waters, and thus they became also works of love.

REPORTING THROUGH ALL FIVE SENSES

As writers reared in this particular culture in which the visual is ubiquitous—movies, videos, glowing electronic screens of all sizes—it's useful to remind ourselves that we have *five* senses. The video screen may offer exciting visual stimuli, often accompanied by music, voices, or other sound effects. But it can't replicate the experience of touch: the rough splintery handle of an old tool, the gooeyness of clayey mud sucking at your boots, the silky sheerness of a nineteenth-century wedding shawl, the smooth heft of an old leather-bound family Bible, the coarse fur of a sled dog, the solid round weight of a railroad pocket watch, the finger-softened brim of an old fedora. These are the things other people have touched, and in touching them yourself you are reliving their intimate gestures and their hard work, feeling the fabric of their world. And the words to express what you feel come immediately with the experience. You handle the object, and you think: *How will I describe this feeling?* And you make a note that will wind up on the page, in the poem or story.

It doesn't stop with touch. Handling an old manuscript, you might catch the unmistakable whiff of cigar smoke imbued in the pages. An original letter may be redolent with perfume. A shop floor may smell of sawdust and varnish and pine resin. All these sensory moments, these physical details, not only connect you emotionally with the subject matter; they also can turn up in the scenes and lines of poetry you write, making the abstract concrete for the reader. The very words themselves are suggested by the sensation.

The sense of smell is our most primitive sense, lodged in our reptile brain, and it can excite powerful and hidden memories of our own experiences. These may be directly related to the item—the faint aroma of your mother's perfume or your dad's aftershave on their clothing as you contemplate your memoir by examining what they have left behind. Or smells may excite correlations, connections, the kind that make for great poems and essays, as the smell of an object calls up a moment in your own life that can now be paired against that object to create a new thing, almost literally redolent with meaning. For me, the odor of hot asphalt recalls powerful memories of my college years, standing beside a highway in the summer heat trying to hitch a ride. The tangy drift of wood smoke from a neighbor's fireplace transports me to that Vermont cabin I inhabited after college, trying to write my first book. And the aroma of fresh-cut grass carries me right back to the soccer field where I guarded a goal against players from South Africa, Greece, Turkey, Mexico, and half a dozen other countries, their chattering voices filling the chilly autumn air with foreign syllables as they scrambled around in the dusk under bare elm trees, week after week, until the snow fell.

And, of course, there's always taste—another sensation absent from the electronic archive. When I moved out on my own at eighteen, my mother gave me a notebook full of index cards bearing all her—and my—favorite recipes, including the coffee can "kulich" bread she used to bake for my many backpacking trips: chunky with raisins, dried apricots and bananas, and chocolate. In the taste of that food resides a good deal of my childhood, and a bite of that sweet dense bread cues it up almost instantly. Taste matters in crafting a true scene, an authentic image—a word that we must free from the merely visual. The cold iron slap of well water, the dry crunch of hardtack, the warm juicy sweetness of an heirloom tomato fresh-picked from the vine—these are the stuff of both truth and art.

I can still recall standing beside a lettuce field near Belle Glade, Florida, and being handed a head of iceberg lettuce by a picker who had just cut it seconds before. I was skeptical—iceberg lettuce? That wilted bland stuff at the salad bar? I bit into it whole, like an apple, amazed at how sweet, juicy, and delicious it was—and how heavy, full of water that spurted onto my shirt front with each bite. I can taste it yet. That moment told me all I needed to know about what happens to fresh food as it is packed and shipped for weeks across the country, across borders—some of that lettuce was bound for a McDonald's in Moscow, Russia—and gave me a radically new appreciation for locally grown produce. Now whenever I write a scene of a character eating, I stop and imagine the texture and taste of the food. Is it fresh, sweet, juicy? Or stale, bitter, and dry? How does the food reflect themes of the story I am telling?

Standing out there in the blazing sun among those migrant workers, even for a few minutes, gave me a glimpse into the rough world they inhabit—living in shacks at the edge of the fields without air-conditioning, bending their backs all day, working long hours in crews that enjoy a deep camaraderie, skillfully harvesting the food that goes onto my table, for a rock-bottom wage. To write about them now would not be to write about some abstraction called "migrant workers" but of a young man of twenty or so with ropy muscled arms, sweat sheening his brow, leaning over a row and slicing free a head of lettuce with a fluid easy motion, then, his dark eyes full of pride, handing it up to us on the raised dirt road, smiling big.

The things of this world have shape, weight, texture, and heft. They are smooth or rough, reassuring or frightening. They inspire a sense of beauty or revulsion. We want to touch them and hold them—or we shy away from their sharp edges or slimy feel. Using them as they are—or were—used by those to whose world they belong requires the writer to enter that world, if only for a moment. It makes the writer's muscles do what the object requires—swing, hold, play, dig, cut, shoot, pump, brush, rake, churn, press, carry, squeeze, or just hang on. They give off odors. Some of them have a distinctive taste. They make sounds. Such an intimate grasping creates knowledge, a visceral and muscular firsthand insight into the lives of the people whose muscles did the same work, rode the same vessel, manipulated the same tool, fastened the same tiny buttons, fingered the same keyboard, carried the same burden.

In researching *The Devil's Highway*, his haunting story of a band of illegal immigrants who come to tragedy in the blistering Arizona desert, Luis Alberto Urrea conducted exhaustive interviews with border patrol agents, investigators, prosecutors, rescuers, and a host of other people on both sides of the border. He also dug through a mountain of reports, legal documents, and other evidence. But just as crucial to his faithful re-creation of the doomed journey of men who walked into the desert toward what they thought was an opportunity for a better life—known to the Border Patrol as the Welton 26—was his own time spent in that same desert. He concludes his author's note:

Finally, although I wasn't with them on the morning when they awoke lost in the Sonoran Desert, I have spent many spring mornings there. I know the smell and sound of the dawn quite well. I know the time of year. And I know the weather conditions in which they found themselves. The Welton 26 had scant time to worry about the nature aspects of their journey. But no story about death and the Devil's Highway could rightly exist without the strong presence of Desolation, in all its intimidating glory.

And Urrea came to know that Desolation firsthand.

At its heart, writing is a passionate exercise in empathy—doing our utmost to inhabit the mind and soul of another, and so to understand experience and choices not our own, as a path to meaning.

Handling—indeed listening to and smelling and even tasting—the thing itself can transport us, and ultimately our readers, into that magic territory.

Prompt #17: "Walking the Ground." In writing as in life, there is just no substitute for being there. Your assignment is to go somewhere you've never been and observe it with all your senses—sight, smell, hearing, touch, even taste if possible. Then write a passage that captures the essence of the place—its soul, dramatic importance, and crucial character. Remember you are not writing brochure copy or a fluffy "destination piece." You are trying to bring a place to life for the reader in a way that serves some larger creative agenda and locates the reader deeply inside it—emotionally as well as sensually. You need not travel to some exotic locale—you can use a place nearby if it serves your project. But capture its significance, which may also mean unearthing its history and human culture.

Prompt #18: "Terra Incognita." Design an experience that will take you out of your familiar comfort zone. (It need not be risky!) Then give yourself to the experience and write a short narrative about what you did and how it felt, physically, emotionally, and intellectually.

Prompt #19: "Handling the Thing Itself." Investigate a subject by handling objects associated with it and write your impression of the experience. In what way was it surprising? Enlightening? What insight does it give you about the people who handled such items?

9 TROUBLESHOOTING, FACT-CHECKING, AND EMOTIONAL COST

I didn't handle it. That was the problem. I was blindsided.
—Kirsten Holmstedt, *Band of Sisters*

The best laid plans can unravel—indeed, it's unusual for any plan to unfold without a hitch. What do you do when a key source bails on an interview? When you are denied access to a crucial person, event, place, trove of information? It can be maddeningly hard to find out the truth of any particular fact beyond a shadow of a doubt. But that's fine—you can use that. Often the most interesting thing the researcher finds is what you don't find, the doubt that hovers over each fact. Time and again, we learn that stories that seem too neat and satisfying are actually bogus. The too-good-to-be-true fact all too often is just that. There is a great satisfaction in loosening our hold on everything we thought we knew for sure. Scientists were once so certain that DDT was harmless, they literally spooned it into their mouths like sugar at press conferences—a cautionary tale if ever there was one about ever being too sure of ourselves.

Research is rarely conclusive. It often teases us, contradicts itself, and leaves the writer with hard choices. Even basic facts—a date on which an event occurred, the names of people involved—can be in dispute. Share some of these choices with your reader, and deepen the drama and impact of your writing. So what do you do when a source throws a monkey wrench into your plans? Suppose you are counting on a key interview, and the person keeps putting you off, and finally becomes unavailable altogether. Or worse, keeps on making dates and then bailing on you at the last minute? You have several options.

First, if this subject is the key to your whole project, you can make one last effort to make him or her understand just how crucial the interview is and at least be available for a phone conversation, which might lead to a face-to-face encounter. Sometimes this can be done through a third party—someone who can vouch for your seriousness and is closer to the individual than you are and can broker a meeting. But if, when all is said and done, this person simply will not cooperate, then you have to figure out if you can complete your project without him or her. Perhaps you can do a version of Gay Talese's "Frank Sinatra Has a Cold," in which, denied access to the famous singer, he builds the piece around interviews with all sorts of people who know Sinatra.

If you really can't imagine a version of your project without the cooperation of this key subject, then it is likely time to cut your losses and move on to some other project. Maybe someday the opportunity will come to chase down that subject, but don't spend your life waiting, and once you've moved on, don't look back. Look forward. If the subject is one of several key interviewees, then arrange the other interviews first, keeping up a steady, gentle effort to enlist this other subject. Perhaps someone who has already agreed to an interview can help persuade the holdout. And it's helpful to figure out, if you can, *why* the person is dodging you. Whenever I've had trouble pinning down a person to an interview, it turned out to be for one of several fairly ordinary reasons:

1. The person I wanted to talk to was just too busy and couldn't—or wouldn't—spare the time. Or our schedules just couldn't mesh because of overseas travel or other obligations.
2. He or she was simply shy or very private, and was uncomfortable sharing thoughts or feelings with strangers. And maybe was very modest, didn't like talking about his or her accomplishments.

3. The subject had recently had a bad experience with a previous interviewer and therefore did not trust any interviewer.

4. Personal matters made the timing very bad. The most common issue was ill health or the death of someone close. Many people just aren't in the mood to talk to strangers during such times. They may be embarrassed by a decline in their faculties or simply under the influence of medication. They may be grieving or preoccupied with settling an estate.

So put yourself in that person's shoes and calculate your options. If it's a matter of overcoming shyness or modesty, gentle persuasion through a letter, e-mail, or phone call may create an opening. If a previous interviewer has fouled the waters, providing your own bona fides might help break the ice—through a trusted third party, perhaps someone that person knows whom you have already interviewed. Your website or Facebook page can make you less a stranger. So can sending along something you have written to demonstrate the kind of writer you are—the narrative intelligence you bring to your craft that will reveal you to be empathetic and trustworthy of their story.

If the person is too busy, don't leap to the conclusion that he is self-important or she is infatuated with her own celebrity. That may indeed be the case, but more often I have found it's just honestly hard for busy people to find extra time in their days. A politician or celebrity might be scheduled wall-to-wall. Maybe your request never even penetrated the layers of insulating personal assistants. Make your request as convenient as possible. Sometimes the only place to catch a busy person is at an airport between planes—a scrap of time in their schedule that might otherwise be wasted.

So again, be gently persistent, and try to penetrate the barrier to the person who can say yes. I spent months trying to arrange an interview with Bill Blass, the clothing designer. I had to approach him through his chain of assistants. It took a while for me to make it clear to them that I was not interested in fashion but in his wartime experience in a top-secret army unit. They had no idea he had even been in the army, since he had never spoken of it publicly. But once Mr. Blass understood that was what I wanted to talk about, he was quite willing

to meet. Then it was a question of fitting me into his extremely demanding schedule.

In the end, someone from his staff called and asked whether I'd
like to meet him at his office in New York City or at his home in Con-
necticut. Of course I chose to visit his home, where he'd be comfortable among his personal things, and where we were less likely to be
interrupted by urgent business matters. We spent hours together
over the course of two days—he was one of the most gracious and eloquent people I've ever met. And we did indeed talk extensively about
his role in the war—but also about Hemingway, whom he knew and
admired; personal style and how it is manifest; camouflage clothing
as high fashion; art and antiques; landscaping with and without trees;
George Washington, who had once stayed in his home back when it
was an inn on the Boston coach road; and what goes into a really good
martini—among many other subjects. It was one of my favorite all-
time interviews.

If illness or some other personal crisis is interfering, your best
bet—if you can—is to wait until it passes. Unfortunately, sometimes
the illness is either chronic or the result of aging, and it won't go away.
Gently persist, but use your humane judgment. I was working on a
piece about Doc Watson, the legendary flat-picking guitar player,
shortly before his death. He was ill and wanted his privacy and de-
clined my request for an interview. I respected his wishes and wrote
the piece from other sources—including oral history–style interviews
in which he describes his upbringing and early life, his musical influ-
ences, and all the rest—exactly the things I would have asked him to
address. It wasn't hard to get his voice into the piece and simply attri-
bute the quotes to the proper sources. In the end, I was very gratified
that I hadn't abandoned the piece. While it was in press, Doc passed
away, and the editor had to literally change present-tense verbs to
past tense. For me, it was not just a feature piece but an essay that paid
tribute to a player who had inspired me. So in some important way,
researching his life and career was also a path into my own musical
beginnings, and the research reached not just into print and audio archives but deep into my memory.

THE ALTERNATIVE SOURCE

If the interview subject is just one of several who can offer the same insight, provide the same center for the piece—either as an exemplar or an expert—simply move on to another one who is more accommodating. If you're writing fiction or poetry—as opposed to nonfiction—bumps in the research road can be less daunting. In those genres, you're more likely searching for authenticity, not literal exactness of fact. There's almost always more than one way to find out what you need to know, especially if what you are after is not a particular set of facts but the felt reality of a place or time or circumstance. So if you're setting your story inside a natural history museum and you had your heart set on spending the night at the Smithsonian, say, and that turns out not to be possible, then just find another good-size museum that will let you. You can extrapolate from the feel of that experience, including specific exhibits at the Smithsonian, if that is your wish, since you can go see them anytime during operating hours.

So it's always helpful to know your goal in interviewing a particular person, visiting a specific site, accessing a specific set of archives, and so on. You want to write a scene on a train in 1890? There are plenty of period steam trains still operating—just choose the one that is most convenient. Need an assembly line scene? Any factory will do. Likewise almost any other setting, contemporary or historic. Don't box yourself in by fixating on one specific location or experience—there are usually alternatives.

Remember that things are often kept in more than one place. It's true that you have to travel to the Smithsonian National Air and Space Museum to see the original Wright Flyer, but there's an exact replica at the visitors' center at Kill Devil Hills, North Carolina, and a half-scale model hanging at the Wilmington, North Carolina, airport. And there are dozens more in other places—including flying replicas in Dayton, Ohio, the Wright Brothers' hometown. You can find a colonial-era Appalachian cabin in the mountains of Virginia. You can also find one in the Ulster American Folk Park—yes, in Northern Ireland. And of course the converse is true: some American folk parks and museums display full-scale artifacts from other parts of the world. Such parks make a practice of finding original artifacts—including whole buildings—and transporting them from their found sites to the grounds, then reconstructing them board by board. Similarly, crucial original documents may rest inaccessible in private archives, but copies—and nowadays often digital facsimiles—might exist in other more public archives.

So there's usually more than one way to find out something you want to know. And again, if it turns out that the essential ingredient of your piece or your book is either unavailable or inaccessible, you have a decision to make. Can you write the thing without it? Don't shy away from this question, or dance around it for months while you gather the low-hanging fruit. Make the call. You'll save yourself time and heartache if you bail out sooner rather than later. If you go forward anyway, map out a clear strategy: What will be your sources instead? How will the piece have to change to take into account this new limitation?

What do you do if it turns out that there is no record of the thing that has captured your imagination—no transcript, no report, no list of passengers, no itinerary, no facts and figures residing in some reliable repository? Again, for a fiction writer, learning that there is no record can be liberating—now you can be free to make up your own. The poet can take equal license, can even call attention to the absence of a record—imagining your way into those missing hours or weeks. That hole in the record may turn out to be the creative heart of the whole project.

In researching Paul Revere, I discovered that almost every minute of his time is accounted for from dusk until dawn of April 18–19, 1775. But after the massacre on the Lexington Green—at which he was present—he disappears until nightfall. A great part of my fascination with his story lies in those missing hours—after he had seen with his own eyes the deadly consequences of delivering the "news" to the militia bands in the countryside. What would he be feeling? What would he do? How would he participate? It opened a whole new opportunity for exploring his character.

The nonfiction writer, however, may be more stuck. All he or she can do is posit what is likely and make clear it is speculation, maybe reflect on why there is no record and how that both confuses and liberates the creative process, and use a lot of words like "probably" and "maybe" and "could have." Or maybe not. Sebastian Junger faced exactly this problem in writing *The Perfect Storm*. His solution was to re-create a meticulous record around the event—all that he could find out about the crew and the sword boat *Andrea Gail* before they sailed off into oblivion, and all that happened in the aftermath of the calamity. Then he could offer a plausible scenario about how events might have played out, always careful to signal the reader which part is verifiable fact and which part possibility. In truth, most important events, public or personal, seem to center on an unknowable mystery at their core, and plumbing this dark absence may bring out the best of a writer's craft and art. Don't be afraid of the dark—explore it.

YOU CAN'T AVOID MISTAKES

Of course, even with an extensive and accessible record, we are human, therefore fallible. We are bound to make mistakes. These can be as simple as the crime novelist having his private eye click off the safety catch of his revolver (by its design, a revolver needs no safety catch) or a poet portraying a Victorian woman hanging her chemise on a wire coat hanger (not invented until 1903). The first is the result of not knowing how a revolver works, the second an anachronism— like automobile tire tracks in old Western movies. We can practice being exact, making sure we are familiar with the props of our stories and poems. Anachronisms are thornier. It's hard to know what people *didn't* know in a given period. It's hard to remember that the household facts of their lives—and therefore the language with which they described those lives—were different. So, for example, it's natural for us to compare any tragedy unfolding with agonizing slowness as happening in "slow motion"—yet that is a cinematic trope invented only in the early twentieth century.

Most of our metaphors and figurative language come from some literal time and place, so it follows that there was a time and place when they weren't yet known or used. The writer needs to live in the time and circumstances of the story or poem. Think about all the terms we have borrowed from just one activity, baseball, invented and made popular in America during the mid-nineteenth century: three strikes and you're out (sentencing laws); hit a home run or knocked it out of the park (delivered an excellent presentation at the meeting); struck out (did not succeed—in romance, business, etc.). Other sports have made their own contributions: The ball's in your court (tennis); a hail Mary pass (football, by way of the confessional); photo finish (horse racing); a marathon not a sprint (track); hat trick (hockey). Be mindful of figurative language. Whenever possible, draw it from the world about which you are writing—don't simply withdraw it from your store of cultural knowledge. All that said, the only way I know not to make mistakes is to not write.

It is wonderful if you can be backstopped by research assistants and fact-checkers, but the plain fact is that, in the end, you the writer are responsible for your own facts. And if you're like most writers, you don't have an assistant to follow up on your work. Book publishers rarely employ fact-checkers. The magazine you write for may not have a fact-checker, or the fact-checker may be inexperienced. In writing a four-year-long series of narratives about the Civil War in North Carolina, I was told up front by the magazine that there was no way a fact-checker could reliably verify all the many facts that would inform my pieces—that would take a full-time Civil War historian. So except for trying to verify basic facts (the dates of a given battle, the age of a certain character), and asking me to provide a catalog of my sources, the responsibility was on me to find the best information out there.

This sounds like only a matter of diligence, but consider that the most basic facts about that conflict (which is simply a very dramatic version of any human conflict you might be writing about—it really was a family feud on a magisterial scale) are in dispute. So, for instance, the most basic number of all—how many men were killed in the war—has changed, and keeps changing. At one time it was accepted that about 620,000 died, 40,000 from my home state of North Carolina. But scholars and various commissions have steadily increased the first number, which now stands at an estimated 750,000–800,000, even as they have decreased the second number to between 30,000 and 35,000.

Many historians agree that in a generation, the number of total dead may reach a million. And yet the war has been over for a century and a half, and all the sources we're ever going to have were available for almost all of that time. Historians tend to illustrate battles with neat diagrams of which regiment was stationed where, with nifty arrows indicating precise movements. But in reality, like so many human endeavors, battle is a mess—chaotic, often accidentally started, full of blunders, conflicting accounts, and unreliable reports written long after the smoke cleared. And even the aftermath is clouded in uncertainty.

Samuel Weaver—the local merchant hired to find the bodies of all the Union soldiers hastily buried during the battle of Gettysburg and re-inter them in the national cemetery—was under strict orders to not allow any Confederate dead to desecrate that sacred ground. He personally supervised the exhumation of more than 3,000 soldiers from shallow graves and mass burials—many just bones—and examined them meticulously. Yet he still mistakenly buried nine Confederates in the Union cemetery. And almost 1,000 of the 7,000 or so bodies left on the field from both armies were never even identified. Others, it is almost certain, were never even found, and lie there still in some farmer's field.

In any story that contains a multitude of facts—of location, number, event, spoken words—it's frustratingly hard to command them all. So on one occasion I had the whole Union army crossing the Potomac instead of the Rappahannock. A colonel traveled a railroad that wasn't yet built. An escaped slave met with President Lincoln in a town he never visited. Sometimes we catch such errors ahead of publication; other times helpful readers point them out. But here's the thing: while some errors are simply unaccountable lapses of attention, others are come by honestly. The escaped slave wrote of the meeting in his memoir and named the place. My mistake was in not backstopping his account by checking Lincoln's itinerary, even if the meeting was a minor footnote to a larger story. I wasn't writing about Lincoln—I was writing about the liberated slave. It was but a brief moment in one man's long saga of stubbornly escaping slavery and fighting for his country, and Lincoln was a bit player, but I should have tracked down Lincoln's itinerary for that period.

There is a sting that comes with being wrong in print. Not long ago I was invited to address a book club. After my presentation, members lined up so I could sign their copies of *Down the Wild Cape Fear*. As I opened one book, I saw that the flyleaf contained a penciled list of items. "What are these notes?" I asked the woman.

She replied, pleasantly, "Mistakes."

The kinds of mistakes I most often make can only be characterized as boneheaded blunders. I will carefully research a person and then, for unaccountable reasons, the wrong first name or middle initial will appear in print. Yet I know I checked and double-checked the copy. Gremlins infest the manuscript.

Some mistakes are just the result of being overwhelmed with facts that change through time. So I had a Confederate colonel traveling on a stretch of railroad tracks that wasn't completed until a few years later. I was working from a good map and assuming the line had all been laid in one sustained effort, but work had been interrupted for a period when funds ran out. Or naming a troop from a county that hadn't yet been carved out of another county. Maps change.

So it's worth keeping in mind: time can change facts. Sometimes the actual geography changes. An event that happened in Virginia in a certain year in a period of a few weeks actually began in Virginia and ended in West Virginia, though the participants never moved: the state moved. The same goes for many counties as they were carved into smaller counties or renamed, and territories that became states. Whole countries shift their borders all the time. Just watch Poland or Ukraine appear and disappear and change shape on the map of Europe over the course of the twentieth century.

In the abbreviated space of an essay or article, it's often maddeningly difficult to sort out the nuances for a reader, so you wind up doing the best you can, focusing on what seems important and not going into a level of detail that would overwhelm the story. And of course, alert readers—often with a personal connection to the story—will never hesitate to call or write to let you know you made a mistake. This is their right, and sometimes it can be useful if the narrative will be reprinted as part of a book. It gives you a chance to correct the mistake, to make the piece that much more truthful. Many magazines will run a correction, if the error is egregious enough. My railroad and Lincoln errors merited such corrections. But sometimes you're just left with egg on your face and all you can do is blush and apologize.

Readers—and some reviewers—will also take you to task for "mistakes" that are not mistakes at all. One reviewer once scolded me for having a character say "Keep on keeping on" in the winter of 1898—smugly asserting that the term didn't come into use until the 1960s. Yet I had a reliable source that credited the saying as a slogan of the Salvation Army, in wide use by 1900. It had simply been rediscovered during the era of civil rights activism.

The Civil War was the most reported war in history—more than two hundred correspondents on both sides ginned up stories for hundreds of newspapers and magazine in America and abroad. And yet the reporting was often sloppy and partisan, so that the story of the war as it emerged in the popular imagination by 1865 was largely a massive fiction. Much of what was and is "known" about the war is simply not true. It is legend, tall tales, partisan interpretation, rumor, and sometimes outright fabrication. And the Civil War is only a very extreme example of how conventional wisdom misinforms our understanding about most public subjects, intermingling mythology and old wives' tales with fact in a stew of "truthiness"—that irritating Zone of Noise again. It is the job of the writer to sort this out.

There are also all those inconvenient facts. You discover a real-life person with a great story and you write about him or her with enthusiasm, even admiration, and then you run across a speech or a letter that clearly shows the person to be a vile racist. Certainly that now informs your tone, maybe darkens a tale that was shaping up to be a story of heroism or strong character in the face of adversity. But you can't sugarcoat it—and, in fact, the new information adds a level of complexity to your subject. He can be compassionate in certain circumstances, morally courageous when it counts, and still be a racist who does harm to innocent people. We're complicated beings, we humans.

I wish I could say that I make fewer mistakes now than in the past, and in one sense that may be true: at least my bar for reliable sources has gotten higher and higher. But I've simply reconciled myself to the inevitable. As long as I am writing, as long as I am ambitious about telling complex true stories full of facts, I will continue to get things wrong. So I will strive as diligently as I know how to make the mistakes as trivial as I can.

FACT-CHECKING

In "Democracy and Things Like That," another essay from *The Partly Cloudy Patriot,* Sarah Vowell writes about how the reporters for the *New York Times* and the *Washington Post* misquoted Vice President Al Gore as he spoke to students at Concord High School in New Hampshire. They changed exactly *one word* of his actual remarks. Gore was making the point that even a single high school student can make a difference. He told his listeners, "I got a letter from a student in west Tennessee about how the water her family was drinking from a well tasted funny." Gore responded by ordering an investigation, which discovered that a chemical company was dumping hazardous waste into a canal and contaminating the groundwater. He told the students at Concord, "I looked around the country for other sites like that. I found a little place in upstate New York called Love Canal. I had the first hearing on that issue and Toone, Tennessee—that was the one you didn't hear of. But that was the one that started it all." The papers quoted him as saying, "But I was the one that started it all." It became a quote of the week in *U.S. News & World Report*. Changing a single word—"that" to "I"—completely distorted both the letter and spirit of his speech. He was giving credit to that high school kid in Tennessee who first brought to his attention the problem of chemical dumping, but in the media he came out having a "Pinocchio problem."

Vowell is quick to offer a personal disclaimer: "And, considering that I am a writer who has publicly misspelled names, confused Sinclair Lewis with Upton Sinclair, and gotten who knows how many things wrong over the years, I am one pot who should not be calling the Gray Lady black. Both *The New York Times* and *The Washington Post* did publish corrections." Much better, of course, is to catch the mistake before it goes into print. Add to your bookshelf *The Chicago Guide to Fact-Checking* by Brooke Borel. It will help you develop your own protocol for getting it right.

Katie O'Reilly is meticulous in her fact-checking regime, both in her writing for print and her radio reporting. For a politically charged piece on a grassroots movement protesting the actions of a state senator and his Republican colleagues for what they saw as their heavy-handed laws to limit women's access to birth control and abortion, defund education, and curtail early voting and require a state-issued ID to vote, she wanted to make sure she got the facts straight. O'Reilly explains her laborious process in service of accuracy:

This brings me to the intensive fact-checking labor my piece is requiring. To specify that information which would require "background checks." I went through the piece with a yellow highlighter. I highlighted any and all fact-checkable information, whether it was included in summary, exposition, scene, or stated through sources' dialogue. After all, in the event that I get something a "character" says wrong, all parties involved (including yours truly) will look bad. Plus, some information consists of facts I would never, under ordinary circumstances, question; however, our brains are unreliable, and if we hear something enough times, we'll assume it to be true. And in some cases during the drafting process, I grabbed information from less-than-reliable outlets such as Wikipedia. This needs to be checked against stronger sources, including experts, university archives, and credible media sources.

She makes important points: repetition makes a thing seem true—just ask any advertiser or political strategist. And small mistakes can destroy credibility in larger ways. O'Reilly explains:

The fact-checking process is ongoing. To check any information I included about sources, I compiled bullet-point lists (which have second homes in Evernote) of every conceivable fact concerning them. This takes the information somewhat out of context, prevents your having to "show" sources pre-published stories (a move many publications consider a fireable offense), yet allows the information to exist in a sort of vacuum where the only question is veracity. I'll be sending each source personalized lists, and they'll be able to simply mark "yes" next to pieces of information—or else make tweaks as they see fit.

It's a lot of work, and she discovered far more than she could ever include in even a long essay about this protest movement. "But of course," she concludes, "this is why research is so rewarding. It's a puzzle and a mystery, rife with opportunities for 'lightbulb moments.' And no matter the topic, it's always guaranteed to make you a lot smarter."

I have to admit that writing a book about research aimed in part at professional researchers and writers gives me sleepless nights. I am bound to commit some boneheaded blunder, include some egregious error that will inspire outrage and ridicule. So I ask the reader's absolution in advance, in the spirit of trying to get it right. As General George S. Patton loved to say (quoting Napoleon Bonaparte): *"L'audace, l'audace—toujours l'audace!"*

Audacity, audacity, always audacity!

Embrace your fallibility. Rather than defend your errors, apologize for your missteps and do your best to make them right, figure out how you might avoid the same misstep in the future, and move on.

Retain the kind of sense of humor about your failings shown by the estimable Benjamin Franklin, whose epitaph reads:

The Body of

B. Franklin, Printer,

Like the Cover of an old Book,

Its Contents torn out,

And Stript of its Lettering and Gilding

Lies here, Food for Worms.

But the Work shall not be lost,

For it will as he believ'd

Appear once more

In a new and more elegant Edition

Corrected and Improved

By the Author.

EMOTIONAL RISK AND LIFELINES

As a researcher, especially one interviewing living individuals, you take one final risk, mentioned briefly in chapter 7: the chance of emotional involvement. I clearly recall such a moment of emotional ambush, driving north on I-95 from Florida home to North Carolina, having spent the past several months interviewing scores of veterans of World War II—all of them then between seventy-four and ninety-two years of age. They were smart, articulate men, funny and wise, gentle and humane in their worldviews, and I would miss them. All at once a kind of grief overcame me. I realized that I would probably never see any of them again. The feeling hit me like a sucker punch and took my breath away for a moment. They were elderly, many suffering from serious illnesses, and they wouldn't live forever. And indeed, in the months after the book was published, my mailbox filled up with cards and letters from widows and family members notifying me that this or that fellow had died—as if they had hung on long enough to tell their story, then passed on.

Before you set out on such a project, throw out a lifeline and anchor it firmly to someone you can reach out to if you need it. I advise my MFA students to visit the campus counseling center at the start of their adventures, just to meet a counselor and give a heads-up about what sort of project they are embarking on. They may never need to come back, but if they do feel overwhelmed, depressed, or emotionally drained by their project, they have someone waiting in the wings to take their call. And by the way, this is not a role that most wives, husbands, significant others, or writing mentors can play very well. We're not trained, and, besides, what you need is someone who is detached from the very emotional turmoil you're trying to sort out. Certainly it is natural to confide your work adventures to loved ones, but they are not equipped to talk you through whatever issue you are handling. For one thing, they are too close—a disinterested third party, someone with professional expertise and training, will typically provide a valuable perspective. And you won't "wear out" friends and family by leaning on them too hard during an extended project.

I asked Kirsten Holmstedt how she handled the emotional demands of interviewing women veterans who had suffered trauma and survived combat. She answered bluntly, "I didn't handle it. That was the problem. I was blindsided." She explains:

One of the most stressful interviews was with a female soldier who was blown up by Al Qaida. As if that wasn't enough, Al Qaida videotaped the explosion and put it on the Internet for everyone, including the victims, to watch. I saw it for the first time in the kitchen of the soldier's house. Her children were playing in another room. I sat on a chair at the kitchen table and she was standing behind me. Even though she had watched the video many times, I could feel her jump at the explosion.

Part of the emotional ambush was seeing what she had not expected. As she relates, "I remember being very stressed out on that trip to Fort Campbell, Kentucky, but it wasn't so much the video that got to me. It was seeing a wounded female soldier for the first time. I had gotten used to seeing wounded men returning from war. This was something new. Women were returning maimed. Those wounds became more personal, which in turn made their stories more personal."

She continued her work in a second book, which took her further into emotionally dangerous territory. She recalls:

The wounds in *Band of Sisters* were primarily physical. It wasn't until I started writing the second book, *The Girls Come Marching Home*, that I started touching on the emotional scars of war. To this day, when I open that book, I hear the cries, anger, and frustration of women returning home. I hear their hopelessness and helplessness. I was told when I started writing this book that I would need a counselor. I don't even think I knew what a counselor was back then. It was the furthest thing from my mind.

But all that changed after so many heart-wrenching interviews, after she had come to share so many harrowing stories of women warriors damaged in such deep and irreparable ways:

I sought counseling after I hit a wall writing CJ Robison's story. I was so filled with the women's emotions I didn't know what to do. I was paralyzed. I shared in their hopelessness because they would tell me their story of near death or betrayal, and I would have no salve for them or myself. "Nice talking to you." That's how the interview ended. That's not the case now. Now I ask them what they are going to do next. I make sure, to the best of my ability, that they have a plan. So if the conversation triggered something about their wartime experience, they will be safe.

The researcher/writer is alone in her quest, and sometimes the burden of carrying other people's troubling stories can be surprisingly heavy, as Holmstedt learned firsthand: "I remember it was near Christmas time one year and I was talking to a Navy nurse. She was screaming and crying into the phone. She wasn't yelling at me. She was venting to whoever would listen. I got off the phone with the intent of sharing what had just happened, but no one in my immediate surroundings wanted to hear about it. So I held on to it, internalized it."

In the postscript to *The Girls Come Marching Home*, Holmstedt writes:

Trauma changes people. It changed CJ Robison and everyone who knew and loved her, including me. I was two-thirds of the way through writing the book when I sat down at my computer one day. I looked at a picture on the screen of Robison in her Army uniform, flanked by her daughter on one side and son on the other. I read the first two paragraphs of her story. I couldn't write. There was no way I could do her story justice. No way. Not after what she'd been through.

"But," she says now, "in hindsight I did do her story justice because I was willing to make myself vulnerable by listening and empathizing." That can be the gift the interviewer gives to the subject: listening with care and attention to a story that perhaps no one has ever before wanted to hear.

The conscientious writer grows though research, both as a writer and a person. "My books have made me more empathetic," Holmstedt says. "I was more of a journalist in the first book, trying to be objective and not get involved emotionally. That was impossible to do with the second book, whose subject is women returning from war. The whole book is about emotions. I dropped my journalism 'act' and dove in. I hear more than I ever heard before. What I mean by that is the words tell the story, but so do actions, appearance, subtle nuances, attitude."

Molly Walling ran into a different kind of emotional ambush in researching and writing a personal memoir that also brought to light the story of a double shooting of two black men in a small Mississippi town—killings in which her father and uncle were complicit. Her publisher describes *Death in the Delta: Uncovering a Mississippi Family Secret* this way:

After a family funeral, Molly Walling learned an awful, unimaginable story about her father. In the 1940s, her father, a prominent Deltan, editor of a newspaper, and scion of a cotton plantation family, settled a score with violence and shot and killed a black man, a fellow veteran of World War II. Discovering this horror started Walling on the investigative quest to find as much of the truth as she could after decades of concerted concealment by locals and relations.

"After I got into it, the story had me," she tells her readers in a video-taped interview to promote the book. She met family members of the slain black men, saw how they experienced "fresh grief" in reliving the story. "If I didn't step up and put this story on the table, I would be colluding with my family to keep this story hidden," she says. "It became an honor trust, in a way."

When I asked her how the family responded to what became a dark southern Gothic tale of racial violence abetted by small-town power brokers, she answered, "Without doubt, Death in the Delta is an example that may be useful to you. It caused a rift in my family that has yet to be resolved. I am attaching a copy of a letter from cousins. It contains a searing reaction—so strong that by reading it, you will get a clear picture of the implications of writing a story like mine. My eyes burned again this morning when I reread the remarks." The letter accuses Walling of publishing sensationalized "theories" of the killings that are untrue and defamatory to the legacy of the men involved, as well as to their descendants living in the same community. Her story hit the third rail of southern culture—sex across racial lines, or, as it was called in the old days, "miscegenation"—in a big way by intimating that her grandfather had a black mistress and fathered at least one child with her, and that the shootings of two black war veterans were partly related to a family dispute about the inheritance of land by a black half-brother. It's a blistering letter, long and detailed, and fraught with emotion. A number of passages are underlined, italicized, or placed in all caps for emphasis. It drives home the point that writing about real people's lives, especially in nonfiction, carries a huge burden of consequence, a ring of shock waves that emanates out from the center and can reach very far indeed.

Walling goes on:

In my immediate family, I encountered the same though less intense reaction. My two daughters have yet to discuss their feelings with me except to say that they felt that writing the book was something I needed to do for myself. Numerous people, including folks in my writing community, suggested—too late—that I would have been well advised to write a fictional account. Without the support of Diana [Hume George] and a competent therapist, I would have walked the solitary road of this journey with little support. However, my belief in the importance of the story—beyond personal gain—was and is still worthy of publication. I felt compelled and inspired to write it.

So inspired that she began working on a sequel, addressing how the families of the African American victims fared in the years following their deaths. It's not clear to me that turning the family story into fiction would have softened the impact on those family members still living in the place where it happened, and sometimes taking on the historical record on its own terms seems the braver course of action.

Not all projects are suitable for novices—unless certain mentoring is available. In the case of undergraduates, the guidance of an experienced teacher can help them determine whether they should undertake a project that is likely to be emotionally fraught. The answer will depend on the level of maturity and experience of the writer, as well as his or her temperament. It's a great opportunity for a mentor to engage the novice writer in a conversation that will resonate for a career.

Research is an adventure, unspooling in its own dramatic arc, and like any good drama, it engages you not just intellectually but emotionally, leading to moments of recognition—who we really are, who our subjects are—and the reversal of expectations and fortunes. And it can result in powerful feelings of catharsis.

Prompt #20: "Just the Facts." Find a paragraph from a nonfiction book or article that contains lots of information and fact-check it. That is, use whatever archives and experts you have available to determine whether the information is accurate.

Prompt #21: "Lifeline." Assume that finding the facts of a chosen project will come with an emotional cost. Draft a short list of available candidates to act as your "lifeline," should you need one—a professional counselor who can offer you a reality check and help you navigate the rough emotional territory you may encounter. Be realistic and practical. This person must be available on reasonably short notice—and affordable.

10 BREATHING LIFE INTO FACTS AND DATA ON THE PAGE

I mean, you look at this beautiful floor or this beautiful piece of furniture. It's a rough piece of wood, it's got splinters all over it, you've
got to do all of the sanding, you've got to do all of the cutting, you
can screw it up. You get splinters in your fingers. You get crap in your
lungs, you've got to blow your nose all the time. And yet when it's
done, it looks like it's this object that came out of heaven.
—Walt Harrington, *Acts of Creation*

There is all the research you need to do to write the book—a lot—and
there's some fraction of it that is what the reader needs to know to
understand and feel emotionally moved by your book. How do you
select that fraction? And when do you stop researching and start
writing? Different writers offer differing answers. It's a fine line, as
illustrated by the following tale of one researcher who delved casually
into her subject and came to be enthralled by it.

Alice Bache Gould was the daughter of an astronomy professor in Cambridge, Massachusetts, who graduated from Bryn Mawr
College in 1889 and went on to graduate study in literature and science. Among other talents, she was an accomplished navigator and
taught the principles and art of celestial navigation to U.S. Navy ca-
dets during World War I. As a girl, she also became fluent in Spanish.

John Noble Wilford recounts what happened next in his provocative book about Columbus, published on the eve of the 500-year anniversary of Columbus's first voyage to the New World: "On her way to Rome in 1911, Gould's ship was detained in Seville. To fill the time, she visited the Archives of the Indies in the former stock exchange, the Casa Lonja, near the port. Examining some old documents, she was annoyed by her trouble in deciphering the archaic Spanish script and determined that she would remain there until she had mastered it."

And so she did. Except for time out to teach navigation, she immersed herself in the archives, dedicated to discovering the names and personal histories of every man who had sailed with Columbus in 1492. Scholars had long put the number of crew at ninety sailors. She succeeded in positively identifying eighty-seven and naming another thirty-one probable crew—before she died of a stroke in 1953—still researching the Columbus archives. The list was finally published posthumously.

Research is seductive. If you're not careful, you can turn into a researcher who always seeks one more fact, one final confirmation of a fact, one last corroborating witness. Who follows one more clue, one more side track, one more fascinating discovery. Human history— private and public—is a web that can trap you so that you never break free, never write the creative work that was the point of the research. At some point, the writer must break free of the gravitational pull of the subject and reenter the creative realm. The Spanish scholar Rolando Lagarda Trias, reviewing Gould's work in 1986, expands on the cautionary tale:

The life of Miss Gould puts squarely before us the problem of whether it is ever possible to reconstruct the past completely. The destructive action by time and man eliminates a good part of the documentation, and to this factor has to be added that many questions asked today were not felt to be important by contemporaries. In sum, archival research cannot give answers to all our queries, which is why we believe that the historian in his reconstruction of the past has to use his imagination in order to fill in the gaps in the documents by hypotheses which are consistent with the facts.

Facts exist first as literal truths, but in the hands of an adroit writer they also resonate with implicit metaphor, a way of capturing a greater truth, a figurative way of thinking about the world. In her poem "Anatomy Lesson," Jill Gerard uses the facts of human anatomy to reach for something even more profound. Her main character in the poem is a cadaver, now offering up his secrets on the lab table:

The cadaver has promised to show me the heart.
I want to see how it breaks, locate the mended seams,
the place where joy resides and sorrow pools.
It's not so simple, he explains.

So opens the first of a cycle of poems in which the cadaver enjoys a second life as a kind of spirit guide and confidant to a woman in search of answers in her own life. She writes:

When I think about my work, I face my obsessions. This group of cadaver poems started so long ago with a trip to the anatomy and physiology lab—a professional development event that I organized for faculty at the school where I taught. For me, it was about facing some deeply seated fear and also a deep curiosity about how the body works. I can still see the student who led the presentation. She explained their work and then "introduced us" to the cadaver. She carefully uncovered the body and lifted the top of his chest away. She picked up his heart and held it carefully in her hands, showing us the mystery. This haunts me still.

The experience sparked a deep creative connection. She goes on, "That moment started a sequence of writing and research projects that would span years. The first writing was in my journal. Pages and pages filled up with wondering. Those journal pages became fodder for poems."

So observation and recording set the stage. "The first cadaver poem focused on that heart," she explains.

But before it could become a poem on the page, I had so much to discover. I started my research with simple talk. I had friends who worked as veterinarians, nurses, doctors. So I asked them to tell me about the heart. I remember one explaining the *chordae tendonae*, literally strings that help the heart to float in the chest. Those "heart strings" that we all pull on to get our way, to charm, to capture attention. The metaphor made real. I visited med school websites and studied diagrams and read and read.

This gave her access to the special language of the body: "The *sulci* rise and fall, visible grooves. The auricle projects from the atrium. When I first heard this term, I heard 'oracle.' My mistake was repaired by the research—but oh how I loved the idea of an oracle living in my chest."

The initial research was not easy emotionally. An observer must be able to detach herself from the cadaver on the table in order to study it and learn from it. "When I started my personal anatomy course, I could only watch the dissection videos through my fingers," she confides. "Literally with hands masking my face, I would peer out. I would often hit the pause button and breathe my way through my anxiety. But the more I watched, the easier it became. Now I still hit the pause button—but only to slow things down to really see what is happening." Her poem goes on:

He tips his head in the afternoon sun,
for a moment the pallor chased away, his face
burnished. I see how handsome he must have been.
Slowly he undoes the buttons of his shirt,
pushes back blue poplin and there his chest.

The incision is a ragged seam, bloodless.
He parts the edges, dips his right hand into the cavity,
pulls out a heart softened with time.
I hold it as it once hung, apex pointed down.
The sulci rise and fall like miniature mountain ranges.

I see no scars, no places where once love rent it, no sign of healing.
I ask about this. *Look here,* he says. *The chordae tendonae,*
heart strings that help the muscle float.
They really can break and cause the heart to flutter.
Here, he says. *These strings broke when she left.*

Here, the puppy that died in my arms. Here
the final ones when I felt the end draw close.
Ultimately we are alone.
He takes his heart back, tucks it into the cavity,
pulls shut the seam.

He says, what I miss most is watching dawn cast peach light on water.
He turns to face the light, raises his arms. The breeze
lifts his hair. He seems alive, in the world again,
skin pulled taut over the planes of his face.

The anatomical research that inspired first one poem and then a cycle of poems began growing into a novel. Gerard writes:

One by one, the cadaver poems were written and the narrative line captured my imagination. Now the poems are one story line in a novel. The research for the novel at times seems endless—and how I long for the extended blocks of time that come when the semesters end. Then you might find me watching dissection videos, working to understand this mystery that is the body.

One discovery leads to another—dissection, terminology, medical history, philosophy. All strands that let this work float in my imagination.

LAYERS OF FACT

There are layers of "factualness," the box of parts from which we construct a creative whole, and the intelligence behind the facts that determines how we shape those parts into meaning. So once you have assembled all the fruits of your research—notes, photos, audio, video, interview transcripts, maps, reports, transcripts, technical data, artifacts, whatever your work has turned up—you must start sifting through it all and beginning its transformation into coherent, resonant, artistic material.

A historical personage—a slave girl in Civil War South Carolina—may now become a lively character; a geographic location—such as a mansion or a crossroads—may serve as the perfect stage of action; the techniques of performing a certain kind of work—carpentry or selling cars, nursing or teaching—may offer a metaphor that reveals character; occupational jargon can serve as a loaded, intentional diction that carries emotion, bias, exclusion of outsiders, history, even humor; mundane or remarkable events become the dramatic context in which characters act to fulfill their desires inside stories; facts of nature—the sound of rushing water, the haunting silhouette of a tree-roosting night heron—provide the imagery that turns to music in a poem.

Katie O'Reilly, whose print and radio pieces are really thoughtful essays based on diligent, sometimes exhaustive reporting, says, "Regarding the actual drafting of the piece, I found it most helpful to let the creative process take over and let myself write, write, write, focusing on story flow, structure, and narrative tension, rather than researched facts (the first time through, that is)." And like any good reporter, she is keenly aware that information overload can kill the energy of a story, that telling too much can sometimes tell you less. "Especially when dealing with unlimited amounts of information," she goes on, "I think it's crucial to be able to turn the research part of your brain off for a given period of time, and, when writing down information that needs to be backed up with research, include bracketed 'notes to self.' You can always go back later and dig up the perfect factoid or quote—but don't let the creative idea get away from you in the moment!"

Poet Lavonne Adams has given a lot of thought to the role of research in poetry. As she puts it, "We have certain expectations when we open a book of history or a biography. We expect 'the truth,' or the closest version possible. So what does it mean if a poet chooses to write about historically based topics? What can this genre offer that isn't already found in biographies and literary nonfiction or textbook presentations?" It's a good question. While biographers and historians often set out to establish the record, most writers are using some part of the record to different creative ends. Adams explains:

I believe that the nature of poetry itself allows the author to present an alternative window into history, one that allows the author to be less bound by facts than a traditional text, more able to make some creative leaps. As a means of liberating myself from the strictly historical, I open my work-in-progress with a poem titled, "I Married Kit Carson's Ghost," thus granting Carson the role of "intimate purveyor" of his stories. This tactic also allowed me the flexibility to create fictional characters within the realm of what was "real," much like someone who writes historical fiction.

Michelle Boyajian addresses the challenge of writing the courtroom scenes that are so crucial to the forward momentum of her novel:

The way this whole entire thing started was reading transcripts online. I knew the issues I wanted to tackle and wanted to see how that would work in reality. It would depend on the state the trial took place in. I wanted *authenticity*, right? I was so worried about the legal stuff, in writing it and getting it perfect. You should paint the picture and it should work, but also your job isn't to become a lawyer in the process, is it. So I had to chill out with that.

The courtroom scenes were essential, but she wasn't writing a legal thriller, and other stages of action commanded her attention as well. So she had to use just the highlights of what she had learned to create the illusion of a long and difficult trial in which all the important moments were captured in her scenes. She says:

It's a matter of overwriting it at first with the research, and then recognizing the instinct that says, "This is not at all interesting in the least," and reading it back and then thinking, "I'm so concerned with getting it right that I'm forgetting the rhythm of sentences." You can be authentic and creative too. And so you have to remember that there's information, but really the information serves the character, right? So you're writing a story about *people*, not about *information*.

Boyajian's observation is one of those that seems so obvious and yet eludes many of us as we become infatuated with what we have learned, even with our own cleverness in finding it out. We too often are tempted to leave the price tag on. Boyajian asks:

So, what is the most fluid way to get it in? The most organic way to get it in? Remembering that even somebody like a DA is accidentally going to spit part of his food when he talks, and that makes him human, and how you get the human part in and just make it flow. It's a matter of being able to say to yourself it wasn't wasted research, it's letting you write like this, and you're going to go in and take four words out of four pages of research, and what comes out is going to be the creative part. But it works because it's authentic. So it's a matter of letting go.

She learned the difficult truth that sometimes you have to master a mountain of information and background to be able to write a short, convincing passage. "It's a subconscious thing," she says. "That's what you hope happens. You are lending a certain authority. . . . You have the authenticity and the authority and you know what? It just lets you write with more confidence—not just the technical stuff. It lets you write the creative stuff because you're not stressing about the technical stuff." Boyajian has a name for the process of knowing a subject so well that the narrator can write about it with complete and unconscious authority: *infusion*. "It works in stuff that I don't even realize it's working in, right? But it's writing with authority, because I *know* it."

In his epilogue to *Acts of Creation*, Walt Harrington reminds us about why he has remained so enamored of the fine craftspeople of whom he writes so lovingly:

Fine craftsmen don't work only to get done, to get paid. They work in the moment. They work for a *feeling* that is rare and beautiful and ineffable. Wanting that *feeling* again and again drives and inspires them. I understand, all right. I get paid to write, but I don't write only to get paid. Remember, I can fiddle with five pages of writing all day long and feel refreshed at the end, feel as if only minutes have passed, as if I have added something of value to the world.

That is finally our goal: to go out into the world and learn from it, then to take what we have learned and craft it into something that adds value to the world. And it is the feeling of the work, the thrill of discovery, that keeps us coming back.

IMAGINING THE SCENE

The hardest thing a writer has to do is to imagine a scene he or she did not witness or participate in. Yet by drawing on a variety of disparate sources, the writer can build a dramatic, believable scene that captures truthfully that event. And remember: the reader must trust us to know, and especially in nonfiction, craves to know how we know it. There are reliable ways to gracefully impart that sense of authority in the writing itself and in how we frame the writing—author's notes, citations, and so on. Which one you use will depend on a number of factors: the house style of the publisher; the extent to which you are in fact creating the record of the people or events; whether the audience is general or specialized by profession; and how much close citation matters to the credibility of the narrative.

One of the great challenges of writing nonfiction from research is the tendency to want to anchor every detail in a source, as if to say, "See? It's really true!" The result can be prose that is stultifyingly dull, clunky and buttressed on every side by citations. Of course the goal is accurate truthfulness. But if you can't tell a good story, the reader won't stay with you long enough to get to the truthful part.

Carrie Hagen came up against this challenge in writing her first book, *We Is Got Him*, the story of the first kidnapping for ransom in American history. She started the project as a high school teacher interested in both history and writing, and pursued the research and wrote a first draft as a student in Goucher College's low-residency MFA program, which like other programs of its kind pairs writers with a series of mentors over the course of several years. Having a seasoned writer appraise your work in progress, with the help of a chorus of others, can be helpful in locating your natural voice, a way to tell the story that holds interest for the reader. Hagen's mentors included Suzannah Lessard, a longtime *New Yorker* writer and author of *The Architect of Desire: Beauty and Danger in the Stanford White Family*, and Richard Todd, a brilliant writer and co-author with Tracy Kidder of *Good Prose: The Art of Nonfiction*, the story of their decades long writer-editor collaboration and a useful guide to the kind of lively writing we're talking about.

One of Hagen's last assignments during her first semester was to write a crucial early scene set on the day in July 1874 when the first ransom note arrives at the Germantown home of four-year-old Charley Ross, last seen climbing aboard a wagon driven by two strange men with his older brother, Walter—who has since escaped his kidnappers. On the same day, the mayor of Philadelphia is dedicating City Hall and the new Centennial Grounds, which will be the site of a grand celebration of the city, attracting tens of thousands of visitors— even as the crime terrorizes the city. Hagen decided to become the most knowledgeable person in the world about her material: What the Centennial Grounds looked like, what the mayor said, what news made the headlines that day, even what the weather was like. Thus she could write with confidence. "I spent *hours* in the archive at the library reading through microfilm to reconstruct that scene," Hagen remembers. "And after drafting and drafting, it just clicked. I felt a surge of excitement and realized I could do it."

Part of her breakthrough came from her own discipline, relentlessly redrafting scenes, pushing her prose to live up to the material. She paid attention to basic matters of clean craft: active voice, clear syntax, dynamic verbs, signature physical detail, provocative juxtaposition of images, logical sequence of events, visual depiction of action, consistent and engaging tone. Hagen says, Todd agreed with our group that I was writing with too much of an academic bent, full of unnecessary details that I was excited to have found in archives, but that fell flat with readers. He really encouraged me to find confidence in my research, and to trust that I was becoming an expert. This eventually— months and months later—made sense, and by allowing myself to speak with more authority, the verbiage faded somewhat. I learned to position scenes for better reading.

So outside readers who would push her past old habits of writing, coupled with a new confidence inspired by that push, and finally the discipline and drive to redraft scenes until they "played" as little movies on the page rather than merely told summaries—all combined to bring a moment of history to life in words. Like many successful writers, Hagen relegated her "B-roll"—historical facts and details, the backstories of people and places—to connecting passages between scenes, where the reader can painlessly absorb them and in effect get better prepared for the next scene, where that information will prove useful.

Hagen learned two important lessons that she carried with her into her second book project. "Patience," she says.

I am struggling to figure out what detail is necessary for the page, and what is necessary for only my research notebooks. I need to tell more of a psychological story, and give less of an academic dissertation. And this is *so hard* to do, even after two years of research. But what gets in my way most is my sometimes feverish desire to get something else out there, to be quite honest. I have had to think about why I want to publish, and what is really driving this research process. If I want to write this book, I have to be more patient, and less focused on the end result. Otherwise, I'll keep spinning.

Just as in the act of interviewing, the book writer must pretend she has all the time in the world to get the story right. The fastest method is to not hurry.

The second lesson: "I have to read more. I studied Erik Larson's endnotes for *Devil in the White City*, and those endnotes helped me think about what to emphasize and how to make well-researched inferences in a way that didn't seem so stymied."

NARRATIVE VOICE: LITERAL AND FIGURATIVE

Reading any scene out loud to hear if it "plays" is another excellent technique—your ear will quickly tell you when a sentence causes your tongue to stumble, or when an image is inexact or an action confusing. Or when a catalog of facts dulls your attention. Listening to a friend or colleague read your words back to you can be even more useful: they will have only the words on the page to clue them in as to tone, pace, and sense—not your secret intentions. The challenge is to take sheer information—facts and ideas—and present them dramatically. Another way of saying that is to imagine how you would film a fact or idea. To show the poverty of a tenement in 1900, what shot would you use? Who would be in it—and saying and doing what?

In prose, you can string together suites of scenes, each one preparing the way for the next, connected as necessary by a perceptive narrator who can duck in and tell us what we need to understand about what we are going to see and hear—never distracting us too long from the action, just occasionally looping an arm around the reader's shoulder and saying, essentially, "Let's ponder what we have just seen, and by the way, you might want to know a couple of things before we continue the story . . ." Thus the narrative intelligence guides the action, helping the reader to make sense of it, maybe explaining customs that are strange or language we are not used to hearing, adding social or historical or family context, then stepping back and letting the next scene play. If you can do this, the reader enjoys the illusion that you've told every last bit of the story—when in fact you have told only the important points, your narrator assuring the reader that he or she hasn't missed anything vital: "For two years, my father was absent, then one day he appeared at the front door holding an old leather suitcase." We glide right by that transition, assuming nothing of note happened during those two missing years, and the story moves on.

In poetry, of course, the writer is after a more elliptical truth, less of a complete narrative than vivid, suggestive moments that capture some fact of the world: the way a redstart perches on a pine bough, the hammer blow of a blacksmith on glowing iron, the embroidered roses on a girl's cotton pinafore on a farm in 1930, the punky odor of a smoldering peat fire in an Ulster cottage. The meaning may lie mostly in the silences between moments, the holes in the story, and whatever narrative we find is the one we imagine by connecting the points of light into the shape of story.

Lavonne Adams wants her poems to speak to the reader not just as reliable documents of our historical and cultural heritage but as works of art. "The challenge with this type of work is how to claim authority over the subject matter, especially if the event(s) occurred well before you were born. The most readily apparent manner is through acknowledging references," she explains. "That meets academic expectations. But real authority is something more craft-oriented—the engagement of the poet with the subject matter." The poet exudes a confidence with the material, born of intimate knowledge, that engenders trust. She just seems implicitly to really know what she is talking about, so we don't stand back skeptically and wonder how she knows what she is telling us. Adams wants to include the real voices of long-dead personages, set in an authentic context that lends inherent credibility to the passage. "Thus, our research represents more than scavenger hunts, or even treasure hunts," she says. "We research in order to provide a more meaningful connection between our work and our readers."

In her Pulitzer Prize–winning collection *Thomas and Beulah*, based on the lives of her grandparents, Rita Dove was passionate about achieving an authenticity of a different kind. In addition to the poems, she includes a chronology. As she told Daniel Bourne in a 2010 interview, "The poems can stand by themselves. Absolutely. But the chronology is also a way of commentary on the lives, insisting upon the veracity of their presence, and to remind us they were real people, and to juxtapose the sense of reality that the reader had just finished experiencing in the poems with the actual reality these people went through." The chronology is a prosaic way of grounding the poems, speaking to the gaps between the moments they illuminate, reminding the reader that those moments exist in the context of long lives, most of which remain unknown and unknowable.

She is after something else. Like good historical fiction, her poems bring to life past events in the context of their times through the experiences of compelling characters. She has written about such diverse historical figures as Rosa Parks, the civil rights pioneer; Ludwig von Beethoven, the canonical composer; and George Bridgetower, an Afro-Polish violinist. But she is also after something different: "Hopefully you will get a sense of the interior life of a George Bridgetower or my version of Rosa Parks that will help to illuminate the facts of the historical 'thing.' But the difference might be that I think my poems will also try to remind you we are not really in that world. They will not let you fall deeply into this feeling, to forget that it is a fiction, or that it is a construct." The reader will experience simultaneously the emotional depth of the poem and the knowledge that it is first, last, and always a poem—a created thing.

Nomi Stone has blended and bent genres in order to create the story she wanted to tell about role-playing warriors. She did two years of preliminary fieldwork and two years devoted full-time to fieldwork observing the war games. "In this new project . . . there is so much buzzing, haunted, and glorious abundance that form is now mutating to accommodate it," she writes in *Jet Fuel Review*. "Still, the book remains a book of poetry. What I am working through now is enabling each piece in the new book to be entirely a creature of its own, not forced into an ill-fitting form." The material itself is helping to guide her into the most effective and artistic form. She is, in an accurate sense, listening to her research.

RE-CREATING THE EVENT

But the challenge for the writer remains: how to re-create a scene that happened far beyond our ability to witness it?

One answer is to assemble the "facts" of the scene from whatever diverse sources and then recombine them intentionally for clarity and drama. In my book *Secret Soldiers*—the true story of a top-secret army unit that used art to manipulate the German enemy in World War II by concocting elaborate ruses—I wanted to write a scene that would both introduce a main character and also establish some of the important themes of the book. The character is Douglas Fairbanks Jr., a swashbuckling Hollywood matinee idol who, as an officer in naval intelligence, champions battlefield deception. Luckily for me, he was also a terrific and vivid writer, and he left behind colorful battle reports and a witty memoir. The scene is the premiere of his new movie, *The Corsican Brothers*—about a week after the stunning attack on the U.S. fleet at Pearl Harbor. The premiere takes place not in Hollywood but aboard the battleship USS *Mississippi*, on which Fairbanks is serving.

From naval records I was able to establish exactly where the battleship was docked that evening on the James River at Norfolk, Virginia. A reference librarian in Norfolk, enlisted by a fellow librarian at my university, tracked down not just the National Weather Service data for that date in Norfolk but also discovered the precise conditions on that part of the river at the time of the showing, so I could set the scene: "The night was clear. The air temperature had dropped to the low forties, and a slight north wind made it seem even colder." I knew where the ship had just come from, and that the men were assembled outdoors for the show, so I could go on: "The men's breath smoked in the damp river air. They had recently returned from Reykjavik, Iceland, so they were used to being outdoors in the cold."

As it happened, the summer I was writing this, the battleship USS *North Carolina*—sister ship of Fairbanks's vessel—was showing old movies on the fantail in exactly the fashion employed in World War II. I also found old photos of such shows on battleships. So I could confidently add:

Officers and chiefs sat in rows of folding slat-seated chairs. Enlisted men sat cross-legged on the immaculate teak deck, slouched against the bulwarks, or perched atop the lower 14-inch gun turret, one of four mounted on the old ship, hanging their legs down the armored face. A sailor lounged astride each of the three massive gun barrels, leaning back against the cool steel slant of the turret, legs crossed or dangling on either side. Others leaned out of anti-aircraft turrets, rubbing their gloved hands to keep warm.

And: "As they waited, they smoked and joshed and some talked in more serious tones about the war." The last was, of course, a small bit of narrative license, but in those days in the service almost everybody smoked, they wouldn't have been silent, and they already knew they were headed out to Pearl Harbor. Because of strict censorship, they hadn't been told much about the devastating toll of the attack, but everyone guessed it must have been pretty bad, so it seemed natural that they would speculate and pass on rumors, as idle sailors are wont to do.

This presented an opportune moment for the narrator to work in a brief bit of information about how many ships had been sunk, how many soldiers and sailors had been killed, then resume the scene: "A movie screen had been rigged from the crane on the fantail. The catapult holding the observation plane was rotated sideways—as if to launch the plane into the clear, starry night—to allow the screen to hang plumb. When it was full dark, the projector flickered, and all at once, the screen came alive as a rectangle of light and moving images." I could then register Fairbanks's delight—as he confided to his memoir, he'd had no idea that his movie was going to be the one shown—and describe his famous dashing smile (visible in every photograph of him). He had been hazed by his shipmates on the outbound voyage on account of his celebrity (from his personal memoir) and took this screening as a sign of acceptance into their brotherhood, so I could write that.

Then I could play the movie for the reader. It was a rare film, and it took me weeks of bidding on e-Bay to snag a copy at an exorbitant price, but I needed it to make the scene come alive. Its gimmicky melodrama would set the stage for more serious technical deceptions on the battlefield.

The movie is a festival of *trompe l'oeil*: Fairbanks plays *both* brothers—stalwart hero and charming rogue. The two were Siamese twins separated at birth by a surgeon's scalpel after their parents have been murdered. Mario is sent to Paris, where he is raised to become a gentleman, Lucien to the mountains of Corsica, where he grows up to be a bandit.

In an inevitable twist of plot, the brothers are reunited twenty-one years later by that same doctor to avenge their parents against Count Baron Colonna, the murderous villain who took their lives and later grabbed power over all of Corsica. He's mistakenly believed that the brothers died at birth, when he burned down their parents' villa.

The brothers meet at the graves of their parents and vow revenge against Colonna. They shake hands, and Mario wonders how they will ever be able to defeat the seemingly invincible baron. Lucien answers him slyly, "No one knows that there are two of us—that will be our sharpest weapon!"

Later, in a rare cinematic love triangle, Fairbanks vies with himself for the hand of the enchanting Countess Isabelle—played by Ruth Warrick.

What makes the film spectacular for the time are not the predictable coincidences of plot but the magical special effects.

In his double role, Fairbanks has to play scene after scene with *himself*—exchanging dialogue with himself, slapping himself, wrestling himself, fighting himself with drawn daggers. In a climactic moment, he even has to pick himself up and carry himself from the baron's castle. It is all done through tricks that fool the eye: Double-exposure, back-projecting one Fairbanks character while the other acts for the camera, using split-screen editing to combine two images of Fairbanks shot in different costumes—all cutting edge stuff in those days.

So the movie portrays very colorfully exactly the sort of tricks these artful soldiers would employ in real life on the battlefield.

Using Fairbanks's own words, I could bring the scene to a fade-out: "Finally the mystery of how I could possibly carry myself in my own arms is explained by my having a plaster life mask made of my face. This was transferred onto thin rubber and fitted onto the face of a double. I thus picked up the double with the mask of my face fitted onto his, and carried him in my arms." So his dual role in the war is established: sailor and trickster, actual person and the image on the screen, the real man and the illusory double. And if I've done my job, the reader sees him as a real and very likable person in the context of a nation heading into a world war, already having suffered an appalling defeat. Thus, the United States was the underdog in need of an edge, an advantage to even the odds. That edge would be deceptive warfare—the stuff I was writing about. And the men who would sharpen that edge were unconventional warriors like Fairbanks.

If I were writing a novel, I'd feel free to create dialogue among Fairbanks and the other sailors. Even delve into the thoughts and feelings of my viewpoint character, add other specific and probable details that would serve the story. And the movie itself would become a fiction within a fiction—again serving the theme of reality versus illusion. A shorter narrative piece might work much the same way, as Walt Harrington's profiles of virtuoso artisans demonstrate. He came away from each encounter with an eyewitness impression of his star character onstage, in action, complete with dialogue that he recorded in the moment, as well as in pre-interviews and follow-ups to furnish more elaborate context and backstory. He had the information of all his alert senses, for he had walked the ground and handled the thing itself. And finally, he was diligent in pursuing his archival homework, so he could adroitly interject background, explanation, history, and context into each scene. In other words, in each encounter he was conscientiously collecting all the elements of a scene so he could reassemble it back in his own workshop.

While still a graduate student, Benjamin Rachlin took on a daunting project: chronicling the long and complicated process by which a wrongfully convicted inmate was at last legally exonerated by the North Carolina Innocence Inquiry Commission. Not only did he have to gain intimate access to Willie Grimes, an African American man who had been locked up for decades, but he also had to simultaneously show how that unique commission came to be. That was another complicated story, requiring access to an unlikely alliance between an idealistic attorney named Chris Mumma and I. Beverly Lake Jr., former chief justice of the state supreme court.

Mumma was something of a crusader for social justice. She had put herself through law school and worked tireless hours for poor clients caught in the gears of a system she came to see as full of inequities. Lake was famously conservative. Yet he also became convinced that too many innocent people were languishing in prison because of institutional failures. They in turn enlisted influential leaders from law enforcement, the justice system, and the political realm and gathered them around a table at Mumma's home—neutral ground.

Rachlin wanted to re-create the drama of that seminal meeting. But it had happened years earlier, and of course he wasn't there to witness it. I asked Rachlin to walk me through his process of research and writing. "In 2002, Chris had helped arrange a kind of summit for leading prosecutors, defense attorneys, judges, law professors, and police officers statewide, to discuss the problems they were all seeing in the justice system," he writes. "A group like that includes deep partisan division, so many of those people had never met, even while they worked in the same field." He tracked some of them down to interview, but he also wanted to visit the actual site of the meeting. "Chris was reluctant," he reports.

I thought I understood: until now we'd only met at her office, and her home was a different thing. Still, I pressed. I didn't want to impose on her privacy, or see her bedroom or anything. Because this meeting had occurred at her house, though, I felt I needed to see it. Was this possible?

We drove there from her office. On the way, she confided why she'd first resisted. It wasn't just privacy—it was that, when strangers saw her house, she worried they got the wrong idea about her. The place was a mansion. It had more than a guest room—it had a guest *house*. They hadn't always lived this way: back when she and her husband, Mitch, had married, Mitch had worked as a CPA, but then he'd left that to experiment in venture capital. This was back when the field was starting, so the choice had been risky: hardly anyone knew what venture capital even meant, much less whether there was any future in it. It turned out there was. Quickly their circumstances had changed, and not just a little. The house Mitch chose was more ostentatious than Chris liked, and even now, years later, she still felt self-conscious bringing people there, what they might assume about her once they saw it.

Rachlin continues:

"You would have greeted them here? They would've walked through this hallway? The meeting was over here?" I scribbled observations in my note-pad: "Foyer/lobby. Wood + tile floor. Lots of windows. CM moved furniture. Mint green paint. Pale green? Big chandelier. Glass double-doors. Hardwood floor—and marble."

I asked lots of questions about the furniture layout, since I knew things might look different today, a decade later. Quickly I sketched a diagram of the room. (I've since learned I can take photographs on my iPhone in a situation like this—but I didn't think of it then, and might not have done it anyway, since I didn't want Chris to feel any more uncomfortable.)

Out front I did the same thing: "Brick, white columns, black shutters. Deck atop front door. Expansively landscaped lawn, iron-railed entrance of curved brick steps, charcoal gray roof shingles. Flagpole at front w/ US flag. Lots of trees (oak?) Yup. Stone-lined driveway. People parked around circle + in back." When I noticed Chris standing there nervously, watching me scribble, I offered to read aloud for her what notes I'd taken. "Very matter-of-fact," she decided.

The project stretched Rachlin beyond what he was used to.

Before this book project, I'd rarely written any scene I wasn't personally there to witness. This raises the degree of difficulty in nearly every way. One thing I noticed, when I began doing it, is the sensation feels unexpectedly similar to writing fiction. Not in making things up, I don't mean—obviously a nonfiction writer commits not to do this. It's just that, if I didn't person-ally witness an event, I need to really concentrate imaginatively to write it well—must *see* the room, *hear* those people talk, *feel* the broken air condi-tioner, or whatever. These are basically fiction muscles I'm using, to imagine such details. If I'm not doing that, or I'm doing it poorly, then all I have is a list of facts. If the scene is to come alive, I need to imagine it into being.

But in the nonfiction genre, allegiance to facts remains a bedrock principle, as he makes clear:

Of course the difference is in fiction those details are invented. In nonfiction they are gathered. I need to find as much primary- and secondary-source material as I can, pester (politely) the real people who were there. What were you wearing? How was the furniture laid out? Were the chairs comfortable? Who in the room were you friendliest with, socially? Did anyone have an accent? Where'd you arrive to that meeting from, and where'd you leave it to? What was the weather outside? What kind of car did you drive then? So the raw materials of nonfiction come from a different place—externally, rather than internally, as in fiction. But the demand on my imagination is much the same.

Sometimes the very details that make the scene so real never make it onto the page but turn out, nonetheless, to be crucial to the writer's understanding. Rachlin recounts:

Near her driveway fluttered a flag with the logo of Duke University, where I knew her kids went—this hadn't flown back in 2002, she told me, so I left it out of my sketch. One of her kids was a student manager for the basketball team there, she remarked, under Coach K [Mike Krzyzewski].

Had Chris ever met him? I wondered. She had. What had she thought? That he'd been inspiring. "I can never decide how I'm supposed to feel about Coach K," I admitted. "On the one hand, there's a lot about him I really like. On the other hand, his mentor was Bobby Knight. And Bobby Knight's so hard to like."

"Yeah," Chris agreed. "But you can learn a lot of important things from people you don't like."

That line of dialogue doesn't appear in the chapter. But it guided everything I wrote.

Here is how the scene appears in his book *Ghost of the Innocent Man* (Little Brown):

They pulled up to Chris Mumma's house at a few minutes after eleven, on a cool, overcast Friday in late November. For days Chris had felt self-conscious about welcoming so many strangers to her home, but finally she'd been forced to admit that it made more sense than anyplace else. She and Beverly Lake had both wanted neutral ground, where no one would feel alienated as soon as they showed up. They couldn't ask prosecutors to come to a liberal university campus, or defense attorneys to go to a sheriff's department. Lake had hoped for a private home, but whose could hold fifteen comfortably? Her own, Chris offered grudgingly, where she and Mitch had moved after his breakthrough in venture capital—Mitch's choice, she insisted, not her own. The two of them and all three kids had once lived in a modest A-frame. Now they owned a ten-thousand-square-foot Georgian Revival, with charcoal shutters and a winding, iron-railed front entrance, whose pillared balcony overlooked a golf course. Between its guesthouse and expansively landscaped lawn unspooled a stone-lined driveway enough for the dozen-plus cars Chris and Lake expected.

Besides Rosen, Newman, Coleman, and Weitzel, from the Center, and one or two colleagues of Lake's, none of the invitees had any idea who she was, Chris knew. They'd come not because they recognized the address on Lake's invitation but because the Chief Justice of the North Carolina Supreme Court had invited them, and now here was some blonde woman, at her porticoed mansion, welcoming the Attorney General inside. Chris worried about impressions. She wondered if some of them presumed she and Lake were having an affair. She'd borne that suspicion before, though it had been wrong then, too: as a young blonde executive at Northern Telecom, more than once she'd considered cutting her hair, or wearing glasses, to downplay the effect of her looks. Finally she'd decided not to. The best way she knew to prove others wrong was to be undeniably good at her job. If for the next thirty minutes or so a handful of police chiefs and district attorneys misperceived her as some restless trophy wife, with some sequined childhood, and this as some hobby luncheon, they would learn quickly enough. The meeting had been her damn idea in the first place. . . .

Now Chris welcomed the invitees into her hardwood and marble and bronze-chandeliered living room, where the previous week she'd dragged aside two embroidered couches and unfolded a rented conference table. Mitch was at work; all three kids were at school; Zeus, their hundred-pound Bernese mountain dog, she'd put in the yard. She'd also paid more than four hundred dollars to a private caterer, guessing that men might stay longer if she fed them, and that if they stayed they might as well choose to talk with one another. Then she'd looked around her house and inhaled deeply. She'd gotten them all in a room. It was impossible to predict what happened next.

Sometimes research has a life of its own, unconnected to any writing project at the time you do it. My father was a World War II veteran of the Army Air Corps who had survived campaigns on Saipan and Okinawa, including the great typhoon of 1945. Years ago, on a visit home, I sat him down at the dining room table and let him talk into a tape recorder for several hours, prodding him to recall his experiences in the war. He talked all afternoon, telling his vivid memories. How one of his jobs was to write the letters home to the families of the airmen killed or missing in action. How the Japanese used to steal down from the hills, hide behind the railroad embankment, and watch outdoor movies shown for the GIs. How one night on guard duty, he was startled by a Japanese soldier and tried to shoot him, but the carbine wouldn't fire—he'd forgotten to flick off the safety—and the Japanese surrendered and my father lived the rest of his life grateful that he'd left the safety on. He told me how the typhoon descended on the island with almost no warning—a sudden change of direction made it defy all predictions. He hunkered down in a steel Quonset hut, the first time enlisted men and officers had ever spent the night in the same billet together. Sometime in the night, half of the structure blew away, leaving the men to shelter in foxholes and air-raid trenches under the whipping wind and black rain. And in the morning, the whole airbase was one giant wreck—except for one item: a carton of eggs siting unscathed on a debris pile, all the eggs unbroken.

I had a vague idea of using his stories in a novel someday, though my first try failed. Then a couple of years ago, I started working on a novel called *The Dark of the Island*, in which two young men—Liam and Tim—from Hatteras Island meet up on Okinawa during the

war. Tim has survived the bloodbath of Tarawa atoll as a navy corpsman, but Liam never made it to the fighting: he spent his war in Ha-
waii teaching navigation to fliers, and he feels deeply frustrated and
ashamed that he never got the chance to fight. The two old friends
take shelter in a Quonset hut that is ripped apart by the wind:

And at last, it happened. The wind lifted the hut and tore it in half. All at
once, men were lashed by stinging rain, pelted by airborne missiles. A
square of sheet metal spun out of the darkness and cut an Army Air Corps
sergeant's throat. A private went down unconscious under a flying chair.

Liam and Tim hit the deck. They crawled through sticky mud and
blundered into an air-raid hole, now full of water. They slid down the sides
and huddled in the wet morass, listening to the typhoon rage over their
heads. It felt like lying between the rails under an eternal freight train, all
roar and racket, the ground shuddering and slopping under them. They
burrowed into the mud, their bodies tucked protectively into each other's,
hands covering their faces. They remained hunkered in that mud hole all
night and all through the next day as the storm squatted over the island.

At dusk, Liam woke to a strange calm, hardly believing he had slept
amid such violent upheaval. The storm had moved north, up the island. Tim
Dant sat facing him, eyes wide open and staring. Liam laid a heavy hand on
his shoulder. They were both covered in muddy slime, their faces blackened
with it. "You and me," he said hoarsely. "You and me."

They helped each other scramble out of the hole. Other men were moving around in dead silence, ghostly figures in slow motion. Their actions
seemed random and aimless to Tim, movement for its own sake. No one
seemed to be doing anything useful.

Tim Dant spied something and began walking toward it, stepping over
and around the debris scattered by the storm: splintered boards, overturned
Jeeps, battered jerry cans, great balled-up clumps of wet canvas. He bent
and lifted something off the ground and held it for Liam to see: a cardboard
carton of eggs. Carefully, as if he were dressing a wound, he opened the lid.
All twelve eggs were intact. He grinned stupidly. Liam cursed.

The typhoon had accomplished in hours what the Japanese could not
in three months. The camp was utterly destroyed. Out on the airfield, B-24

bombers lay overturned, their great nose wheels pointed to the sky. The smaller observation planes, PBYs, were in a pile at the far end of the runway, as if pushed there by a giant plow. And it was the same all over the island. Hardly a building remained standing.

The island had been blown clean of tents. Men had died. Villagers in the countryside had been swept away. A dozen ships had been overwhelmed by thirty-five-foot waves and lost at sea. Hundreds more had been driven aground, and a hundred landing craft were lost.

Liam took the carton of eggs from Tim. *The cruelest piece of wreckage*, he thought, *to survive unscathed*. He smashed the eggs on the ground.

Clearly I wanted the eggs to be more to the story than a mere curiosity. For Liam, they become the embodiment of his own safety amid the carnage of a war that has taken, among so many others, two of his brothers. When he flings them to the ground, it's almost an act of self-destruction. I have my father's photos of his wrecked squadron of Liberators and overturned Jeeps, and because I weathered several hurricanes at home and a typhoon in Hong Kong, I could imagine pretty accurately the terrifying sound of the wind.

TURNING FACT INTO DRAMA

Learn to listen to your material, to let it suggest the kind of story it can tell, one that may not be apparent as a clean narrative plot. Tracy Kidder writes, " 'I don't have a book,' the young writer says when the events don't deliver the kind of obvious drama in which everyone recognizes a story. But usually what's missing isn't a story. What's missing is a broader way of thinking about what makes for a good story."

One way to begin to achieve that broader vision is to write parts: a description of a place that seems to matter; a careful reconstruction of an event or action you witnessed; a word-picture of a scene or object you encountered—all of these using "thick" description, a term borrowed from the anthropologist Clifford Geertz. Thick description gathers up all those images and actions that have cultural connotations. The usual example to illustrate this is that while the observer may notice both an inadvertent eye tick and a deliberate wink, only the latter carries cultural information because it is intentional. Such observed moments come already freighted with meaning, resonating outward like rings from a stone thrown in to a pond. A wink can be conspiratorial, flirtatious, ironic, threatening, inappropriate, or inclusive—and some or all those things at once.

Gather up enough moments, enough parts, and they often begin to suggest a pattern. They comment on one another. And as soon as parts start relating, you the writer are on the way to meaning. The images and scenes you have encountered in your research present obvious images and scenes for the page. Dry facts, information, or statistics can be harder to handle. So some rules of thumb for turning fact into drama:

Use Original Language

Specific details you've gathered from your research can get you past formulaic prepackaged ways of relating a fact or event. Don't write, "Another *brutal, senseless* murder," as if there were some other kind; instead address some especially abhorrent specific fact about the murder or the motive of the killer: "A couple of teenaged boys got bored one night and killed a random stranger just for the thrill of it." Don't fall back on "brochure-speak": "The town is *nestled* in a *postcard* valley . . ."; say, "You can follow the gravel river road for miles along the flat valley floor, and suddenly the town looms against the blue shadows of the hills at the western end." Forget squishy verbs: "They were *involved* in a plot to manipulate the stock market"—involved how, manipulate how? I can be "involved" in an auto accident if I am the drunk driver who caused it, the pedestrian who got run over, or the cop who investigates it. So be exact. Don't resort to "history-speak": "*Casualties were comparatively light.*" The guys who are killed and wounded don't think so. Figure out a fresh way to present facts,

events, information. Think. Build the scene from scratch. Don't bor-
row generic phrases wholesale. Part of the satisfaction of discovering
facts is figuring out a lively way to put them into words the reader
doesn't expect.

Practice Distillation

Digest the reams of information from your research, and tell the
essence of it clearly and vividly. For instance, I got tired of reading
reports of World War II battles that said, "A tank got knocked out."
What did that term "knocked out" even mean? I reached out to an intelligence analyst at Fort Belvoir, and he provided me with more than
forty pages of documents, some of them previously classified, including graphic pictures of tanks hit by German 88s—named for the cali-
ber of their bore or muzzle diameter (88 mm)—and the grisly wounds
they caused, called "spall wounds." I then wrote about two paragraphs
describing how a cocktail shaker-size projectile would pierce the thin
armor of the American tanks and explode inside, and described the
horrific wounds inflicted by the shrapnel ricocheting around inside
a steel shell, as well as the fact that the gasoline-driven tanks often
caught fire—so their five-man crews ironically nicknamed them
"Ronsons" after the popular cigarette lighter. So "knocked out" was a
deceptive term that indicated a kind of bloodless removal from inventory, when in fact the men in those tanks endured horrible wounding
and an agonizing death. That's a more useful truth to me: they knew
that was the risk, and they did it anyway.

Humanize the Abstract

When describing distance or dimension, amount or weight, put the
quantity in human terms. For instance, for the average adult, an object two feet away is just within arm's reach—and within reach of a
fist. Thus you can communicate the fact of distance with a dramatic
gesture in the scene. Likewise you can tell us an old leatherback tur-
tle crawling ashore on the beach to make a nest is eight feet long and
weighs 2,000 pounds, or you can say, "Imagine a barnacle-encrusted

creature as big as a Smart car emerging from the surf and trenching its way through the sand to dig a nest deep as a grave."

Decode Statistics

Press the numbers until they yield a human consequence. Whenever you write "24% of this" or "87% of that," your reader's eyes tend to glaze over. Tell us instead that if you were the mother of four kids, the odds are that one them would be stricken with influenza. Or that in a high school class of thirty, it's likely that six of the kids are gay—or whatever true figure your research yields. Put faces on the numbers, human consequences on the arithmetic.

Employ Outside Supplementary Knowledge

Use what you know to be generally true to give the scene texture and authenticity. If you know, for instance, that a certain town in 1885 was lit by gas lamps (which you may have discovered from Sanborn-Perris insurance maps, many available online now, color-coded to indicate brick or wood buildings, gas and electric lines, water mains, and so on), and your character is walking an unpaved street late on an October evening, and you know (from National Weather Service records, say) it was a drizzly night, you can describe the dim, shadowy quality of the light around her—especially if you have walked that street yourself or one nearby. If you know the street had no wooden sidewalk, then you can reasonably infer that the road was muddy and full of puddles. If she claims to witness something that happens a block away in such uncertain light, as the reader we can be aware that her testimony is suspect. In any case, you can vividly describe her walking along the shadowy street, even if her own account makes no mention of gas lamps or rain.

Write Specifically and Concretely

To convey a sense of the politics or mood of a time and place, avoid generic statements, especially if they float around in large blocks of equally abstract statements: "The townspeople were rabidly anti-union." Instead show us—with details from your research—a political rally in which you can describe action, quote a snippet of a "rabid" speech; take us to the polls, where thugs armed with brickbats keep out the union organizers, or whatever moment captures the essence of the political divide. Your narrator can gently guide us through the issues in well-placed sentences between moments of action or description.

Let the Resonant Part Stand for the Whole

There's usually no need to give us the entire history of an event, or the complete biography of a character. Pick the salient detail, the revelatory moment, the colorful quote that carries all the rest along with it. I can tell you that the outdoors author Colin Fletcher (*The Complete Walker*) was obsessed with how much the things in his backpack weighed, and I can provide you an inventory of all the many things he carried on his overland treks. Or I can tell you that he filed off the end of his toothbrush because he thought it weighed too much.

Set the Stage of Action

If place is important to your story—and it usually is, whether it's a tenement slum in Baltimore in 1902, a mountain town in Colorado in the 1960s, present-day Rwanda, or the suburb where you grew up—don't feel that you need to give us a tour first, before telling the story. Think of it as a stage of action, and, just like a theatrical stage or a movie set, its parts and functions will reveal themselves as the characters move around inside it. We'll climb narrow stairs with them, or slog through mud, or notice the snowcapped peaks rising in the distance. We'll smell the stench of open sewers, or the musty smell of cabbage boiling, or the sharp bite of wintry air. We'll touch rough handrails, lean against hot tin siding, avoid shady characters lurking in alleyways. We'll hear the music of street vendors, the clangor of traffic, the eerie soughing of wind through the aspens. Place will enter the story or, more exactly, we as readers will enter the place of the story alongside the characters. We will map it with our senses just as they do.

Remember That Dialogue Is Not Conversation

It is the highlights of conversation: the line that succinctly distills a big idea, the colorful description that betrays attitude, the humorous take that deflates a subject character. For the nonfiction writer, hours of interviewing might yield only a few resonant lines to include in the piece—but those lines make all the difference. They were spoken after lots of conversation, after trust was earned, as the speaker's imagination slipped into high gear. Listen for those lines. They typically do not include social introductions ("Hello—I'm John Smith") or long explanations of facts or events, since the narrator can handle both much more economically. Instead they add energy or an emotional charge to the moment. Even in nonfiction, lines of dialogue from an interview or immersion experience need not be presented in the order in which they were heard; it is up to the writer to cast them in a sequence that lends meaning to the encounter without distorting the truth (in letter or spirit) of what was spoken. You're going to select a very few lines anyway, so you have to arrange them in a way that accurately captures what the subject was trying to say and also provides a dramatic movement to the piece. For the fiction writer and poet, the same kind of distillation applies, but you can also feel free to recast the line, to combine parts, to steal the best phrases and idioms and use them shamelessly to create interest.

Select Your Facts

There is all that you need to know to write the book—and a much smaller percentage of that material that the reader needs to know. Most of your research won't be expressed directly on the page. This is as it should be. A doctor spends years in medical school and residencies so she can deliver a precise and accurate diagnosis. You don't need to attend classes in gross anatomy—you just need to listen to her distill her comprehensive study into particular knowledge that is useful to you at that moment. That's what you are doing for your reader.

Be Vividly True

And always, we're trying to do what the best poets routinely do instinctively with personal material: find and express that one piece of an event or life, as concretely and with exactly the right sensory detail, that will bring the full truth of it into clear relief.

Of course, not all writers are trying to create full-fledged scenes, at least not all the time. In all genres, there are moments when the writer uses a select detail to suggest an idea or provoke a thought related to her themes. In an essay, the writer has wide latitude to explore ideas as they are connected to events and people, and often the point is not to reach a firm conclusion but to awaken interest in the ideas and the way the ideas cross-reference and contradict each other—often using very concrete episodes and images to embody the force of the idea. As essayist Michelle Orange put it in a lecture to MFA students at Goucher College, "The essay is a mixture of the conversational and the coherent," meaning that the personal voice of the savvy narrator can lead the reader through a skein of logic and impression that connects many disparate things into a whole, related piece.

So in "What He Said There," one of the pieces that make up *The Partly Cloudy Patriot*, Sarah Vowell can incorporate her research into the writings of Abraham Lincoln into a moment of personal epiphany, inside an essay that meditates, in a manner both lighthearted and serious, about the meaning of the Gettysburg Address in contemporary America: "Abraham Lincoln is one of my favorite writers. 'The mystic chords of memory.' 'Better angels of our nature.' 'The father of waters flows vexed to the sea.' All those brilliant phrases I'd admired for so long, and yet I never truly thought of him as a writer until I visited the David Wells house in Gettysburg's town square." The house, that is, where Lincoln composed, or at least polished, his famous little speech.

She concludes in typical conversational fashion, drawing on her "artsy craftsy" experience in school, where she and her fellow students encountered Lincoln as part cartoon and part saint: "How many of us drew his beard in crayon? We built models of his boyhood cabin with Elmer's glue and toothpicks. We memorized the Gettysburg Address, reciting its ten sentences in stovepipe hats stapled out of black construction paper. The teachers taught us to like Washington and to respect Jefferson. But Lincoln—him they taught us to love." Think of how many facts we have just read: quotes, a historical location, and a variety of facts from her personal history that mimic "facts" from popular lore and media imagery. Yet her tone is conversational—she is talking across the table to us, fellow explorers in this world of historical whimsy, never down to us, combining the various elements of her essay, each impression leading to the next and shaping an overall idea: why Lincoln holds her in such imaginative thrall.

The past, the unwitnessed, the forgotten, the invisible—all are made of the things people say and do in particular places and the tools and props at hand. They happen in weather and time, in political or personal context. They are moments in a sequence of other moments, and sometimes it matters a lot what happens just before and just after. You have to find as many of the pieces as you can in all the disparate boxes where they have been discarded and reassemble them in some artful fashion that tends toward meaningfulness. Construction paper hats, Elmer's glue and toothpicks, crayons and the real interior of a farmhouse—mystic chords of memory, indeed.

Prompt #22: "Interrogating the Dead." Ever visit an old cemetery and been intrigued by the bare facts of a person's life and death as recorded on a cryptic gravestone? No? Then this is the perfect opportunity. I suggest a cemetery that has plenty of old graves. Find the name of a dead person who interests you for some reason and about whom you know virtually nothing. Track down all the information you can on the deceased and present a brief profile, creating a living character of dramatic interest to your reader. Do this by using the facts to re-create the person's story.

Prompt #23: "The Art of Re-creation." Choose a brief scene that interests you but that you did not witness. It may be contemporary or historical, private or public, related to your own life or to those of strangers. Assemble as many facts of the event as you can from any source you can find. Then write one page of scene in which key people say and do something meaningful.

AFTERWORD

To write is to talk to strangers. You want them to trust you.
—Tracy Kidder and Richard Todd, *Good Prose: The Art of Nonfiction*

I borrowed the structure of the prologue to this book from an inspiring book by the late Larry Brown, who was a fine writer and story-
teller. His memoir *On Fire* tells the story of how he became a writer,
and it starts with the romance he had with an earlier job, that of firefighter in Oxford, Mississippi. His opening chapter reminded me of
two things. First, that simple forms often work the best. One test of
that is that such a form can be emulated by others to serve an entirely
different content. Brown's memoir is a valentine about being a firefighter. "I love what I do with my hands and with the hose," he begins,
and the rest of that first chapter is a catalog of all the things he loves
about the job—the tools, the feeling, the pride, the camaraderie. I
wrote of being "on fire" in a different way, and the love of craft that
inspires.

The second thing he reminded me of is that we writers too rarely
celebrate the things we love. True, our mission is often to explore the
dark places of the earth (thanks, Joseph Conrad), to delve into poverty, abuse, crime, war, all the ways in which we do each other harm
emotionally and physically, all the suffering of innocents, all the in-
justice of the world, all the heartbreak of its tragedies. But it is equally
urgent to recognize beauty, loyalty, friendship, love, endurance, the
value of honest work, family, community, self-sacrifice, altruism,
generosity—all the things that transcend the drudgery of workaday

lives with the glint of something finer. So we begin this journey of research with a reminder: it is an adventure. It is meant to be rewarding, fulfilling, maybe even—if we do it right—a lot of fun.

We have an honorable excuse to go out into the world to the places we find most interesting, then talk to the most fascinating people we can find about the things we most urgently want to know. We actually get to do this. I love it—and reminding myself that I love it always gets me through the rough patches and makes me bless my luck. This is my job. As I writer, I get to go out from the tribe and bring back the news, the facts, the truth. Whether you're a veteran researcher or a writer who is ready to strike out into new territory, as you set out on your own adventure of discovery, remember: finding out the truth, engaging the world on its own terms, is a daring enterprise fraught with emotional ambush and, sometimes, physical risk. You take that small risk because it can lead to exhilarating breakthroughs in your writing.

As discussed in chapter 9, in addition to all the archivists and other professionals you recruit to your cause, a good researcher has a support network in place—not just somebody to call if you wind up stranded in a remote place, but also somebody to talk to about those matters that trouble you, prey on your emotions. This is obviously true for war correspondents and police reporters, who deal with trauma regularly. But it can also be true for the memoirist confronting long-hidden truths, the interviewer with whom a subject has just shared a heartbreaking story, the novelist immersed in the upheaval of history. Craft an exit strategy, and secure a lifeline. The researcher is like a mountain climber, and you need some reliable people back at base camp, a quick radio call away.

The good news is that the act of research, the process and practice of putting yourself out there, can work wonders on your writing, inspiring fresh ideas and leading you in productive directions you never would have found trapped in your own head.

Teaching has much in common with writing, including this lucky facet: teaching your passion helps to nurture and fulfill it. So to teach writing is to engage a passion for language and stories, for the architecture of sentences. Some years ago I began designing and teaching a research course for writers that allowed me—required me—to engage my passion for research. And the creative dynamic of pursuing research is precisely why the research class is so satisfying to teach: the writers create their own epiphanies, and through sharing them with the rest of us, expand our own experience. I always come away feeling as if I've gotten the best of the deal—they do so much hard work, and I always learn something new. In other words, the credit belongs to them, not me.

Teaching research has given me the privilege of working with many fine writers at an early stage of their careers, and the act of creative research challenges them to enlarge their vision and infuses their work with a deep seriousness that continues to pay off over the long haul.

Since they have taken me up on my dare to venture out into the world to find their stories and poems, it's only fair to give them a chance to report on how that turned out.

One of them, Catherine Shubert, is exploring the nature of silence in a collection of poems in which she seeks to understand silence both as an enforced condition of women and as a chosen opportunity. What does it mean to have a voice, and is silence just the absence of sound or something more profound and complex? She writes, "The 'walking the ground' assignment in particular taught me to think about silence as a *place* I can seek out—by way of traveling to extreme silence-scapes, such as the beach, float tanks, woodland paths, solitude, sanctuaries, and more. This assignment broadened the scope of my project and allowed for place to more centrally figure in my process, ultimately leading me to posit silence itself as an ecotone." An ecotone is that middle ground between two habitats, the place where water meets shoreline, where savannah turns into forest, a place of both danger and opportunity. Shubert writes, "Those two main branches are an enforced, oppressing silence that censors and endangers its subjects; and a positive, inward, centering silence that allows for creativity and opportunity. Thus silence is an ecotone, not the opposite of sound, but existing at its edge, occasionally allowing us access to the unknown—or at least, to the stance and sites we need to negotiate the unknown."

Another poet, Emily Wilson, has been tracking down her Czech ancestors, whose activities and origins have remained somewhat elusive, and she has come to terms with the fact that there are some things she will just never be able to find out. She writes:

My poetry-manuscript-in-progress now has a trajectory, an arc of revealed information that creates a journey. The starting point of that journey was a state of unknowing, and I haven't yet reached the ending point—because there isn't one. The progression of my manuscript will flow from unknowing to unknowing a little less. And this is okay. The research process taught me *unknowing* is not an acceptable excuse for being inactive but that *active unknowing* is also okay. That is a wonderful lesson; it is a wonderful gift.

"Active unknowing"—what a resounding phrase. The writer is a seeker and finder only of a partial truth, but more truth than she previously had.

Heather Hammerbeck, working on a memoir of ranching in South Dakota, writes, "I now have a greater confidence that when I'm ready, I have the tools to grow a project, letting it mature organically, chasing the threads, until I have a story I want to write. This is a pretty thrilling idea, and brand-new for me. Before now, I've been writing from the other direction; waiting for something to happen that I thought I could write about. Now I can cultivate the project. It seems so simple, but is really very empowering." She goes on:

Another thing this process has done for me is to drill in how incalculably important the small details are. For example, I was recently looking through some video of me and my sister joyriding in the six-wheeler at the ranch with her kids, and amid all the bouncing and laughing, I caught a glimpse of erosion above a creek. Now, a year later, I can go right back to that spot and compare and contrast changes. Will the erosion be worse or will our grazing practices over the last year have helped to heal that spot?

Diane Sorensen came away from her extensive research in New York and Nebraska transformed by the experience. She writes:

I began with an amorphous idea, the "concept" of some vague historical novel. I end with a box full, a computer full, and a head full of not only facts and information but also ideas—the puzzle pieces—for my novel. I have a growing cast of characters; I have an understanding of setting; I have lists of scene ideas and historical events that will feed the plot. Maybe most important, this research journey has imbued me with a commitment to the project. No longer a vague "someday" idea, my novel is now a living, breathing work-in-progress.

Sorensen continues, "I've made some discoveries about myself and about the research process." She cites three in particular: "Getting out in the field suits me. . . . For me, the field trip is incredibly stimulating and a way I can collect not just information but experiences to directly feed the fiction. People who were once mere names and dates have sprung to life. Family dynamics have emerged that will make great plot complications. I am building an understanding of 'place,' so I can create setting. The weather is almost a character in Nebraska. Fieldwork feels like the immersion method for learning a new language." Her second insight: "The scientific model works great for fiction." She describes it thusly: "Define the question (What do you want to know and why?). Data collection (Gather information). Analysis (Cull through your data and figure out what it means)." In sum, Sorensen admits, "I'm a total convert. Now when writers in workshop say: 'I don't like to research,' I hear: 'I don't like new ideas. I only want to listen to what's already inside my head.'"

Michelle Boyajian, hard at work on a new novel, has this advice for writers new to research: "Over-research. Seriously over-research." She explains:

Man, the second you start to go out, you get fired up. You have six hours of research, and twenty minutes of it was *unbelievable*. And that alone teaches you two things. One, sometimes I have to do six hours of research to have twenty minutes of happiness, but also, oh, I have to find a way to find the time to do this. And also to be prepared that people aren't waiting for me on *my* timeline to talk to me, and there are going to be some flubs when they can't meet, and so if I have deadlines. . . . And it taught me, Holy Mother of Pearl, I've got a lot of research to do! Because research kept leading to research and it was a big uncomfortable tangle at first. But if you want to write a book, and you want to write the fiction part, you have to head right into the tangle. But you know what? It's a blast in a lot of ways.

Yes—head right into the tangle.

Here I am reminded of an obsolete usage for the term "research," cited by musicians into the late nineteenth century. To them, the "research" was the prelude or introductory passage in which the composer sought out the themes and harmonies that would find later expression in the formal work. In one form, it was an extemporaneous exploration, a joyful moment of playing and listening as the music came back from the instrument, guiding the player toward an understanding of the music he was creating, showing her the elements of her art, suggesting how they might combine into something meaningful and beautiful.

Exactly.

ACKNOWLEDGMENTS

It is always a privilege and a joy to write about a thing you love, as I love the act of research. One of the special joys of writing this book has been the excuse to reach out to fellow writers and students past and present to mine their wisdom. The following were especially generous in sharing their insights on the research process and how it informs their writing: Lavonne J. Adams, Stephen Anim, Erin Armendariz, Paul Austin, Andrea Barillo, Jacob Bateman, Larry Blakely, Sheri Booker, Michelle Boyajian, Valerie Boyd, Mary Campbell, Joseph Connolley, Cathy Day, Bronwen Dickey, Carolyn Forché, Tom French, Sabrina Garity, Diana Hume George, David Gessner, Liz Granger, McKenzie Gritton, Carrie Hagen, Heather Hammerbeck, Stephanie Harcrow, Walt Harrington, Silvia Hawkins, Jason Hess, Kirsten Holmstedt, Emily Isaacs, Thomas Jones, Joe Mackall, Mathias Marchington, Charlotte Matthews, Honor Moore, Jason Mott, Brenda Nicholas, Michelle Orange, Katie O'Reilly, Seth Photopoulous, Lydia Plantamura, Benjamin Rachlin, Autumn Rankin, Caylee Reid, Bob Reiss, Beth Roddy, Leslie Rubinkowski, Joanna Sherron, Catherine Shubert, Diane Sorensen, Nomi Stone, Morgan Thompson, Joanna Tine, Richard Todd, Molly Walling, Derek West, Emily Wilson, and Laura Wright.

In addition, I am grateful for the help and support of my colleagues in the Department of Creative Writing at the University of North Carolina Wilmington and my colleagues and mentees in the

Goucher College Low-Residency MFA Program in Nonfiction. And Mary Laur, senior editor at the University of Chicago Press, both understood the value of this subject right from the start and helped to shape it in smart and useful ways. Thanks also to my manuscript editor, Erin DeWitt, for her smart and conscientious guidance; to Lauren Smith for her clean interior design and vivid, elegant cover; to Susan Hernandez, who crafted the index; and to Skye Agnew in production and Lauren Salas in marketing for their hard work.

Finally, my heartfelt thanks to my wife, Jill Gerard, a gifted writer and editor, as well as resourceful researcher, who inspires my best work and tirelessly helps sort out the practical details to make it come true.

The original version of the prologue, "On Fire for Research," first appeared in *River Teeth: A Journal of Nonfiction Narrative* in Spring 2013. "Anatomy Lesson" was published in *Something Yet Unseen* (Finishing Line Press, 2009) and is used by permission of the author.

SELECTED SOURCES FOR QUOTATIONS AND
CONCEPTS ADDRESSED IN THIS BOOK

Books

Adams, Lavonne J. *Through the Glorieta Pass*. Long Beach: Pearl Editions, 2009.

Austin, Paul. *Beautiful Eyes: A Father Transformed*. New York: W. W. Norton, 2014.

———. *Something for the Pain: Compassion and Burnout in the ER*. New York: W. W. Norton, 2008.

Booker, Sheri. *Nine Years Under: Coming of Age in an Inner-City Funeral Home*. New York: Penguin, 2013.

Boyajian, Michelle. *Lies of the Heart*. New York: Penguin, 2010.

Boyd, Valerie. *Wrapped in Rainbows: The Life of Zora Neale Hurston*. New York: Lisa Drew/Scribner, 2003.

Brown, Larry. *On Fire: A Personal Account of Life and Death and Choices*. Chapel Hill, NC: Algonquin, 1993.

Conover, Ted. *Rolling Nowhere: Riding the Rails with America's Hoboes*. New York: Viking Penguin, 1984.

Cox, Mark. *Smoulder*. Boston: David R. Godine, 1989.

Dove, Rita. *Thomas and Beulah*. Pittsburgh: Carnegie Mellon, 1986.

Earley, Pete. *Crazy: A Father's Search Through America's Mental Health Madness*. New York: G. P. Putnam's Sons, 2006.

French, Thomas. *Unanswered Cries: A True Story of Friends, Neighbors, and Cold-Blooded Murder*. New York: St. Martin's, 1991.

———. *Zoo Story: Life in the Garden of Captives*. New York: Hyperion, 2010.

Gerard, Jill. *Something Yet Unseen*. Georgetown, KY: Finishing Line Press, 2009.

Gerard, Philip. *The Dark of the Island*. Winston Salem, NC: John F. Blair, 2016.

———. *Secret Soldiers: How a Troupe of American Artists, Designers, and Sonic Wizards Won World War II's Battles of Deceptions Against the Germans*. New York: Dutton, 2002.

Harrington, Walt. *Acts of Creation: America's Finest Hand Craftsmen at Work*. La Jolla, CA: Sager Group, 2014.

Hemley, Robin. *Do-Over!* New York: Little Brown, 2009.

Holmstedt, Kirsten. *Band of Sisters: American Women at War in Iraq*. Mechanicsburg, PA: Stackpole, 2007.

Irving, Washington. *The Life and Voyages of Christopher Columbus*. New York: G. & G. & H. Carvill, 1829.

Kidder, Tracy, and Richard Todd. *Good Prose: The Art of Nonfiction*. New York: Random House, 2013.

Laine, Kristen. *American Band: Music, Dreams, and Coming of Age in the Heartland*. New York: Gotham/Penguin, 2007.

Madariaga, Salvador de. *Christopher Columbus*. London: Hollis and Carter, 1949.

Matthews, Charlotte Hilary. *Green Stars*. Oak Ridge, TN: Iris Press, 2005.

Mott, Jason. *The Returned*. New York: Harlequin, 2013.

Orlean, Susan. *Rin Tin Tin: The Life and the Legend*. New York: Simon and Schuster, 2011.

Rachlin, Benjamin. *Ghost of the Innocent Man*. New York: Little Brown, forthcoming.

Reiss, Bob. *The Road to Extrema*. New York: First Glance Books, 1992.

———. *Salt Maker*. New York: Viking, 1988.

Resnick, Susan Kushner. *Sleepless Days: One Woman's Journey Through Postpartum Depression*. New York: St. Martin's, 2000.

Schacter, Daniel L. *Searching for Memory: The Brain, the Mind, and the Past*. New York: Basic Books, 1993.

Stone, Nomi. *Stranger's Notebook*. Evanston, IL: Triquarterly, 2008.

Sullivan, John Jeremiah. *Pulphead: Essays*. New York: Farrar, Straus and Giroux, 2011.

Urrea, Luis Alberto. *The Devil's Highway*. New York: Little Brown, 2004.

Vowell, Sarah. *The Partly Cloudy Patriot*. New York: Simon and Schuster, 2002.

Walling. Molly. *Death in the Delta: Uncovering a Mississippi Family Secret*. Jackson: University Press of Mississippi, 2012.

Welty, Eudora. *One Writer's Beginnings*. Cambridge, MA: Harvard University Press, 1983.

Wilford, John Noble. *The Mysterious History of Columbus: An Exploration of the Man the Myth, the Legacy*. New York: Alfred A. Knopf, 1991.

Essays, Stories, Poems

Bourne, Daniel. "Changing the Whole Neighborhood: A Conversation with Rita Dove." *The Artful Dodge*, October 2010. http://artfuldodge.sites.wooster.edu/content/rita-dove.

Conover, Ted. "Rolling Nowhere, Part Two." *Outside Magazine*, June 10, 2014.

Davis, Jim, et al. "Interview with Nomi Stone." *Jet Fuel Review*, no. 5 (Spring 2013).

Gerard, Jill. "Anatomy Lesson." *Something Yet Unseen*. Lexington, KY: Finishing Line Press, 2009.

Mershon, Erin. "New Web Suffixes to Enter Market," *Politico*, December 30, 2013. http://www.politico.com/story/2013/12/new-web-suffixes-set-to-enter-market -101601.html.

Miller, Brenda. "A Braided Heart: Shaping the Lyric Essay." In *Writing Creative Nonfiction*, ed. Carolyn Forché and Philip Gerard. Cincinnati: Story Press, 2001.

Moore, Honor. "Twelve Years and Counting: Writing Biography." In *Writing Creative Nonfiction*, ed. Carolyn Forché and Philip Gerard. Cincinnati: Story Press, 2001.

Stone, Nomi. "Poet of the Month: Nomi Stone." *PoetryNet*. April 2015. http://poetrynet .org/month/intro.html.

Talese, Gay. "Frank Sinatra Has a Cold." *Esquire*, April 1966.

Wolfe, Tom. "The Last American Hero Is Junior Johnson. Yes!" *Esquire*, March 1965.

Wright, Richard. "I Have Seen Black Hands." In *Richard Wright Reader*, ed. Ellen Wright and Michel Fabre. New York: Harper & Row, 1978.

Archive

John F. Schrank Letters, SC/MS/148, Special Collections, William Madison Randall Library, University of North Carolina Wilmington.

INDEX

Acts of Creation (Harrington), 103, 117–19, 177–78

actuality of an event, 5–8, 59

Adams, Lavonne J., 2–3, 131, 142–43, 175–76, 182

American Band (Laine), 85

"Anatomy Lesson" (Gerard), 172–74

Architect of Desire, The (Lessard), 179

archives: audio, 61; availability and variety of, 57–59; electronic (*see* electronic archives); experiential (*see* handling the object; walking the ground); living (*see* living archives); of memory and imagination (*see* archives of memory and imagination); origin of the word, 62; paper (*see* paper archives); prompts for, 96–97; visual, 60–61

archives of memory and imagination: accessing your imagination, 85–86, 91–92; basis of memoir, 83, 87; connections made through imagination, 91–92; definition of memory, 87; emotions' impact on memory, 87–88, 89; expertise from personal experience, 92–94; fickleness of, 87–89; information gained from the way an event is misremembered, 89; inspiration from dreams, 90–91; mining the archive of memory, 91–92; plausibility and imagination, 89–90; power of reawakening your memories, 84–85; prompts for, 96–97; triggering memory, 83–84, 92; types of, 61–62

Arctic Dreams (Lopez), 4

artifacts, 3, 58, 80, 143, 154. *See also* handling the object

artists and research, 3, 131

Attucks, Crispus, 135–36

audio archives, 61

Austin, Paul, 92, 95

Band of Sisters: American Women at War in Iraq (Holmstedt), 30, 122, 139–40, 165

Beautiful Eyes (Austin), 92

Beloved (Morrison), 4

Big Thing, The (blog), 67

binoculars, 48

Bixby, Horace, 4

Black American Lives at the Turn of the Twenty-First Century (Kenan), 4

Blass, Bill, 127, 151–52

Blonde (Oates), 4

Booker, Sheri, 31

Borel, Brooke, 161

Bosque Redondo, New Mexico, 142–43

Bourne, Daniel, 182

Boyajian, Michelle, 35, 36, 116, 120–21, 176–77, 207–8

Brown, Larry, 203

cameras, 40–42

Cape Fear River, 41, 43, 44, 55, 78, 130, 140, 158

Chicago Guide to Fact-Checking (Borel), 161

China Syndrome, The, 89

Circle of Hanh, The (Weigl), 93

Circus in Winter, The (Day), 66

Civil War, 3, 4, 7, 8, 69, 70, 80, 156–58, 159

Cold Mountain (Frazier), 4

Comeback Season (Day), 66

Complete Walker, The (Fletcher), 198

Conover, Ted, 4, 51–52

Corsican Brothers, The (film), 184

Country Between Us, The (Forché), 2, 84

Cox, Mark, 114

Craddick, Ged, 137

Crane, Stephen, 3

creative research: advantages of writing from research, 16–17; anachronistic language and, 155–56; artists and writers who engaged in research, 1–5; author's excitement about, vii–xiii; creative value in data, 17–18; described, 11; difficulty of discerning the truth, 6–7; diversity of experience of writers, 13; drawing from the contemporary world, 156; emotional risks inherent in, 163–68; ethical dimension of research, 18; fallibility of memory, 9–10; finding an outward connection, 19–20; first principles for starting a story, 12–13; goal of nonfiction writers, 5; imagination and, 13, 20; inevitability of mistakes, 157–60, 162–63; meaning of "true" in a story, 8, 10; methods for pursuing a story, 12; narrative intelligence and, 15–16, 181–83; personal experiences and (*see* handling the object; walking the ground); planning the research (*see* research plan); primary sources and, 5, 7, 10; prompts for finding a writing topic, 20–21; qualities of pursuable facts, 21; relationship of sources to Actuality, 7–8; role of research, 18; secondary sources and, 5–6, 7; serendipity and, 14, 69–70; syntax of a story and, 8–11; temptations of research, 18; time's influence on facts, 158; value of diligence and commitment in, 14–15; verifying facts, 156–58, 160–63, 167–68; Zone of Noise and, 6, 59, 73, 159

Creef, George Washington, 143–44

Dark of the Island, The (Gerard), 192–94

Day, Cathy, 66–67

Death in the Delta (Walling), 85, 166–68

Devil in the White City (Larson), 180–81

Devil's Highway, The (Urrea), 147

Dickey, Bronwen, 10

Dickinson, Emily, 4

Didion, Joan, 4

Dogpile.com, 103

Dove, Rita, 1, 182–83

Down the Wild Cape Fear (Gerard), 158

Drum-Taps (Whitman), 4

Duffy, Tim and Denise, 101–2

Duncan, Lee, 70–71

electronic archives: bias due to political agendas and, 76–77; challenges from the volume of information, 80–81; evaluating the source, 75–76; prompts for, 82; tests to apply to sites, 73–74; types of, 60; value of electronic communications, 81–82; vetting a site for reliability, 78–80; Wikipedia and, 74

essayists, 17, 200

Evernote, 40, 46, 53

experiential archives: dynamic of geography, 133–34; immersion in the research (*see* handling the object; walking the ground); reenactments, 104, 135; rewards from pursuing experiences, 130–31, 138–42; types of, 62

fact-checking research, 160–63

Fairbanks, Douglas, Jr., 184, 185

fiction writers, 3–4, 5

Fletcher, Colin, 198

Forché, Carolyn, 2, 84, 109

Franklin, Benjamin, 163

Frazier, Charles, 4

Freedom of Information Act (FOIA) Reference Guide, 63

French, Thomas, 26, 47, 95, 104, 110–12, 114–15, 128, 136–37

Geertz, Clifford, 194

Gerard, Jill, 46, 172–74, 184

Gerard, Philip: Cape Fear River research, 43, 55–56; childhood example of the unreliability of memory, 88–89; course of research in Poland, 14; excitement about research, vii–xiii; exploring personal relationships for research, 31; insight gained from riding in a handmade boat, 143–44; interview with a blues musician, 100–102; on making mistakes, 159–60; power of smell and taste, 145–46; re-creating the event for a war story, 184–87; Revolutionary War research, 133–36; ride-alongs with police, 137–38; securing an interview with Bill Blass, 151–52; ship piloting experience, 140–41; using imagination and research to write about historical figures, 85–86; using research to turn fact into fiction, 192–94

Ghost of the Innocent Man (Rachlin), 190–91

Girls Come Marching Home, The (Holmstedt), 165, 166

Going After Cacciato (O'Brien), 93

Good Prose: The Art of Nonfiction (Kidder and Todd), 15, 179

Google, 103

Google Books, 67

Gore, Al, 160–61

Gould, Alice Bache, 170–71

Granger, Liz, 45

Grimes, Willie, 187

Guterson, David, 4

Hagen, Carrie, 30–31, 178–81

Hammerbeck, Heather, 206

handling the object: connecting to events by handling objects, 134–36, 143–44; connecting to events by visiting the location, 136–37; insight gained from tactile experiences, 144–45, 146–47; value of hands-on research, 141–44

Harrington, Walt, 103, 117–19, 121–22, 177–78, 187

Hemley, Robin, 32

Holmstedt, Kirsten, 29–30, 122, 124–25, 138–40, 164–66

Hughes, Langston, 4

ICANN (Internet Corporation for Assigned Names and Numbers), 75

iCloud, 54

imagination. *See* archives of memory and imagination

Internet. *See* electronic archives

Internet Corporation for Assigned Names and Numbers (ICANN), 75

interviews: allowing for an open agenda, 100, 123–24; creating a sense of trust, 108–9, 111, 124–25; dealing with technical problems, 121; editing decisions and, 101–2; element of curiosity and, 128; emotional and ethical concerns, 122–24; empathy and, 110–11; exploring the drama of the ordinary, 111–15; formats for, 99; incorporating material into your work, 107–9; listening and, 111, 113, 166; locating sources for, 103–5; location selection, 116–19; moving on to an alternative source, 153–54; points of human contact and, 113–15; preparing for, 116, 119–21; prompts for, 128–29; questions to ask, 102–3, 127; reasons people are sometimes hard to interview, 150–51; reasons to interview people, 115–16; recording protocol, 105–6; research plan and, 31–32; respecting the interviewee's identity, 109–10; silence and, 111, 123–24; strategies for confronting a lie, 125–26; strategies for getting passed the superficial, 127; strategies for when a source is difficult to schedule, 150–52; technological aids, 106–7; tools for, 38; transcribing, 54, 107; treating the interview as a privilege, 121–22; using to complement a narrative, 186–87; value in, 98–99; written release forms, 106

iPads, 40

Ironing Board Sam, 100–101

Irving, John, 93

John Locke Foundation, 76–77

Johnson, Robert Glenn "Junior," 119

Jones, Tanya, 69

Junger, Sebastian, 155

Kelly, Ellsworth, 108–9

Kenan, Randall, 4

Keneally, Thomas, 4

Kidder, Tracy, 4, 15, 179, 194

Laine, Kristen, 85

Lake, I. Beverly, Jr., 187–88, 191

Land of the Free (MacLeish), 4

Larson, Erik, 180–81

Leaves of Grass (Whitman), 4

Lessard, Suzannah, 179

Library of Congress, 64

Lies of the Heart (Boyajian), 35, 116

Life on the Mississippi (Twain), 4

Lincoln, Abraham, 200–201

living archives: expert consultants, 35, 99, 103, 116, 153, 180; expertise derived from first-person experiences, 92–94; language of expertise and, 95–96; memory and imagination (*see* archives of memory and imagination); mining expertise through language, 95–96; observations (*see* walking the ground); personal interviews (*see* interviews); types of, 60

Lonesome Dove (McMurtry), 4

Lopez, Barry, 4

Louis Round Wilson Library Special Collections, 64

MacLeish, Archibald, 4

magnifying glasses, 48–49

maps: capturing spaces with, 42–45; creating and using, 43–45; creating your own spatial representations, 44–45; insights offered by, 44; time's influence on facts, 158

Matthews, William, 5

McMurtry, Larry, 4

memory and imagination. *See* archives of memory and imagination

Miami (Didion), 4

Morrison, Toni, 4

Mott, Jason, 89, 91

Mumma, Chris, 187–92

museums, 3, 28, 49, 63, 75, 76, 143, 153, 154

Music Maker Relief Foundation, 100–101

narrative intelligence, 15–16, 181–83

National Archives and Records Administration (NARA), 66

National Archives website, 63

National Oceanic and Atmospheric Administration, 44

Native Son (Wright), 93

Navajo American Tribes, 142–43

New York Times, 67

Nine Years Under: Coming of Age in an Inner-City Funeral Home (Booker), 31

nonfiction writers, 3, 4, 5, 8, 15, 99, 126, 155, 189, 199

Oates, Joyce Carol, 4

O'Brien, Tim, 93

O'Keeffe, Georgia, 3, 131

One Writer's Beginnings (Welty), 71–72, 86

On Fire (Brown), 203

"Open Boat, The" (Crane), 3

Optimist's Daughter, The (Welty), 87

Orange, Michelle, 200

O'Reilly, Katie, 119–20, 161–62

organizing the research: choosing a system, 54–55; digital and actual filing cabinets, 54; fallibility of memory and, 53; imperative of, 52; labels and notes, 53; storage tips, 55; transcribing interviews, 54, 107

Orlean, Susan, 70–71

paper archives: accessing special collections, 63–66; arranging to visit, 63–64; attitude when querying about, 69–70; being alert for the unobvious, 66–70; copying documents, 65–66; labels and hidden data, 67–68; locating private archives, 68; making the most of your time inside, 65; National Archives website, 63; online catalog review, 64–65; origin of the word "archive," 62; prompts for, 72; research plan and, 30–31; responding to a request for credentials, 66; strategies for locating material, 65; types of, 59–60, 63; vividness of lives shown on paper, 70–72; what to expect, 65–66

Partly Cloudy Patriot, The (Vowell), 8, 160, 200–201

Perfect Storm, The (Junger), 155

personal experience. *See* living archives

Pit Bull: The Battle over an American Icon (Dickey), 10

poets: advantages of writing from research, 17; goal for their writings, 5; narrative voice and, 182; role of research in poetry, 175–

76; value in interviews, 99; writers who engaged in research, 1–3, 4–5
primary sources, 5, 7, 10
priority in the syntax of a story, 9
Pulphead (Sullivan), 131

Rachlin, Benjamin, 187–92
re-creating the event: assembling the facts of the scene, 183–84, 188–90; interjecting realistic detail, 184–85, 187, 191–92; setting the stage, 185–86; using interviews to complement the narrative, 186–87; using research to turn fact into fiction, 192–94
Red Badge of Courage, The (Crane), 3
Reiss, Bob, 14, 33, 35, 51, 89
relationship in the syntax of a story, 9
research plan: archives use (*see* archives); basic questions to ask, 26; benefits of having, 22–23; budgeting for costs, 27, 28, 32, 33; drafting a timeline, 27; establishing a schedule, 25, 31, 33; exploration of possible subjects, 23–24; finding emotional support for yourself, 168, 169; finding something to write about, 20–21, 37; finding yourself in the subject, 25–26, 163–68; flexibility and, 29, 32, 37; gaining access and, 35–37, 63–66; going where the facts lead you, 29–32; imagining the scene with credibility, 178–81; knowing when to stop researching and start writing (*see* writing from your research); lessons for, 180–81; locating specific tasks, 27; locating the subject, 24–25; moving on to an alternative source, 153–54; prompts for, 168; repetition's influence on the truth, 162; for speculative fiction, 34–36; steps in formulating and sample follow-through, 26–29; strategies to use when a source is difficult to schedule, 150–52; tools for research (*see* tools of researchers); what to do if there is not record of a thing or event, 154–55
Resnick, Susan Kushner, 92–93
Returned, The (Mott), 89, 91
Revolutionary War research, 133–36
Rin Tin Tin (Orlean), 70
Rolling Nowhere (Conover), 4, 51–52

Salt Maker (Reiss), 35, 89
Schacter, Daniel L., 87, 88
Schindler's List (Keneally), 4
Searching for Memory (Schacter), 87
secondary sources, 5, 7
Secret Soldiers (Gerard), 184
sequence in the syntax of a story, 9
Seward, Michael, 121
shad boat, 143–44
shorthand, 48
Shubert, Catherine, 205
Skype, 40
Sleepless Days (Resnick), 93
smartpens, 45–47
smartphones, 40, 45–47
Snow Falling on Cedars (Guterson), 4
Something for the Pain (Austin), 92
Song of Napalm (Weigl), 93
Sorensen, Diane, 43, 53, 131–33, 207
Soul of a New Machine, The (Kidder), 4
South of Heaven (French), 47–48
speculative fiction research, 34–35
Stieglitz, Alfred, 3
Stone, Nomi, 94–95, 109–10, 183
Sullivan, John Jeremiah, 131
syntax of a story, 9–10

Talese, Gay, 150
technology for researchers: multi-function devices, 40; paper notebooks, 39–40; photography, 40–42, 44; recording devices, 40–41
Things They Carried, The (O'Brien), 93
Thomas and Beulah (Dove), 1, 182–83
Through the Glorieta Pass (Adams), 2–3, 131
Todd, Richard, 15, 179
tools of researchers: for archival work, 38–39; audio devices, 40, 45–46; capturing spaces in images and maps, 42–45; choosing your tools, 38–39, 55–56; creating and using maps, 43–45; creating spatial representations, 44–45; credentials and reputation, 49–50; dressing for the situation, 50–52; formal shorthand, 48; general purpose items, 39; getting permissions, 41, 106; habit of noticing and, 38; insights offered by maps, 44; for interviewing, 38; lim-

tools of researchers (*continued*)
  itations of electronics, 46–47; low-tech
  options, 47–49; magnifying glasses, 48–49;
  non-physical tools, 49; for observation of
  sites, 39; organizing the research, 52–55;
  photography and, 40–41, 44; prompts for,
  56; smartpens, 45–47; technology options
  and considerations, 39–42; unexpected
  usefulness of, 18
Trias, Rolando Lagarda, 171
turning fact into drama: achieving a broader vision, 194–95; conversation versus dialogue,
  199; decoding statistics, 197; distilling the
  information, 196; employing outside sup-
  plementary knowledge, 197; facts selection,
  199–200; humanizing the abstract, 196–97;
  language choice and use, 195–96; picking
  salient details, 198; seeking the full truth,
  200–201; setting the stage, 198–99; writing
  specifically and concretely, 197–98
Twain, Mark, 3–4

URLs (uniform source locators), 74–75
Urrea, Luis Alberto, 147
U.S. Census Bureau, 77

visual archives: artifacts, 3, 58, 80, 143, 154;
  maps, 42–45; museums, 3, 28, 49, 63, 75,
  76, 143, 153, 154; types of, 60–61
Vowell, Sarah, 8, 160, 161, 200–201

Walking on Water (Kenan), 4
walking the ground: authority and plausibility
  through experiences, 141–42; discovery of
  an emotional investment, 131–33; empathy
  gained by, 147; experiencing situations
  yourself, 130–31, 137–38; power of smell
  and taste, 145–46; prompts for, 148;
  reporting through all five senses, 144–48;
  ride-alongs, 105; understanding made
  possible by, 133–34, 143–44
Walling, Molly, 85, 166–68
Watson, Doc, 152
Weaver, Samuel, 157
Weigl, Bruce, 93
*We Is Got Him: The Kidnapping That Changed
  America* (Hagen), 31, 178–81
Welty, Eudora, 71–72, 86, 87
Whitman, Walt, 4
Wikipedia, 74
Williams, Brian, 126
Wilson, Emily, 206
Wolfe, Tom, 119
Woodman, Don, 137
World According to Garp, The (Irving), 93
Wright, Richard, 93
writing from your research: authenticity
  and, 180, 182–83; basic elements of good
  writing, 179, 180–81; chronologies use,
  182–83; imagining the scene with credibility, 176–77, 178–81; inspirational nature
  of research, 172–74, 178, 179; letting the
  creative process take over, 175–78; narrative voice and, 181–83; prompts for, 201–2;
  re-creating the event (*see* re-creating the
  event); role of research in poetry, 172–74,
  175–76; seductive nature of research, 171,
  177, 178; shifting through the layers of
  facts, 174–75, 180; turning fact into drama
  (*see* turning fact into drama)
written release forms, 106

YouTube, 80–81

Zone of Noise, 6, 59, 73, 159
Zoo Story (French), 47, 95, 136–37